BRAIN GAMES FOR SMART KIDS

Challenging Fun Brain Teasers and Logic Puzzles for Smart Kids

K. Murdle

ISBN: 979-8-9886895-8-4

Copyright © 2023 by SmartKid Press
All rights reserved.

Contents

Welcome to the Ultimate Brain-Teaser Adventure!

 Hey there, young puzzler! Ready to dive into a world of mind-bending challenges and brain-teasing adventures? You've just opened the door to a fantastic journey of wit, logic, and fun all Packed in this almost 200 Pages.

Inside these pages, you're going to encounter a thrilling variety of puzzles—everything from the classic games of Hangman and Sudoku to intriguing challenges like Nurikabe, Kakurasu, and Shikaku. Whether you're a fan of number crunching with Calcudoku or navigating intricate Mazes, there's something for everyone here!

But what makes this book extra special? The sweet satisfaction every five pages! That's right, you won't be left scratching your head for too long because the solutions are placed conveniently near their puzzles. It's the perfect balance to test your skills and still enjoy every moment.

Designed with an Easy-Medium to difficulty level, this collection is ideal for young minds craving some fun, without feeling overwhelmed. Whether you're on a rainy afternoon indoors, on a road trip, or just looking to unwind after a long day, these puzzles are your perfect companions.

So, sharpen those pencils (or pens if you're feeling confident!) and get ready to challenge your brain. The world of puzzles awaits!

Happy Solving!

Tic-Tac Logic

HOW TO PLAY

Tic-Tac-Logic is a single player puzzle based on tic-tac-toe. Each puzzle consists of a grid containing X's and O's in various places.

The object is to place X or O in the remaining squares so that

1. there are no more than two consecutive X's or O's in a row or column;

2. the number of X's is the same as the number of O's in each row and column; and

3. all rows and all columns are unique.

TIC TAC LOGIC - 1

0		0			1
	1			0	0
1			1		
	0	1		1	1
0	1		1		
		1		0	1

TIC TAC LOGIC - 2

			0	1	
1	1		1	0	
	0	1			1
0		1		0	
	1		0		0
1		0		0	

TIC TAC LOGIC - 3

	0		1		
1		0		1	0
	1	0			
1			1		0
1	1			1	0
	1	1		0	

TIC TAC LOGIC - 4

0		1	0		0
	1			1	
0			1	0	
0		1			
		0		0	0
1	0		1		

TIC TAC LOGIC - 5

0		1		0	
		0	0		
0	0		1		1
	1	0		1	
1		1		0	0
	0		1		

TIC TAC LOGIC - 6

0	0		1		1
	0	1		0	
			0		0
0	1		0	0	
	0				0
	1			1	

TIC TAC LOGIC - 7

			0	1	
1	0		1		0
	1	0		0	
1			0		0
	0	1		0	
1		1		1	

TIC TAC LOGIC - 8

1		0	1		1
	1		1	1	
0					1
		1		0	
	0	0			0
0	1			1	

TIC TAC LOGIC - 9

		1	0		0
1		1		1	
			1		1
0	1				
	0		1	0	
0			0		1

TIC TAC LOGIC - 10

0		1		1	
	0			0	1
	1			0	
0		0	0		1
0		1		0	1
	0		1		

TIC TAC LOGIC - 11

1		0		1	
	1	0		1	1
0	0		1		
		0		0	0
0		1			
	0		1		0

TIC TAC LOGIC - 12

	0		1		1
1	0			0	
		0	0		
0			0		1
	1	0		0	
0		1			0

TIC TAC LOGIC - 13

0		0	0		1
	1		0		
	0	1		0	1
0		1	0		1
	1				
	0		1		0

TIC TAC LOGIC - 14

	1	0			1
			1	1	
0	0			1	
	1		1		0
0		1	0		
	0	1			1

TIC TAC LOGIC - 15

	0	1		1	
	0			0	0
1		0	1		
	1			1	1
1		1	1		
		0	1		1

TIC TAC LOGIC - 16

1		0		0	
	1		1	0	
0	1				0
1				0	
	0			1	1
1		1	0		0

TIC TAC LOGIC - 17

1			0		0
	1	0		1	
0		1	1		1
	1		1	0	
0	0				1
		1	1		

TIC TAC LOGIC - 18

	1		0		
0		1	1		1
	0			1	1
1			1		
	1	0		1	
1		1	1		0

TIC TAC LOGIC - 19

1			0		0
		1		1	
1	0			0	1
		0			0
		1	0		
1	0		1	0	

TIC TAC LOGIC - 20

0		1			0
1		1		1	0
	0				
0		0		1	1
	0		1	0	
0				1	1

TIC TAC LOGIC - 21

	1		1		0
0		1		1	
	0	1			1
	0		1		
0			1	1	
1		1		0	

TIC TAC LOGIC - 22

1		0			1
	1			1	
	0		0		1
1		1		0	
1	1		0		0
	1	1		0	

TIC TAC LOGIC - 23

0	1		0		0
			0	1	
	0	1			
0	1			0	1
		0	1		0
	0	0		0	

TIC TAC LOGIC - 24

		0			1
0	1		1		
0	1		0		0
		1		0	0
0			0	1	
1	1				0

TIC TAC LOGIC - 25

1	0		1		1
	0		1	1	
		0		1	
1	0		1	1	
		1			1
0	1			1	

TIC TAC LOGIC - 26

	0		1	0	
0		1			1
0	1		1		1
		0		1	
	1		0		1
1		0		1	

TIC TAC LOGIC - 27

1		0			1
		1	0		
1	1			0	
	1	0		1	0
			1		1
0		1		1	

TIC TAC LOGIC - 28

0		0		1	
	0		1		1
1			1		0
	1	1		1	
0		0	1		1
	0			1	

TIC TAC LOGIC - 29

1		0		1	0
	1		0		
1		0		1	0
	1		1		
0		1	0		1
	0			0	

TIC TAC LOGIC - 30

		1		1	
1			1		1
	1	0			
0		1		1	0
	0			0	1
1			0		

TIC TAC LOGIC - 1
(Solution)

0	1	0	0	1	1
1	1	0	1	0	0
1	0	1	1	0	0
0	0	1	0	1	1
0	1	0	1	1	0
1	0	1	0	0	1

TIC TAC LOGIC - 2
(Solution)

0	1	1	0	1	0
1	1	0	1	0	0
0	0	1	0	1	1
0	0	1	1	0	1
1	1	0	0	1	0
1	0	0	1	0	1

TIC TAC LOGIC - 3
(Solution)

0	0	1	1	0	1
1	0	0	1	1	0
0	1	0	0	1	1
1	0	1	1	0	0
1	1	0	0	1	0
0	1	1	0	0	1

TIC TAC LOGIC - 4
(Solution)

0	1	1	0	1	0
1	1	0	0	1	0
0	0	1	1	0	1
0	0	1	0	1	1
1	1	0	1	0	0
1	0	0	1	0	1

TIC TAC LOGIC - 5
(Solution)

0	1	1	0	0	1
1	1	0	0	1	0
0	0	1	1	0	1
0	1	0	0	1	1
1	0	1	1	0	0
1	0	0	1	1	0

TIC TAC LOGIC - 6
(Solution)

0	0	1	1	0	1
1	0	1	1	0	0
1	1	0	0	1	0
0	1	1	0	0	1
1	0	0	1	1	0
0	1	0	0	1	1

TIC TAC LOGIC - 7
(Solution)

0	1	0	0	1	1
1	0	1	1	0	0
0	1	0	1	0	1
1	1	0	0	1	0
0	0	1	1	0	1
1	0	1	0	1	0

TIC TAC LOGIC - 8
(Solution)

1	0	0	1	0	1
0	1	0	1	1	0
0	1	1	0	0	1
1	0	1	0	0	1
1	0	0	1	1	0
0	1	1	0	1	0

TIC TAC LOGIC - 9
(Solution)

0	1	1	0	1	0
1	0	1	0	1	0
1	0	0	1	0	1
0	1	0	0	1	1
1	0	1	1	0	0
0	1	0	1	0	1

TIC TAC LOGIC - 10
(Solution)

0	1	1	0	1	0
1	0	1	0	0	1
1	1	0	1	0	0
0	1	0	0	1	1
0	0	1	1	0	1
1	0	0	1	1	0

TIC TAC LOGIC - 11
(Solution)

1	1	0	0	1	0
0	1	0	0	1	1
0	0	1	1	0	1
1	1	0	1	0	0
0	0	1	0	1	1
1	0	1	1	0	0

TIC TAC LOGIC - 12
(Solution)

0	0	1	1	0	1
1	0	0	1	0	1
1	1	0	0	1	0
0	0	1	0	1	1
1	1	0	1	0	0
0	1	1	0	1	0

TIC TAC LOGIC - 13
(Solution)

0	1	0	0	1	1
1	1	0	0	1	0
0	0	1	1	0	1
0	0	1	0	1	1
1	1	0	1	0	0
1	0	1	1	0	0

TIC TAC LOGIC - 14
(Solution)

0	1	0	1	0	1
1	0	0	1	1	0
0	0	1	0	1	1
1	1	0	1	0	0
0	1	1	0	1	0
1	0	1	0	0	1

TIC TAC LOGIC - 15
(Solution)

0	0	1	0	1	1
1	0	1	1	0	0
1	1	0	1	0	0
0	1	0	0	1	1
1	0	1	0	1	0
0	1	0	1	0	1

TIC TAC LOGIC - 16
(Solution)

1	0	0	1	0	1
0	1	0	1	0	1
0	1	1	0	1	0
1	0	1	1	0	0
0	1	0	0	1	1
1	0	1	0	1	0

TIC TAC LOGIC - 17
(Solution)

1	1	0	0	1	0
0	1	0	0	1	1
0	0	1	1	0	1
1	1	0	1	0	0
0	0	1	0	1	1
1	0	1	1	0	0

TIC TAC LOGIC - 18
(Solution)

1	1	0	0	1	0
0	0	1	1	0	1
0	0	1	0	1	1
1	1	0	1	0	0
0	1	0	0	1	1
1	0	1	1	0	0

TIC TAC LOGIC - 19
(Solution)

1	1	0	0	1	0
0	0	1	0	1	1
1	0	0	1	0	1
0	1	0	1	1	0
0	1	1	0	0	1
1	0	1	1	0	0

TIC TAC LOGIC - 20
(Solution)

0	1	1	0	1	0
1	0	1	0	1	0
1	0	0	1	0	1
0	1	0	0	1	1
1	0	1	1	0	0
0	1	0	1	0	1

TIC TAC LOGIC - 21
(Solution)

1	1	0	1	0	0
0	1	1	0	1	0
0	0	1	0	1	1
1	0	0	1	0	1
0	1	0	1	1	0
1	0	1	0	0	1

TIC TAC LOGIC - 22
(Solution)

1	0	0	1	0	1
0	1	0	1	1	0
0	0	1	0	1	1
1	0	1	1	0	0
1	1	0	0	1	0
0	1	1	0	0	1

TIC TAC LOGIC - 23
(Solution)

0	1	1	0	1	0
1	1	0	0	1	0
0	0	1	1	0	1
0	1	1	0	0	1
1	0	0	1	1	0
1	0	0	1	0	1

TIC TAC LOGIC - 24
(Solution)

1	0	0	1	0	1
0	1	0	1	0	1
0	1	1	0	1	0
1	0	1	1	0	0
0	1	0	0	1	1
1	0	1	0	1	0

TIC TAC LOGIC - 25
(Solution)

1	0	0	1	0	1
0	0	1	1	0	1
1	1	0	0	1	0
1	0	0	1	1	0
0	1	1	0	0	1
0	1	1	0	1	0

TIC TAC LOGIC - 26
(Solution)

1	0	1	1	0	0
0	0	1	0	1	1
0	1	0	1	0	1
1	0	0	1	1	0
0	1	1	0	0	1
1	1	0	0	1	0

TIC TAC LOGIC - 27
(Solution)

1	0	0	1	0	1
0	0	1	0	1	1
1	1	0	1	0	0
1	1	0	0	1	0
0	0	1	1	0	1
0	1	1	0	1	0

TIC TAC LOGIC - 28
(Solution)

0	1	0	0	1	1
1	0	0	1	0	1
1	0	1	1	0	0
0	1	1	0	1	0
0	1	0	1	0	1
1	0	1	0	1	0

TIC TAC LOGIC - 29
(Solution)

1	1	0	0	1	0
0	1	1	0	0	1
1	0	0	1	1	0
0	1	0	1	0	1
0	0	1	0	1	1
1	0	1	1	0	0

TIC TAC LOGIC - 30
(Solution)

0	0	1	0	1	1
1	0	0	1	0	1
1	1	0	1	0	0
0	1	1	0	1	0
0	0	1	1	0	1
1	1	0	0	1	0

LOGIC SQUARES
HOW TO PLAY

The game is played on a grid that's 9 squares
- You are X, the other player is O.
- Players take turns putting their marks in empty squares.
- The first player to get 3 of her marks in a row (up, down, across, or diagonally) is the winner.
- When all 9 squares are full, the game is over.

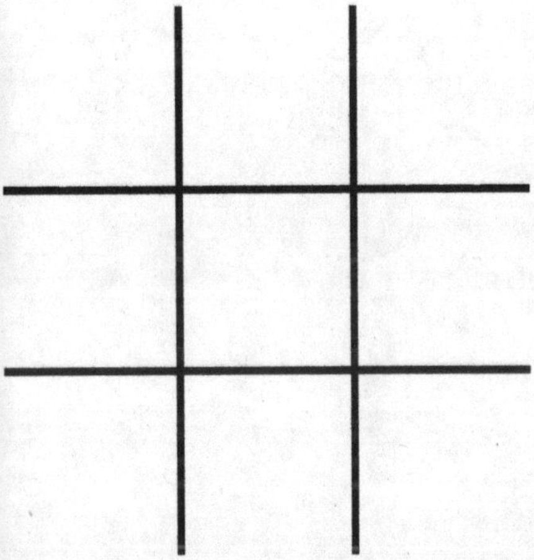

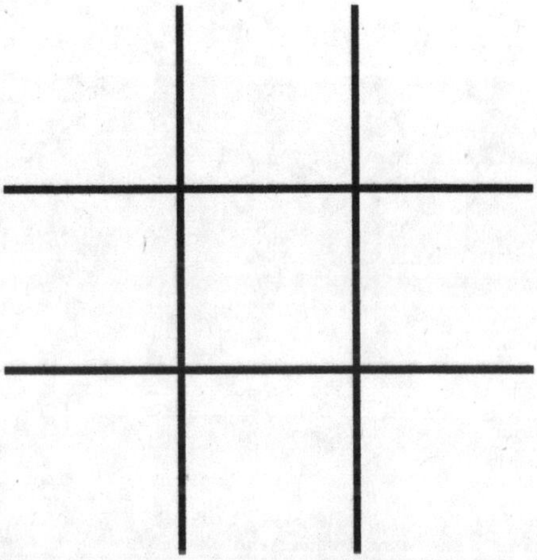

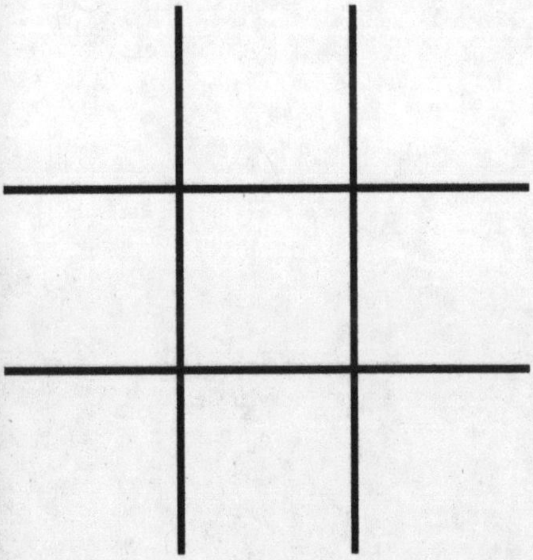

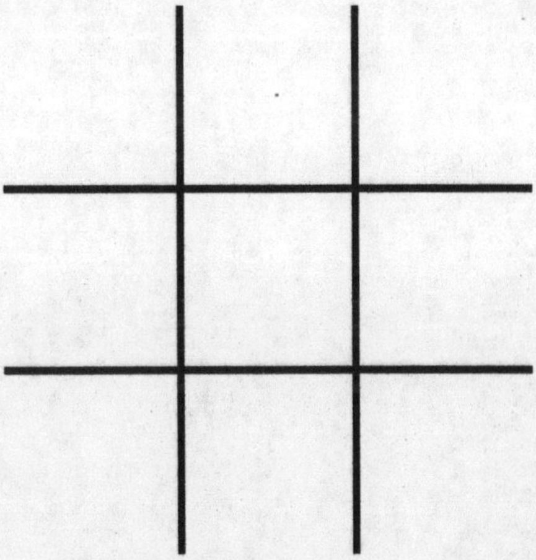

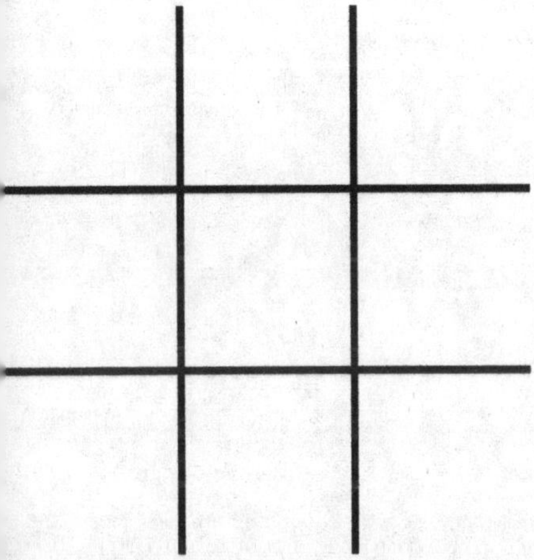

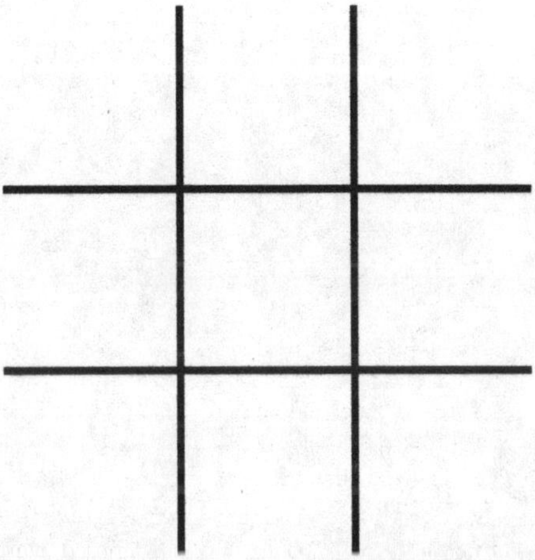

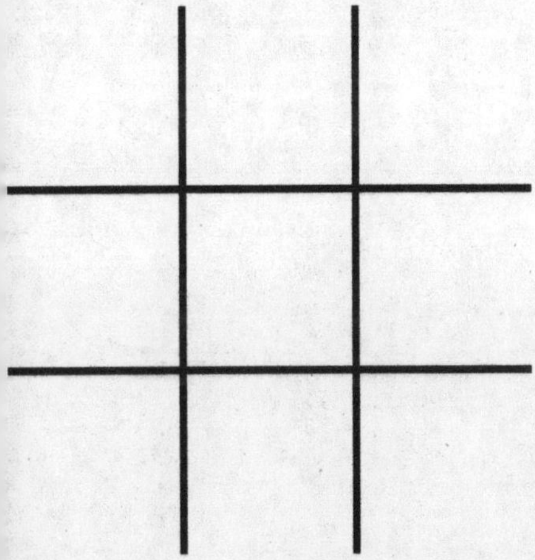

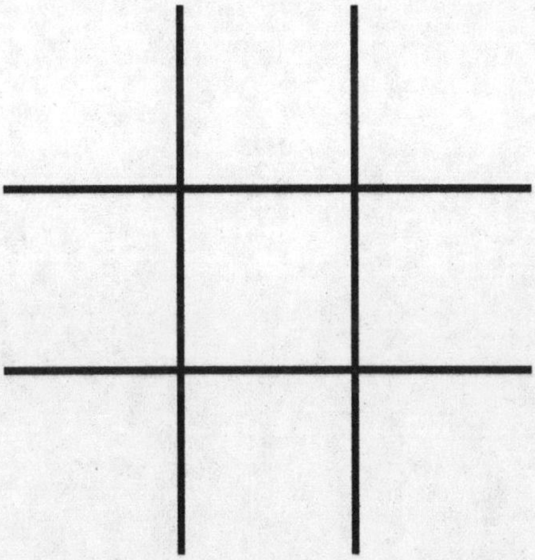

NURIKABE
HOW TO PLAY

Each puzzle consists of a grid containing clues in various places. The object is to create islands by partitioning between clues with walls so

- Each island contains exactly one clue.
- The number of squares in each island equals the value of the clue.
- All islands are isolated from each other horizontally and vertically.
- There are no wall areas of 2x2 or larger.
- When completed, all walls form a continuous path.

NURIKABE - 1

NURIKABE - 2

NURIKABE - 3

NURIKABE - 4

NURIKABE - 5

NURIKABE - 6

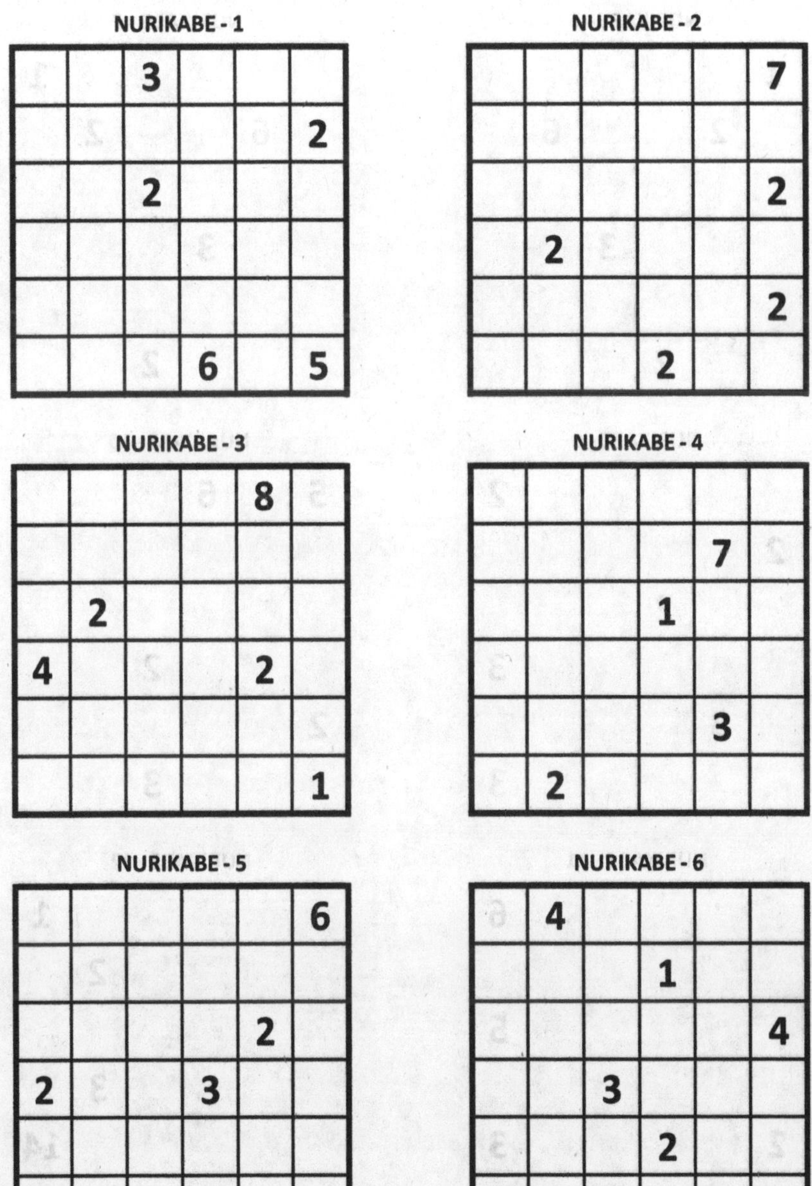

23

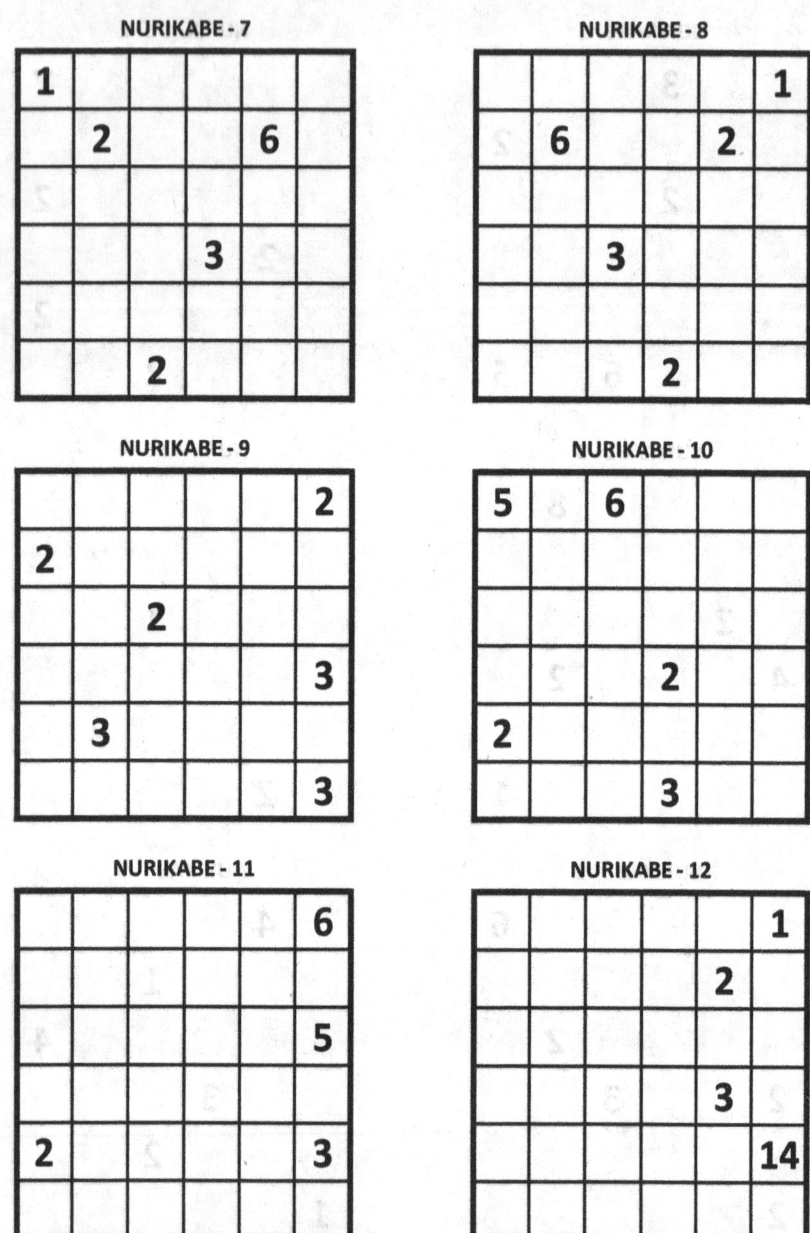

NURIKABE - 7

1					
	2			6	
			3		
		2			

NURIKABE - 8

					1
	6			2	
		3			
			2		

NURIKABE - 9

					2
2					
		2			
					3
	3				
					3

NURIKABE - 10

5		6			
			2		
2					
			3		

NURIKABE - 11

					6
					5
2					3

NURIKABE - 12

					1
				2	
				3	
					14

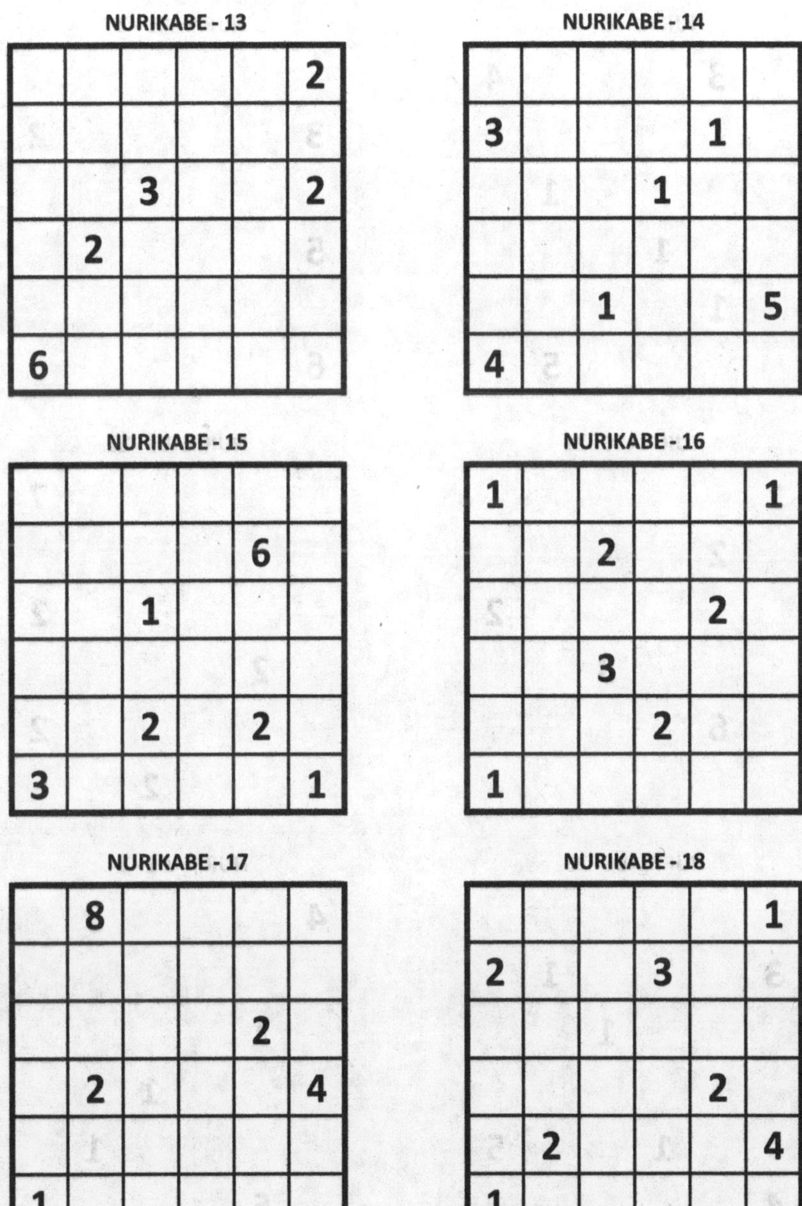

NURIKABE - 13
NURIKABE - 14
NURIKABE - 15
NURIKABE - 16
NURIKABE - 17
NURIKABE - 18

NURIKABE - 19

NURIKABE - 20

NURIKABE - 21

NURIKABE - 22

NURIKABE - 23

NURIKABE - 24

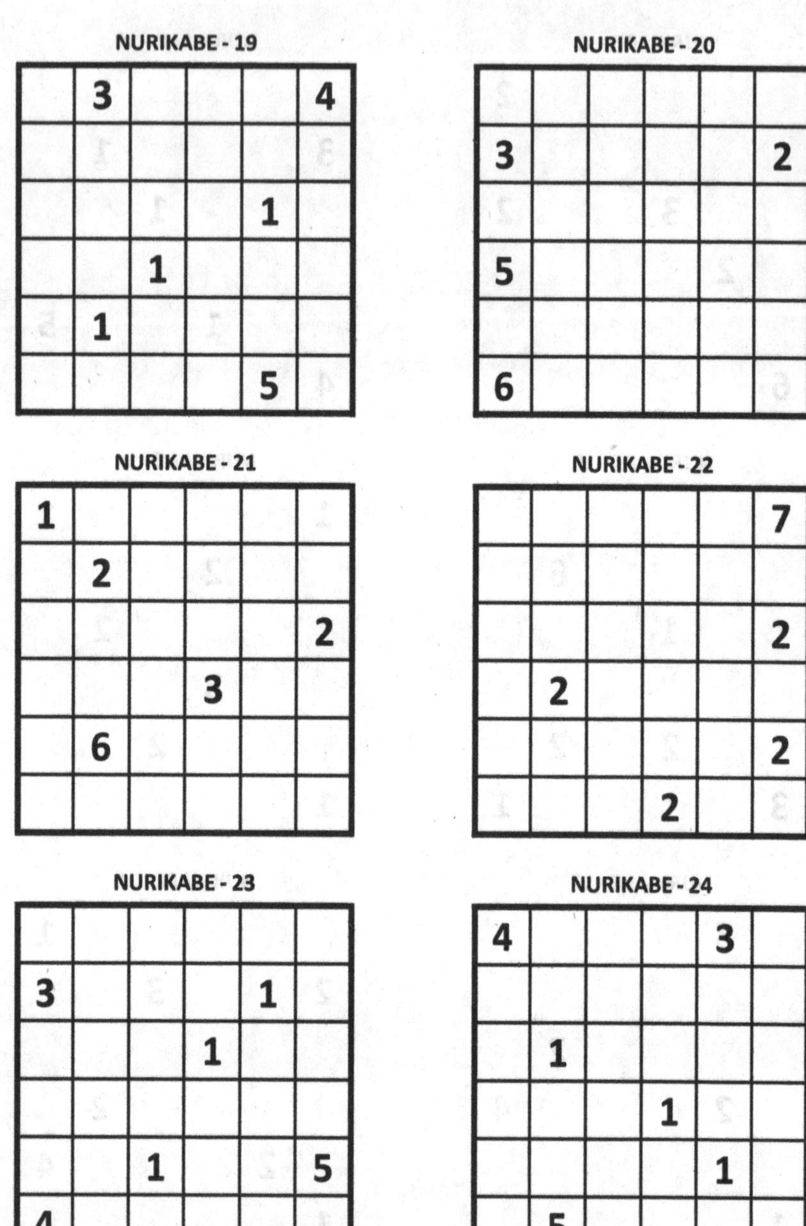

NURIKABE - 25

1					3
	2		2		
			1		
	6				

NURIKABE - 26

6					
5					
3					2

NURIKABE - 27

	5				
				1	
			1		
	1				
4				3	

NURIKABE - 28

					2
			1		
	7			3	

NURIKABE - 29

	2		2		7
2					
		2			

NURIKABE - 30

6					
5					
3					2

NURIKABE - 1 (Solution)

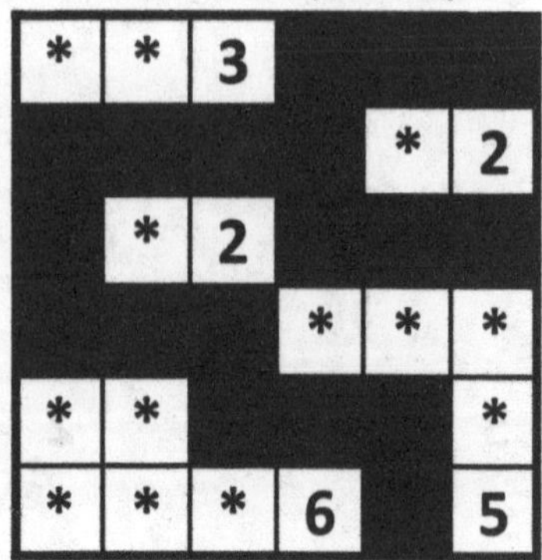

NURIKABE - 2 (Solution)

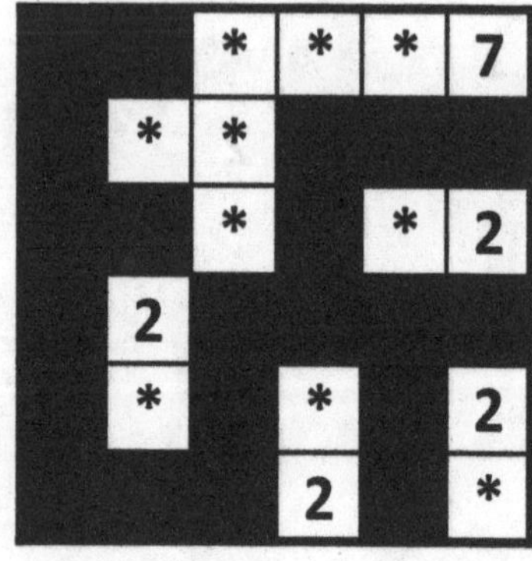

NURIKABE - 3 (Solution)

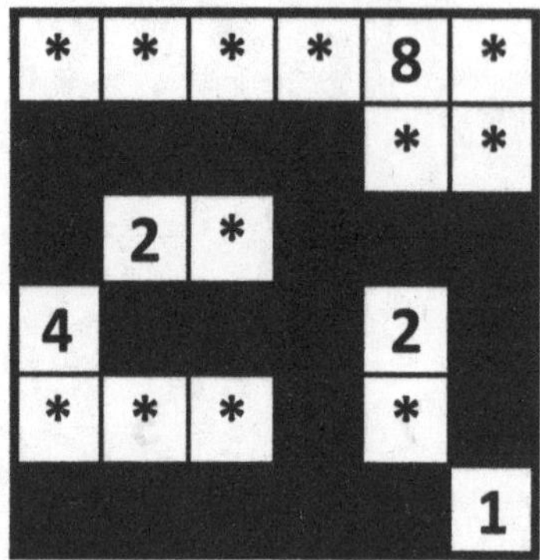

NURIKABE - 4 (Solution)

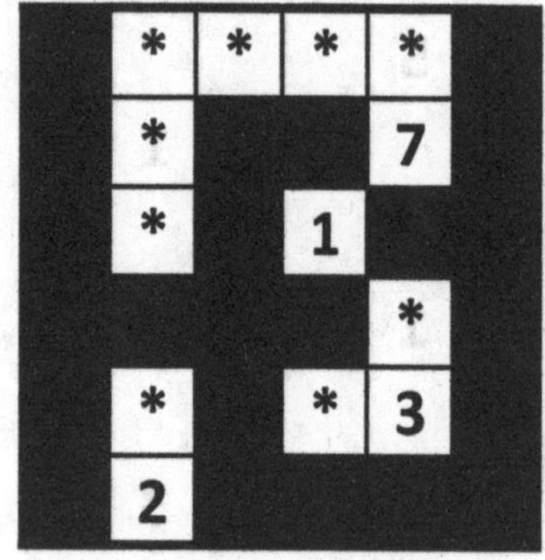

NURIKABE - 5 (Solution)

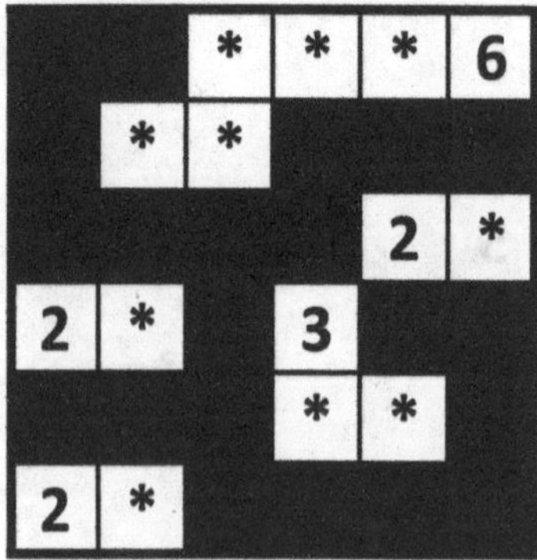

NURIKABE - 6 (Solution)

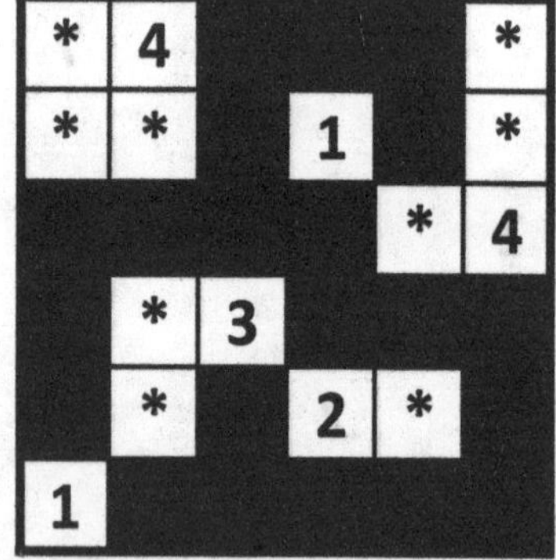

NURIKABE - 7 (Solution)

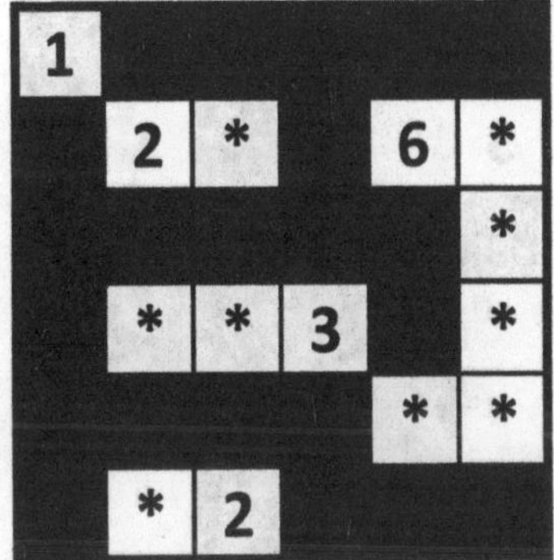

NURIKABE - 8 (Solution)

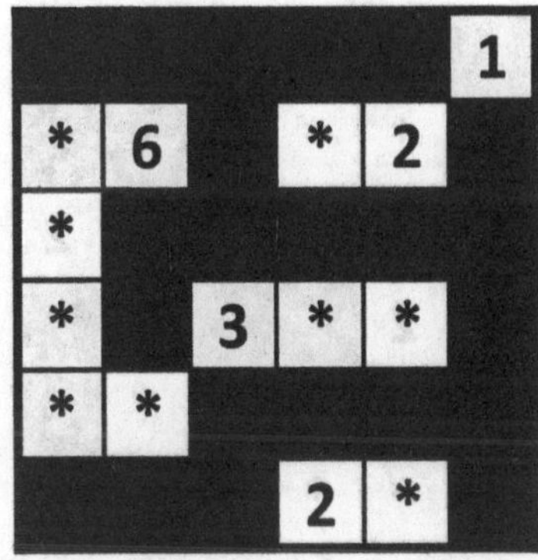

NURIKABE - 9 (Solution)

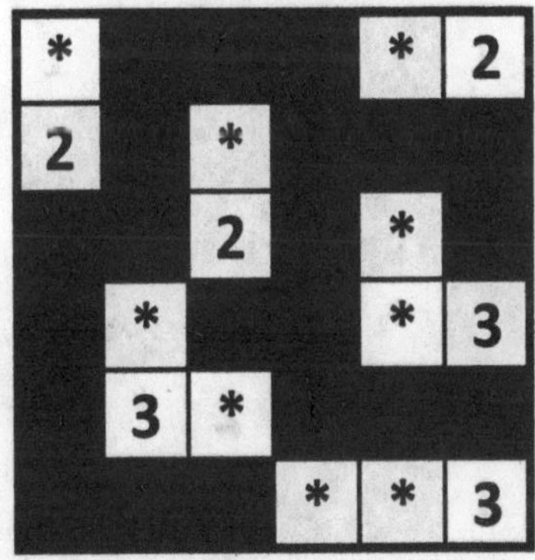

NURIKABE - 10 (Solution)

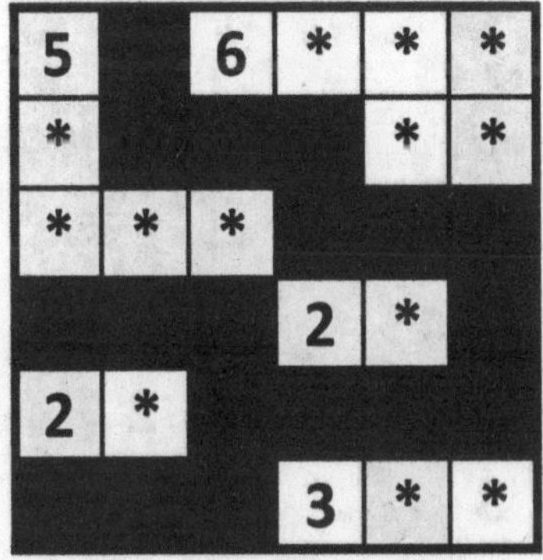

NURIKABE - 11 (Solution)

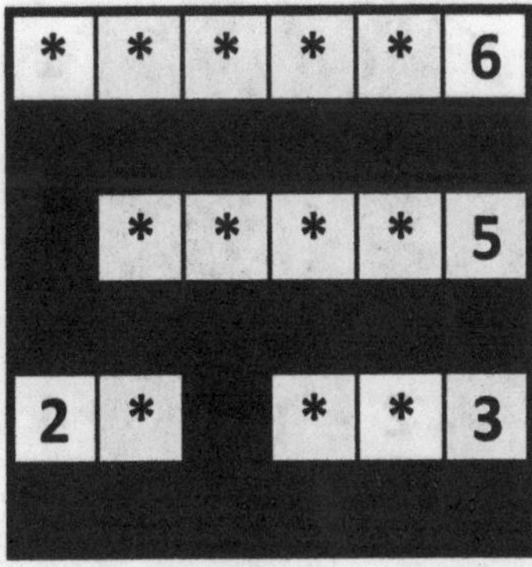

NURIKABE - 12 (Solution)

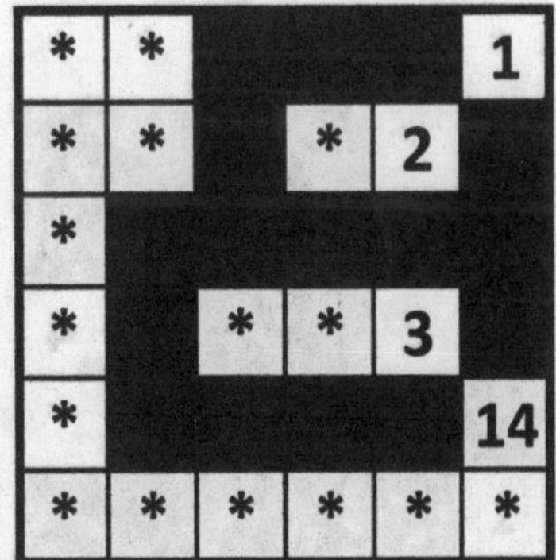

NURIKABE - 13 (Solution)

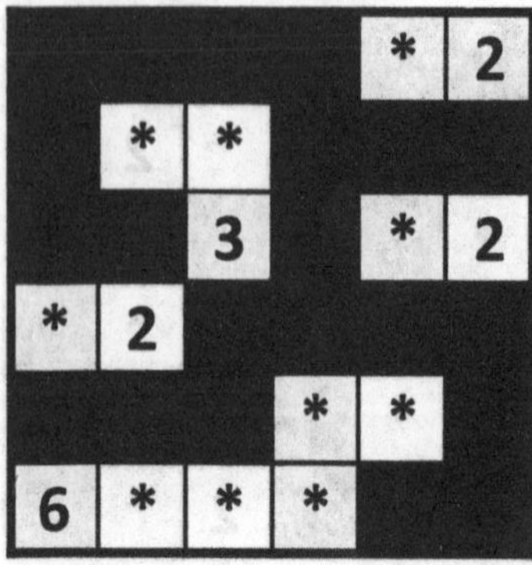

NURIKABE - 14 (Solution)

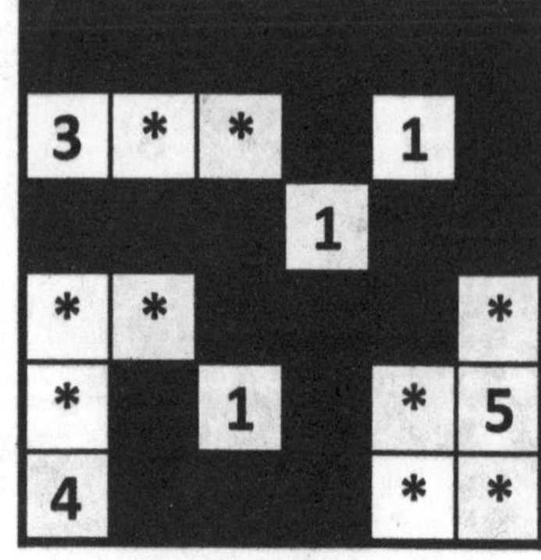

NURIKABE - 15 (Solution)

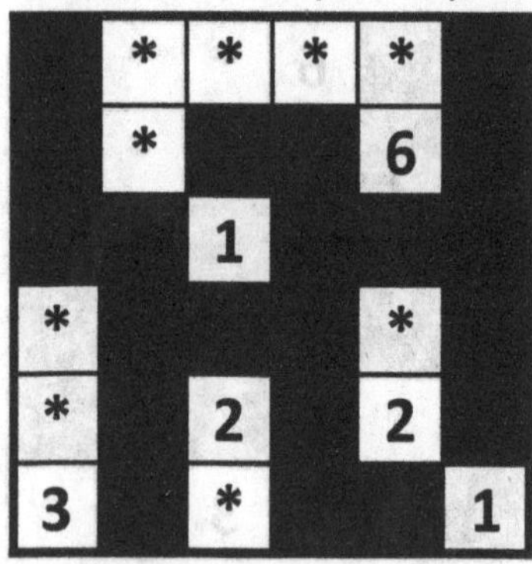

NURIKABE - 16 (Solution)

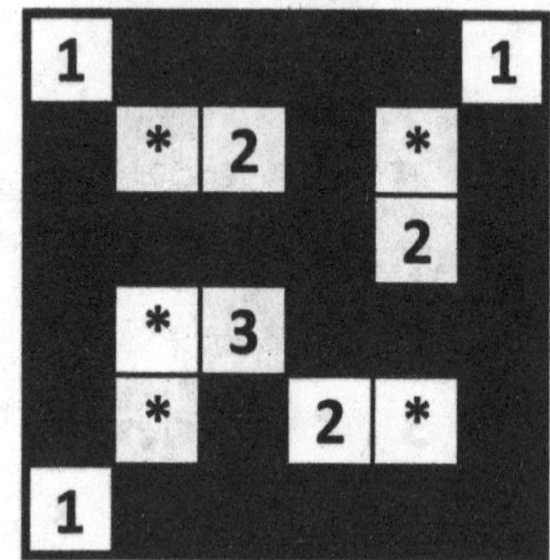

NURIKABE - 17 (Solution)

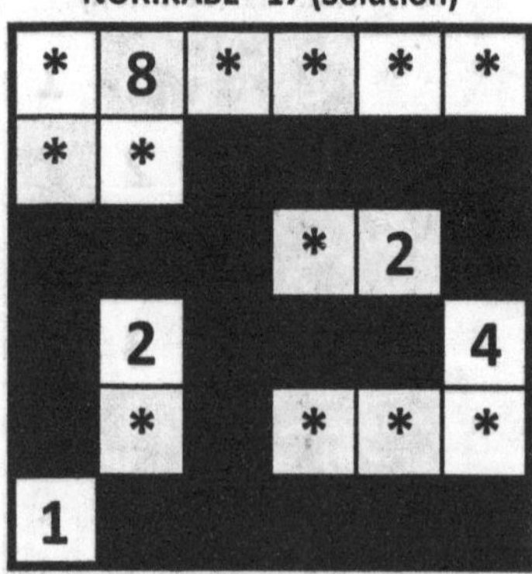

NURIKABE - 18 (Solution)

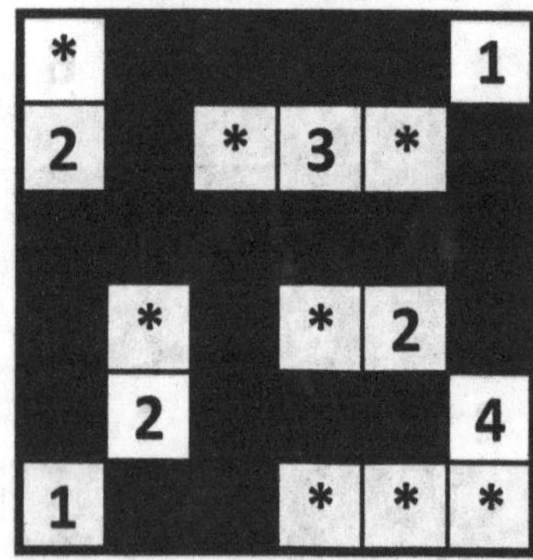

NURIKABE - 19 (Solution)

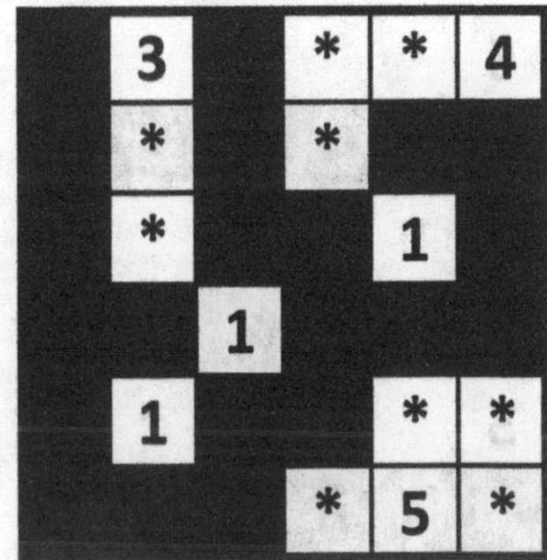

NURIKABE - 20 (Solution)

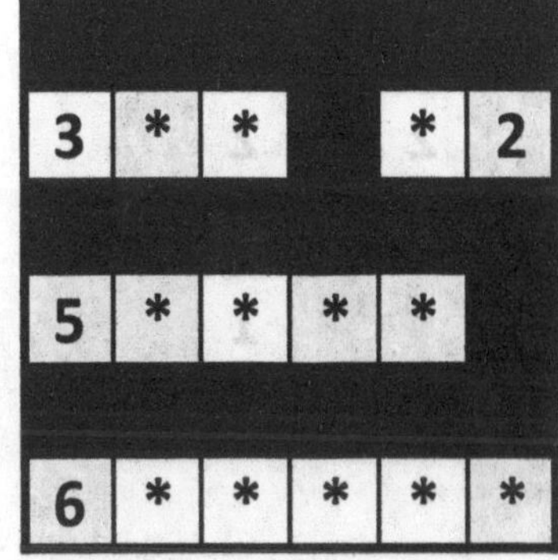

NURIKABE - 21 (Solution)

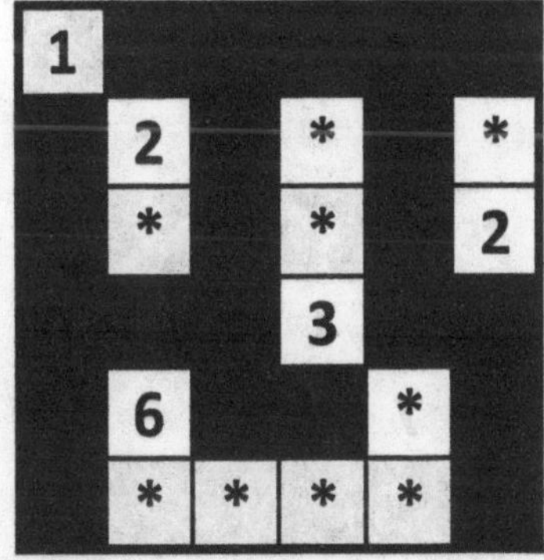

NURIKABE - 22 (Solution)

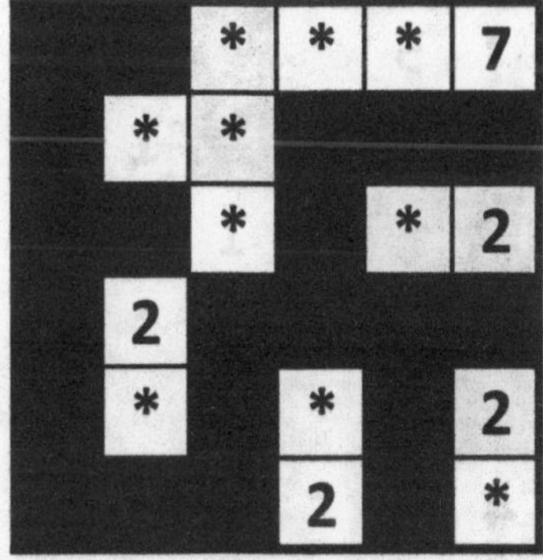

NURIKABE - 23 (Solution)

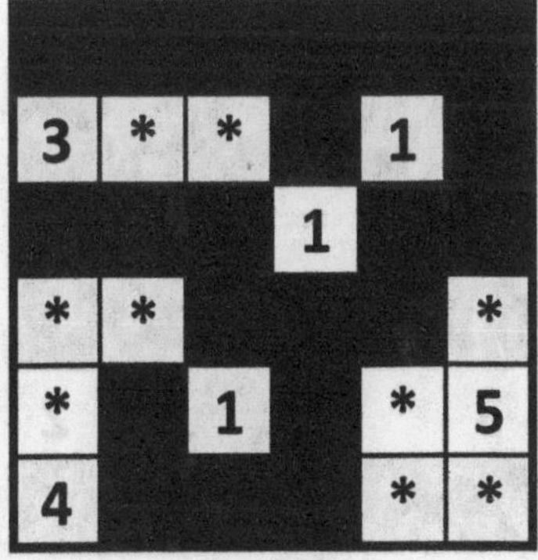

NURIKABE - 24 (Solution)

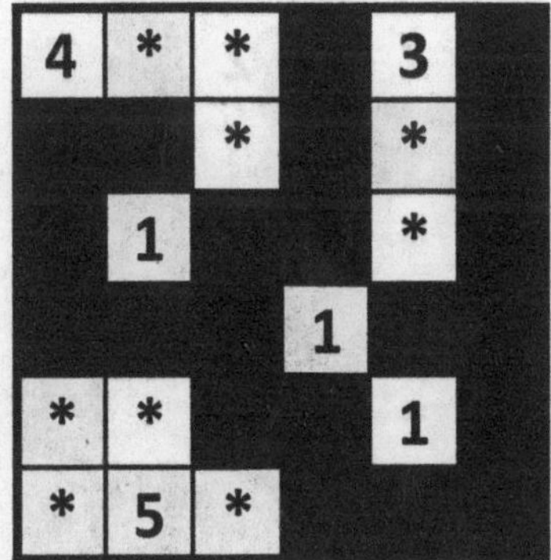

NURIKABE - 25 (Solution)

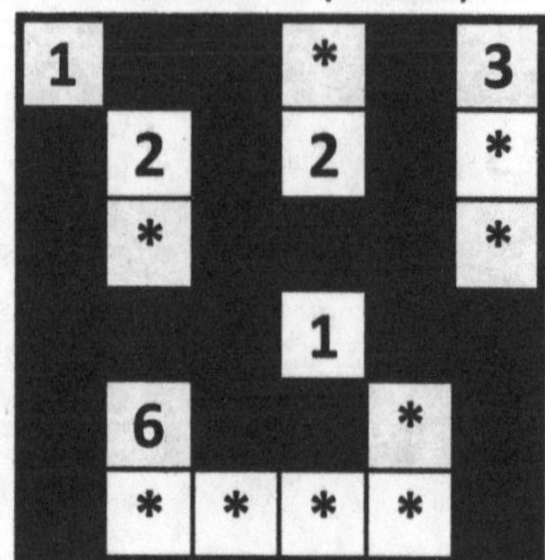

NURIKABE - 26 (Solution)

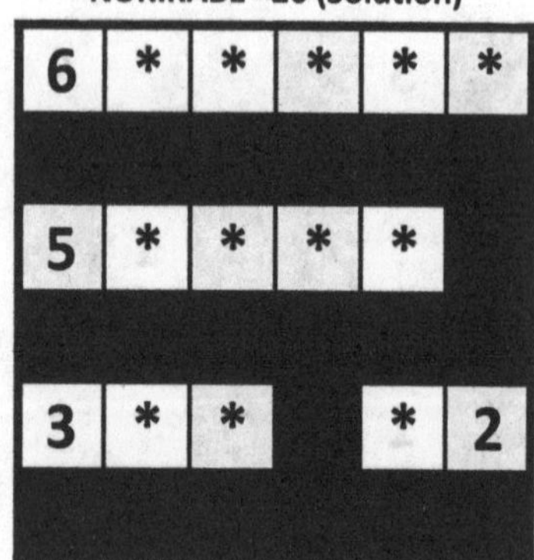

NURIKABE - 27 (Solution)

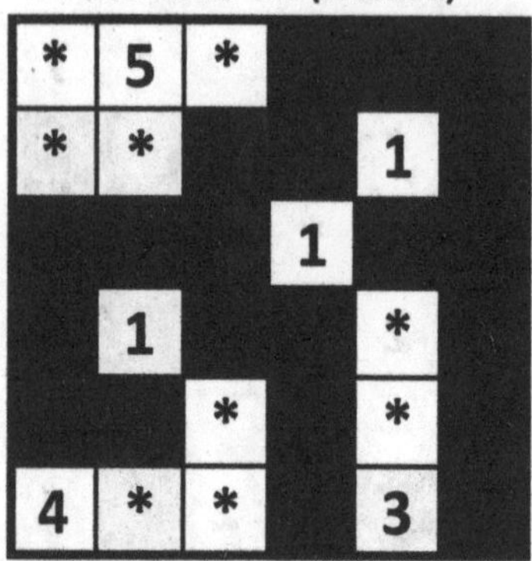

NURIKABE - 28 (Solution)

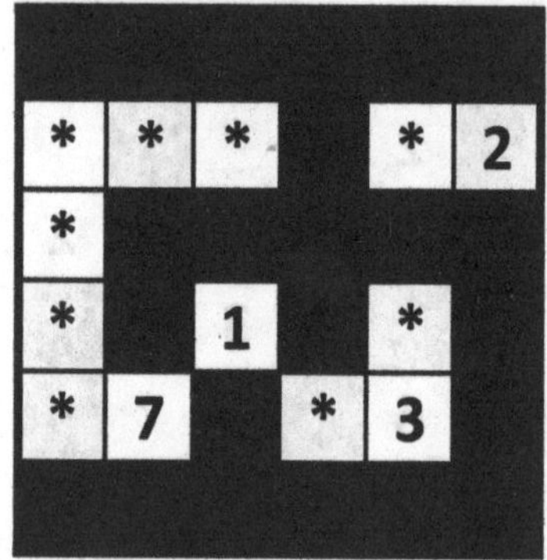

NURIKABE - 29 (Solution)

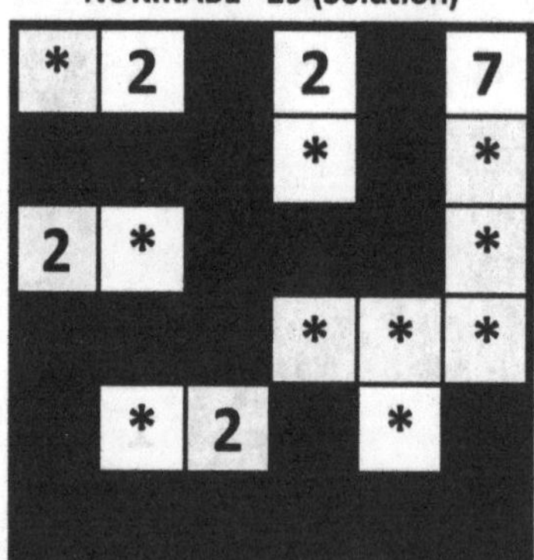

NURIKABE - 30 (Solution)

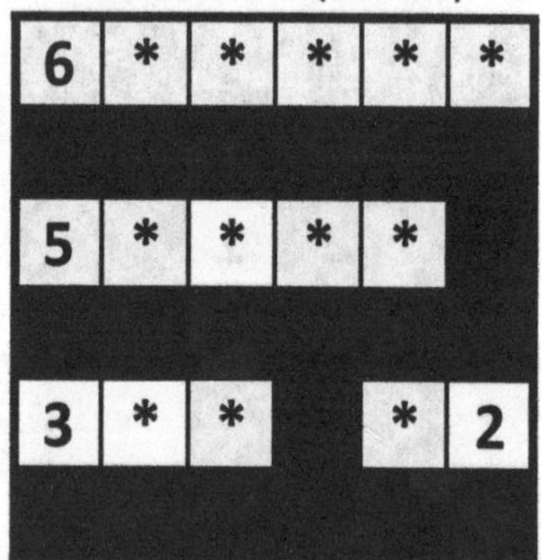

BRAIN TEASER HITORI

HOW TO PLAY

Each puzzle consists of a square grid with numbers appearing in all squares.

The object is to shade squares so

- No number appears in a row or column more than once.
- Shaded (colored) squares do not touch each other vertically or horizontally.
- When completed. all un-shaded (white) squares create a single continuous area.

HITORI - 1

2	1	2	4
3	2	4	1
4	3	3	2
1	3	2	3

HITORI - 2

3	3	1	1
2	1	4	3
1	2	3	4
4	4	1	2

HITORI - 3

3	1	1	4
4	1	3	2
2	3	4	1
1	4	3	3

HITORI - 4

1	4	1	3
4	4	1	2
3	2	4	4
3	1	3	4

HITORI - 5

2	3	3	4
4	2	4	1
1	4	2	4
3	1	3	2

HITORI - 6

4	3	3	2
4	4	3	1
1	4	4	2
3	1	2	4

HITORI - 7

1	4	1	1
2	3	1	4
1	1	4	3
4	1	3	2

HITORI - 8

1	2	1	1
2	4	3	1
3	1	4	2
1	4	2	4

HITORI - 9

2	4	4	2
1	2	3	4
2	3	4	1
3	1	2	3

HITORI - 10

1	3	1	2
1	4	1	3
3	1	4	1
2	1	3	4

HITORI - 11

1	2	1	3
4	3	2	1
3	3	1	1
2	1	3	4

HITORI - 12

4	3	1	2
1	1	4	3
3	1	2	2
2	4	3	1

HITORI - 13

4	3	1	2
3	1	4	2
1	3	2	2
2	4	3	1

HITORI - 14

1	3	2	4
3	3	4	4
2	4	3	1
4	1	1	3

HITORI - 15

3	4	2	2
3	3	1	4
1	2	4	3
2	1	3	2

HITORI - 16

3	3	2	1
1	4	3	1
3	1	1	4
2	1	4	3

HITORI - 17

3	1	4	1
1	4	2	3
4	1	3	4
4	3	4	2

HITORI - 18

2	3	4	1
3	2	3	1
4	1	2	3
3	3	1	3

HITORI - 19

1	2	3	3
3	1	2	1
4	3	1	4
2	3	3	4

HITORI - 20

1	4	4	2
4	1	3	2
4	3	1	4
3	4	2	1

HITORI - 21

1	1	4	3
4	1	3	3
2	4	2	1
2	3	1	2

HITORI - 22

2	4	3	3
3	1	4	2
1	1	3	1
4	3	2	1

HITORI - 23

1	3	3	4
3	2	4	1
4	1	4	3
1	4	3	2

HITORI - 24

3	4	4	1
1	3	3	4
4	3	3	2
2	1	4	3

HITORI - 25

1	3	4	4
4	4	3	2
2	4	1	3
3	2	4	2

HITORI - 26

2	1	4	1
1	2	3	3
4	1	4	3
4	4	1	2

HITORI - 27

3	1	2	4
1	4	3	4
3	2	1	3
2	3	4	1

HITORI - 28

3	2	2	4
1	4	2	3
3	1	3	2
2	3	3	1

HITORI - 29

4	4	3	2
2	3	1	4
1	4	2	3
3	2	1	1

HITORI - 30

1	3	4	4
4	3	3	1
2	4	1	4
2	1	2	4

HITORI - 1 (Solution)

2	1	2	4
3	2	4	1
4	3	3	2
1	3	2	3

HITORI - 2 (Solution)

3	3	1	1
2	1	4	3
1	2	3	4
4	4	1	2

HITORI - 3 (Solution)

3	1	1	4
4	1	3	2
2	3	4	1
1	4	3	3

HITORI - 4 (Solution)

1	4	1	3
4	4	1	2
3	2	4	4
3	1	3	4

HITORI - 5 (Solution)

2	3	3	4
4	2	4	1
1	4	2	4
3	1	3	2

HITORI - 6 (Solution)

4	3	3	2
4	4	3	1
1	4	4	2
3	1	2	4

HITORI - 7 (Solution)

1	4	1	1
2	3	1	4
1	1	4	3
4	1	3	2

HITORI - 8 (Solution)

1	2	1	1
2	4	3	1
3	1	4	2
1	4	2	4

HITORI - 9 (Solution)

2	4	4	2
1	2	3	4
2	3	4	1
3	1	2	3

HITORI - 10 (Solution)

1	3	1	2
1	4	1	3
3	1	4	1
2	1	3	4

HITORI - 11 (Solution)

1	2	1	3
4	3	2	1
3	3	1	1
2	1	3	4

HITORI - 12 (Solution)

4	3	1	2
1	1	4	3
3	1	2	2
2	4	3	1

HITORI - 13 (Solution)

4	3	1	2
3	1	4	2
1	3	2	2
2	4	3	1

HITORI - 14 (Solution)

1	3	2	4
3	3	4	4
2	4	3	1
4	1	1	3

HITORI - 15 (Solution)

3	4	2	2
3	3	1	4
1	2	4	3
2	1	3	2

HITORI - 16 (Solution)

3	3	2	1
1	4	3	1
3	1	1	4
2	1	4	3

HITORI - 17 (Solution)

3	1	4	1
1	4	2	3
4	1	3	4
4	3	4	2

HITORI - 18 (Solution)

2	3	4	1
3	2	3	1
4	1	2	3
3	3	1	3

HITORI - 19 (Solution)

1	2	3	3
3	1	2	1
4	3	1	4
2	3	3	4

HITORI - 20 (Solution)

1	4	4	2
4	1	3	2
4	3	1	4
3	4	2	1

HITORI - 21 (Solution)

1	1	4	3
4	1	3	3
2	4	2	1
2	3	1	2

HITORI - 22 (Solution)

2	4	3	3
3	1	4	2
1	1	3	1
4	3	2	1

HITORI - 23 (Solution)

1	3	3	4
3	2	4	1
4	1	4	3
1	4	3	2

HITORI - 24 (Solution)

3	4	4	1
1	3	3	4
4	3	3	2
2	1	4	3

HITORI - 25 (Solution)

1	3	4	4
4	4	3	2
2	4	1	3
3	2	4	2

HITORI - 26 (Solution)

2	1	4	1
1	2	3	3
4	1	4	3
4	4	1	2

HITORI - 27 (Solution)

3	1	2	4
1	4	3	4
3	2	1	3
2	3	4	1

HITORI - 28 (Solution)

3	2	2	4
1	4	2	3
3	1	3	2
2	3	3	1

HITORI - 29 (Solution)

4	4	3	2
2	3	1	4
1	4	2	3
3	2	1	1

HITORI - 30 (Solution)

1	3	4	4
4	3	3	1
2	4	1	4
2	1	2	4

SOLVE KAKURASU

HOW TO PLAY

The goal is to fill (color) some cells to satisfy the clues.

The numbers across the bottom and down the right are the clues. and equal the row and column totals for the colored cells.

The numbers across the top and down the left are the values for each of the cells in the rows and columns (the first cell in a row or column is worth 1. the second 2. the third 3. etc.).

KAKURASU - 1

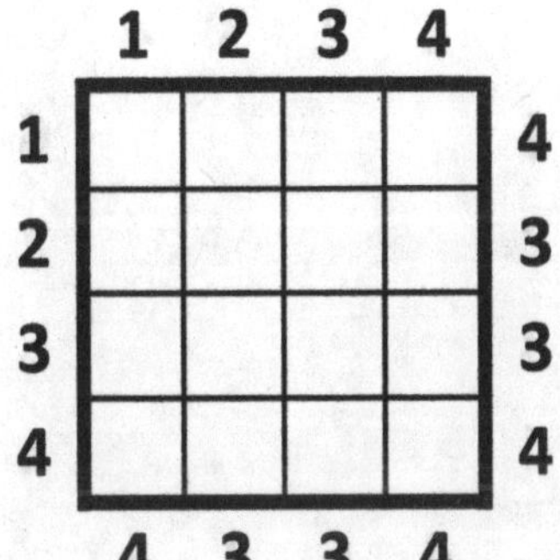

KAKURASU - 2

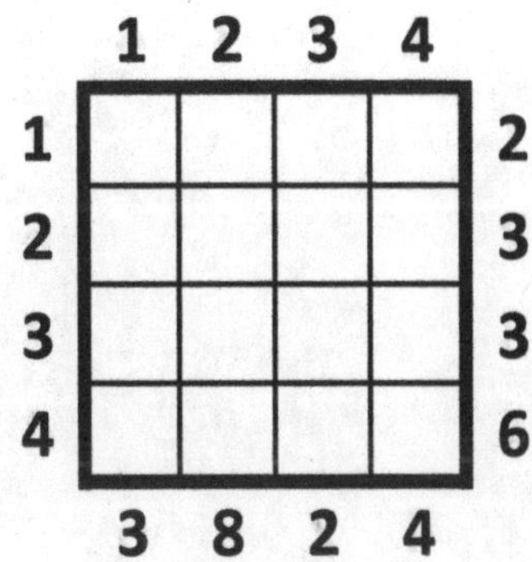

KAKURASU - 3

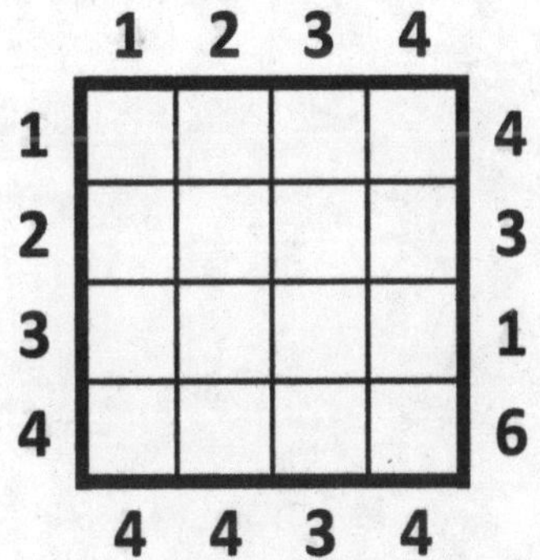

KAKURASU - 4

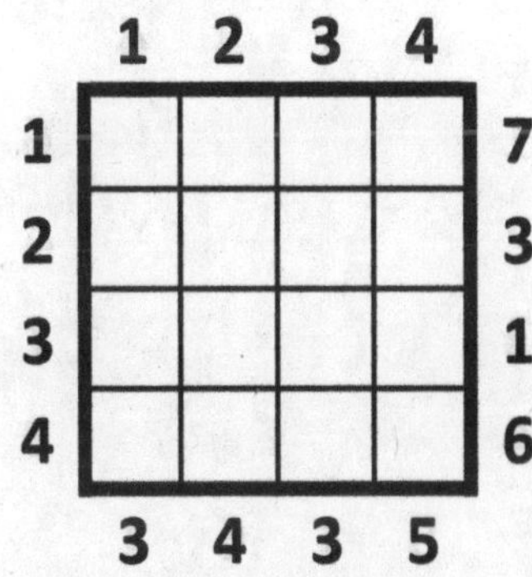

KAKURASU - 5

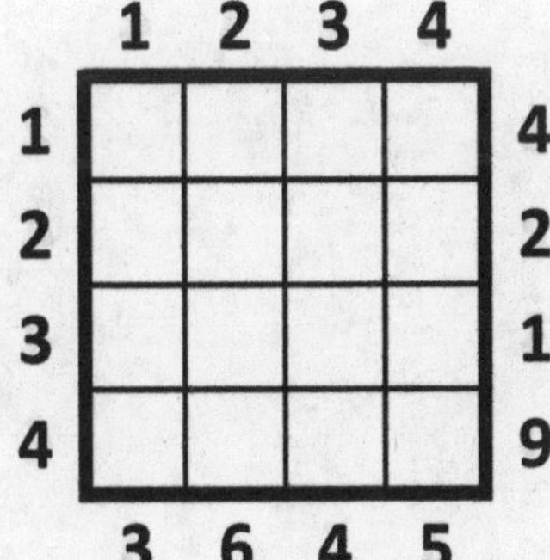

KAKURASU - 6

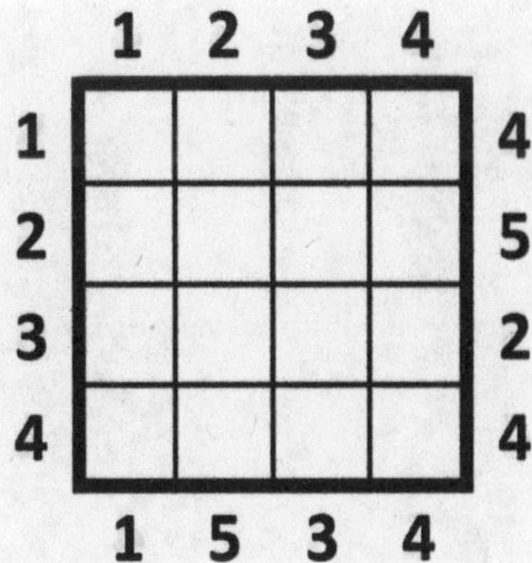

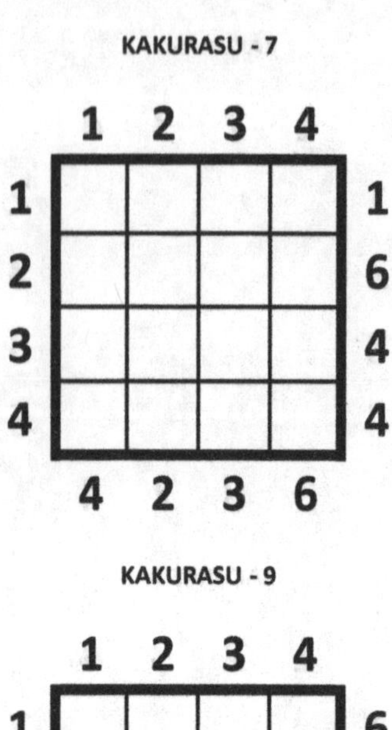

KAKURASU - 7

	1	2	3	4	
1					1
2					6
3					4
4					4
	4	2	3	6	

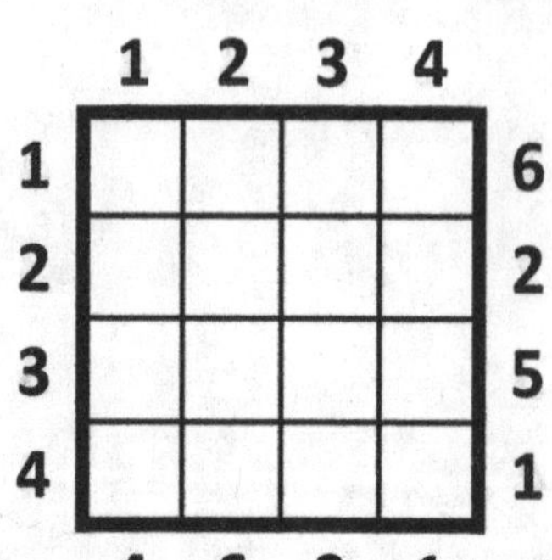

KAKURASU - 8

	1	2	3	4	
1					6
2					2
3					5
4					1
	4	6	3	1	

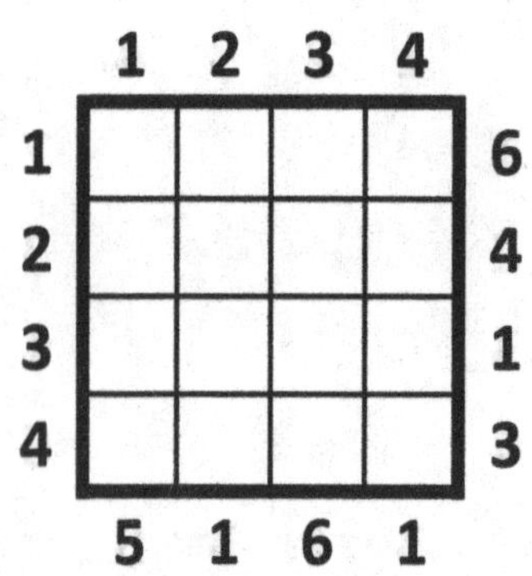

KAKURASU - 9

	1	2	3	4	
1					6
2					4
3					1
4					3
	5	1	6	1	

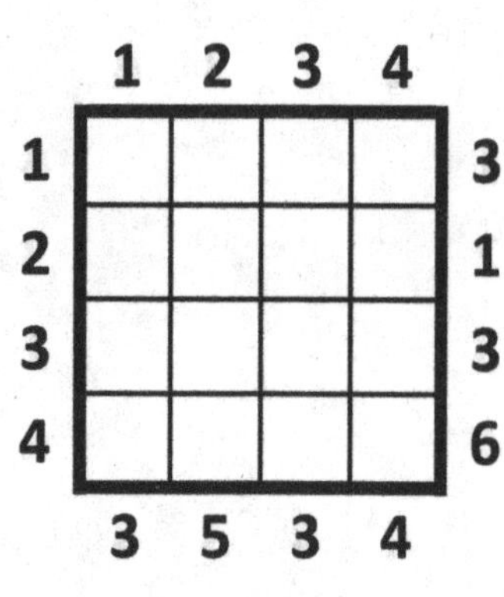

KAKURASU - 10

	1	2	3	4	
1					3
2					1
3					3
4					6
	3	5	3	4	

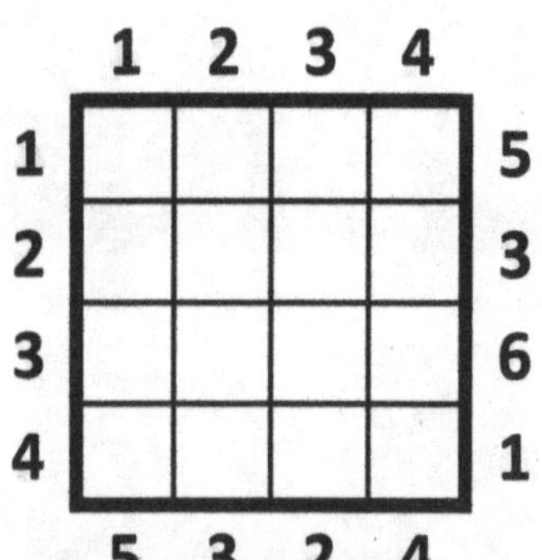

KAKURASU - 11

	1	2	3	4	
1					5
2					3
3					6
4					1
	5	3	2	4	

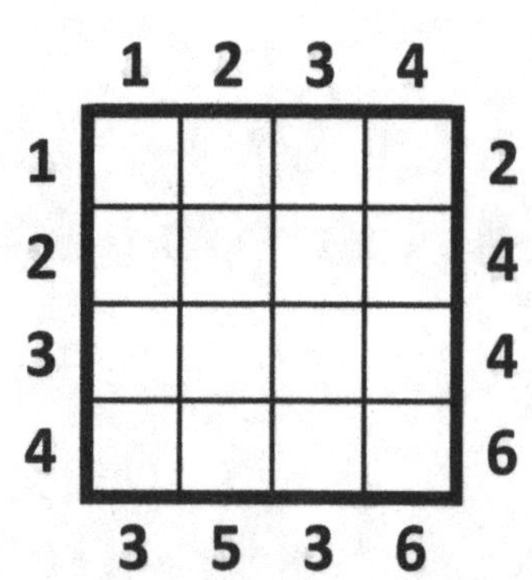

KAKURASU - 12

	1	2	3	4	
1					2
2					4
3					4
4					6
	3	5	3	6	

KAKURASU - 13

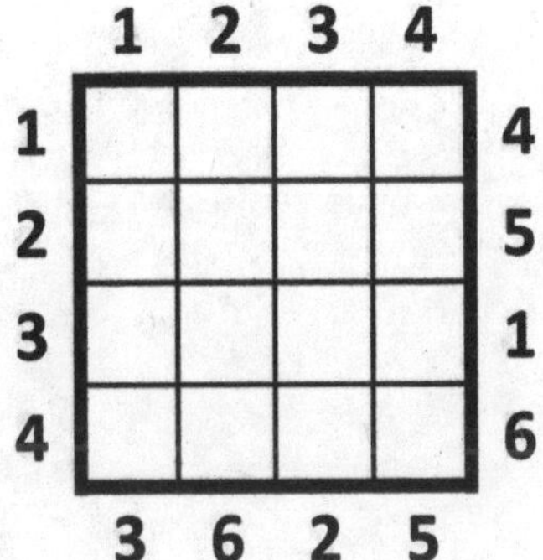

KAKURASU - 14

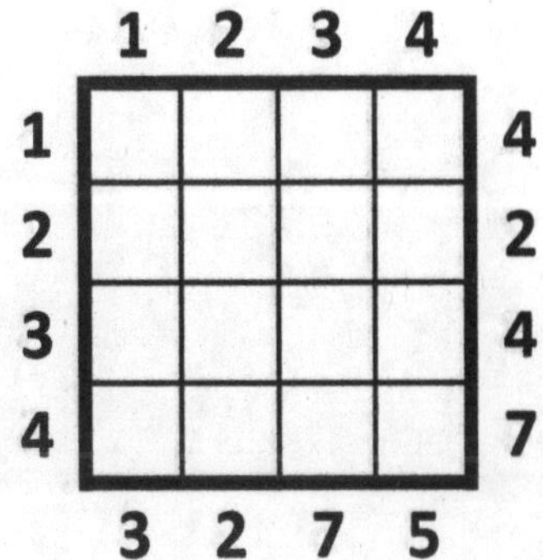

KAKURASU - 15

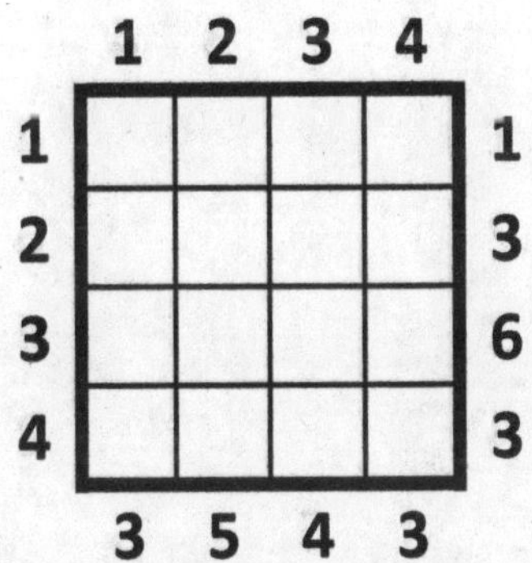

KAKURASU - 16

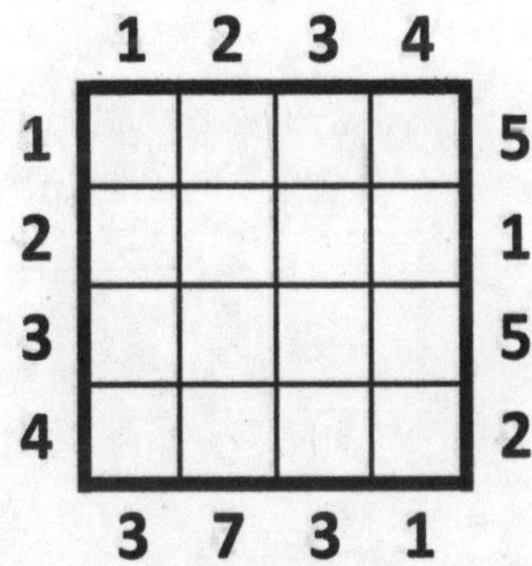

KAKURASU - 17

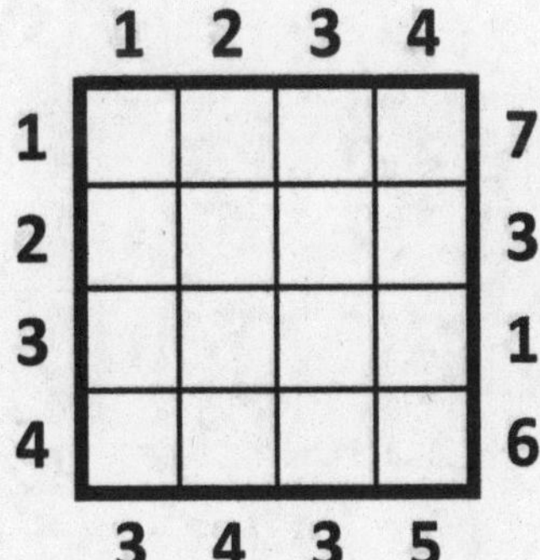

KAKURASU - 18

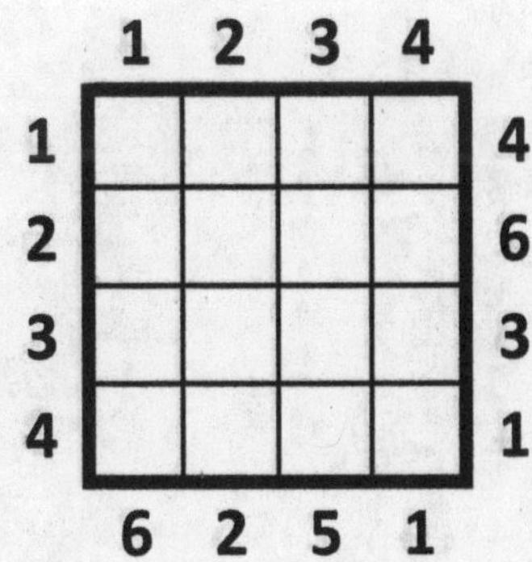

KAKURASU - 19

KAKURASU - 20

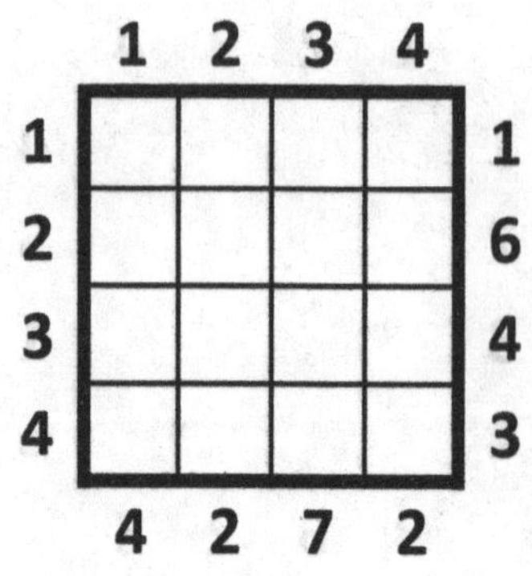

KAKURASU - 21

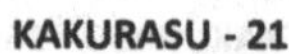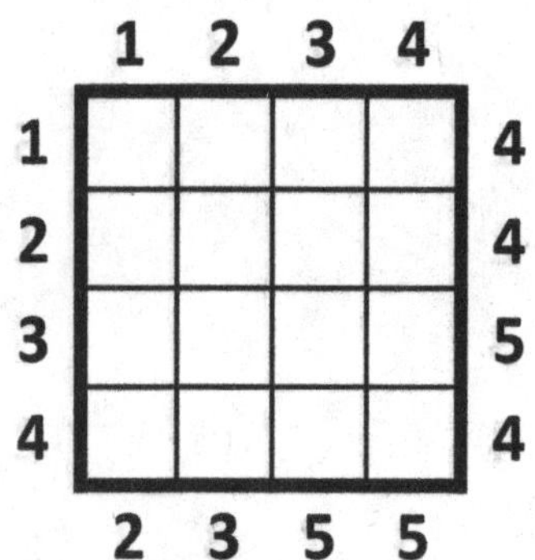

KAKURASU - 22

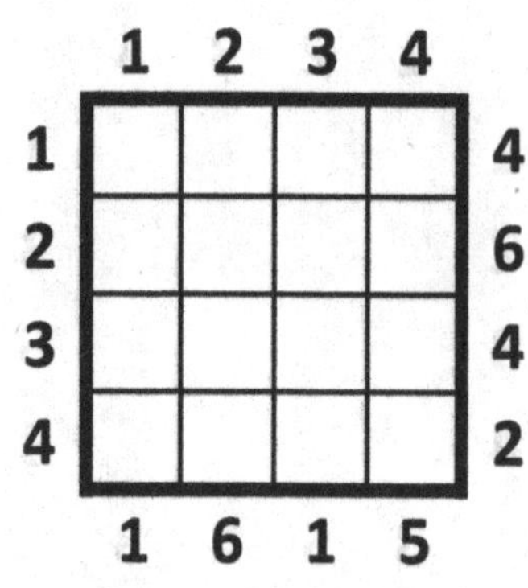

KAKURASU - 23

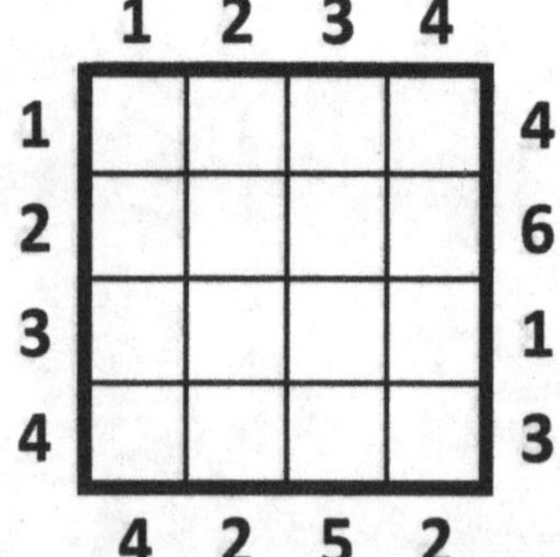

KAKURASU - 24

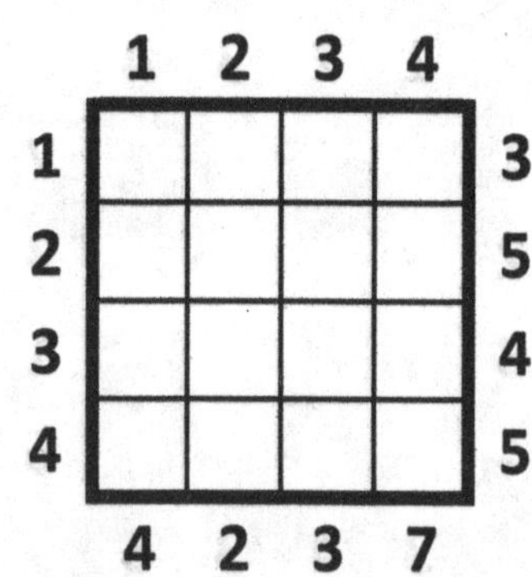

KAKURASU - 25

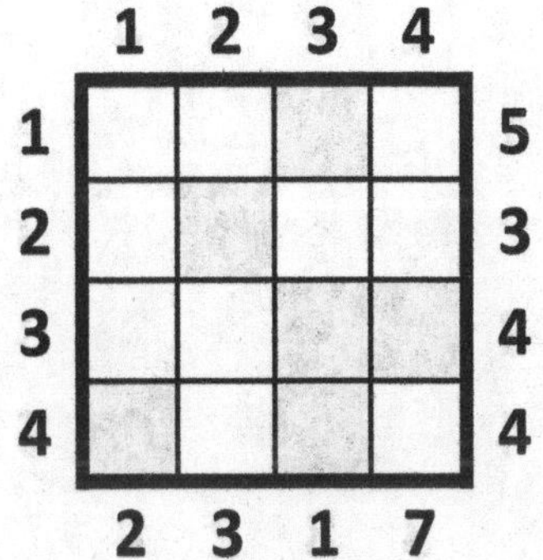

KAKURASU - 26

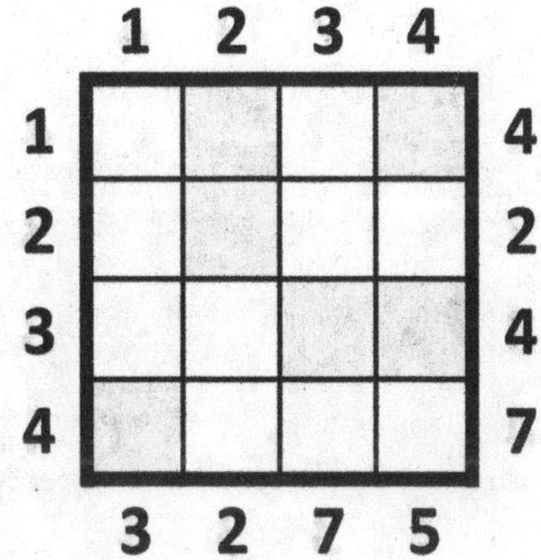

KAKURASU - 27

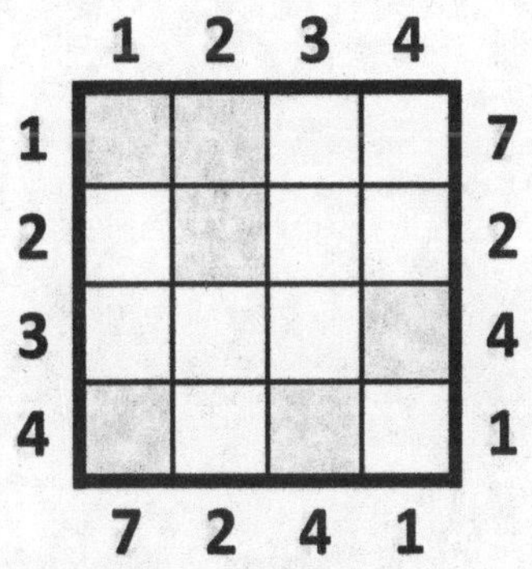

KAKURASU - 28

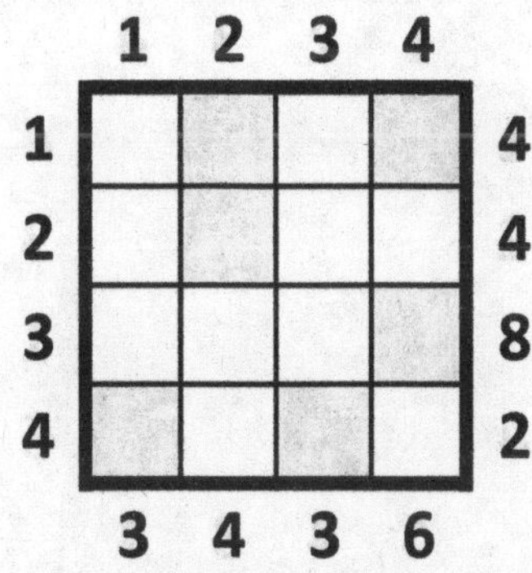

KAKURASU - 29

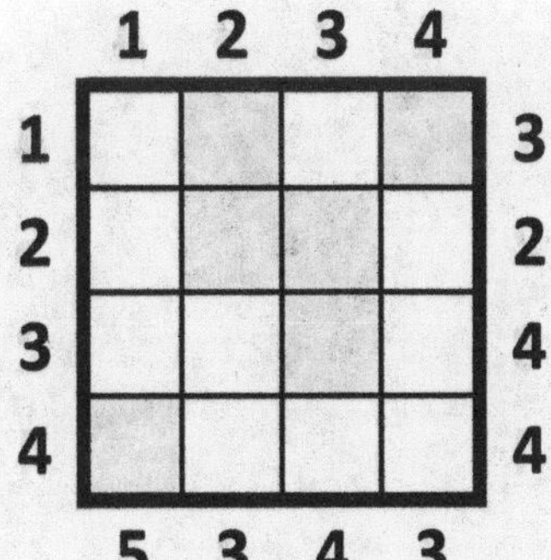

KAKURASU - 30

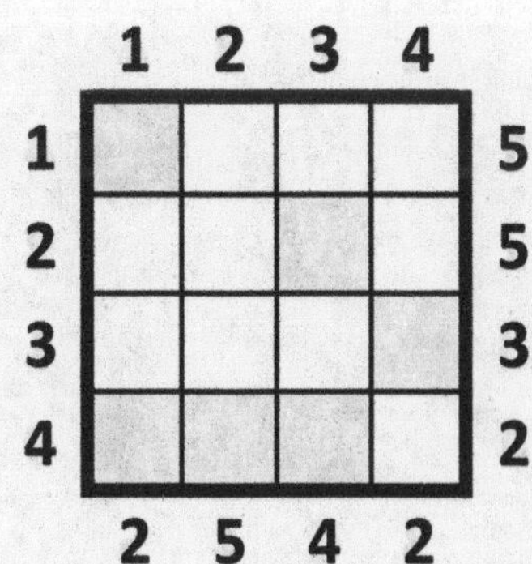

KAKURASU - 1 (Solution)

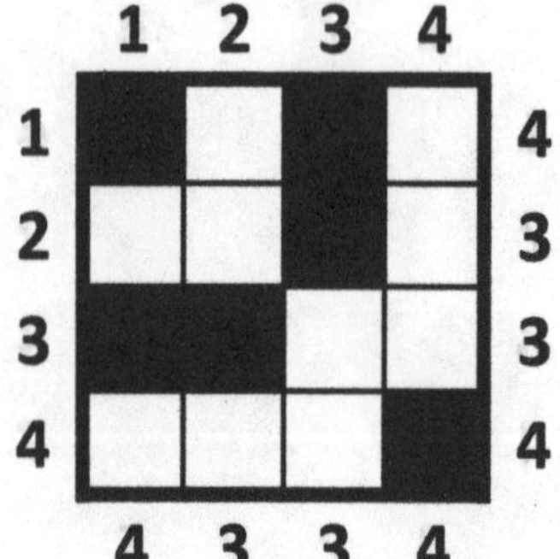

KAKURASU - 2 (Solution)

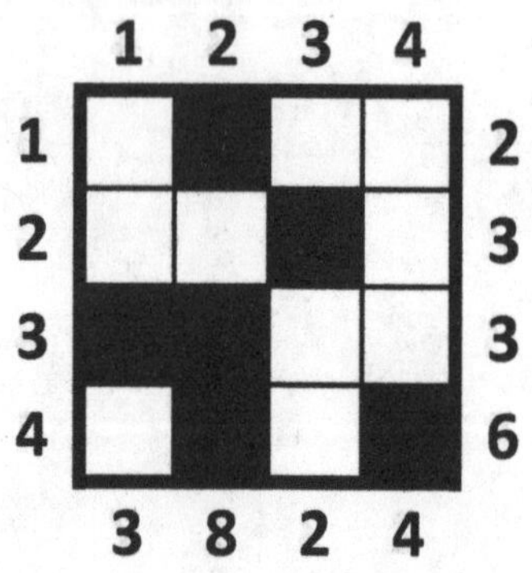

KAKURASU - 3 (Solution)

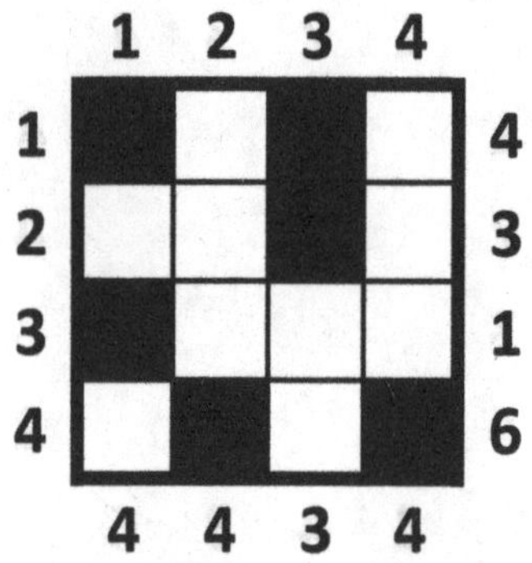

KAKURASU - 4 (Solution)

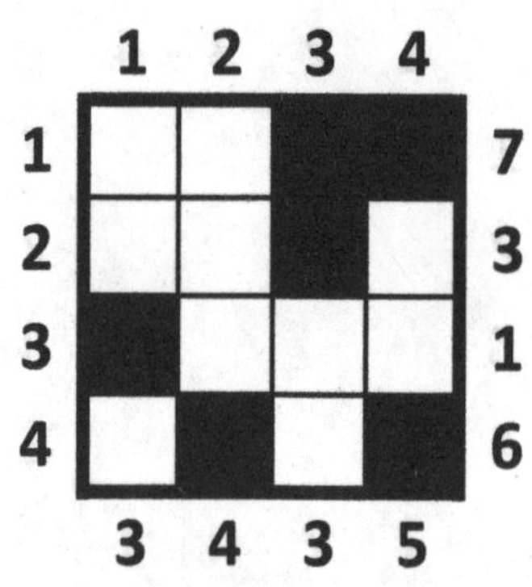

KAKURASU - 5 (Solution)

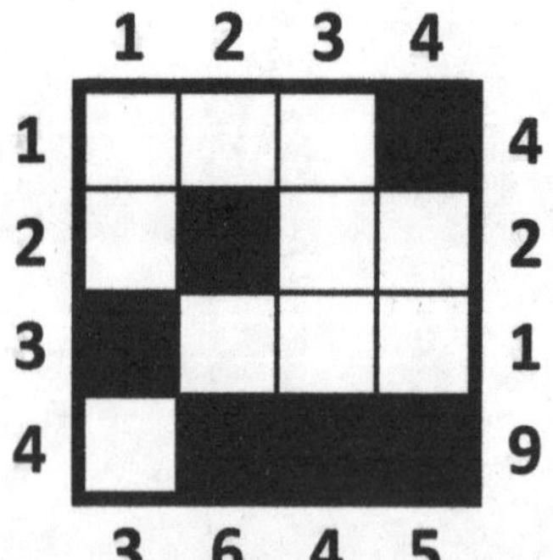

KAKURASU - 6 (Solution)

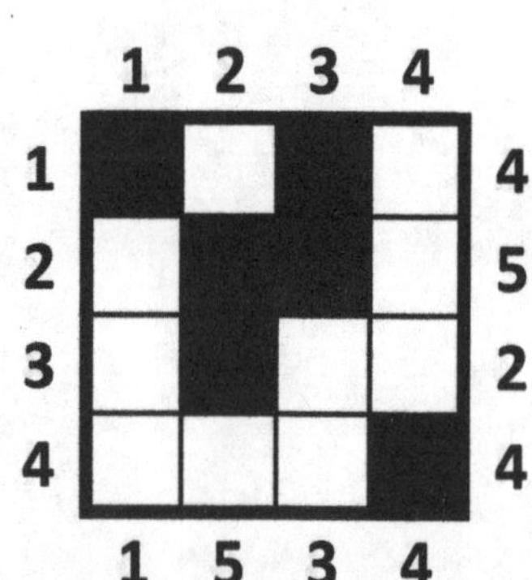

KAKURASU - 7 (Solution)

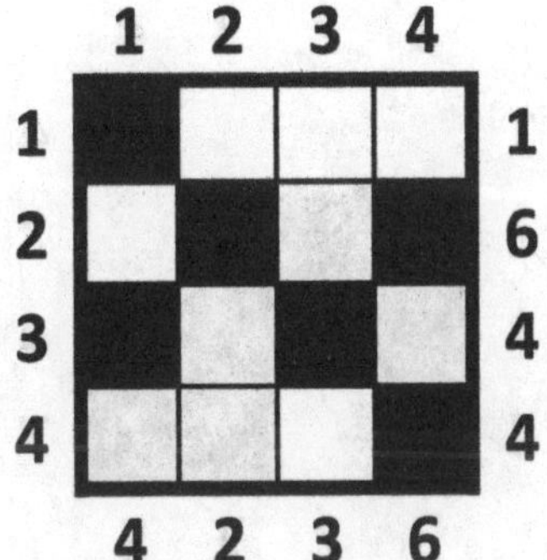

KAKURASU - 8 (Solution)

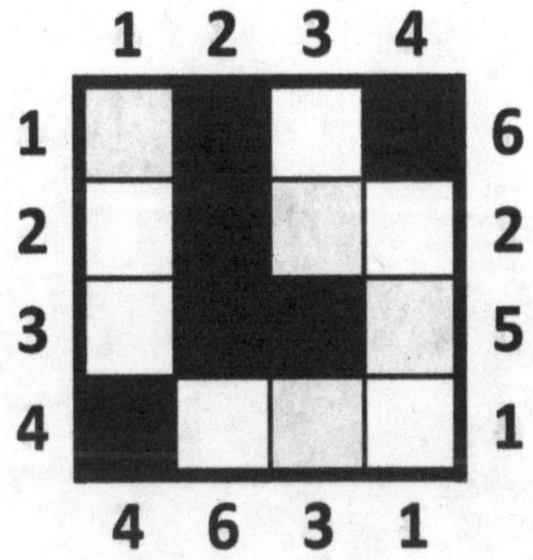

KAKURASU - 9 (Solution)

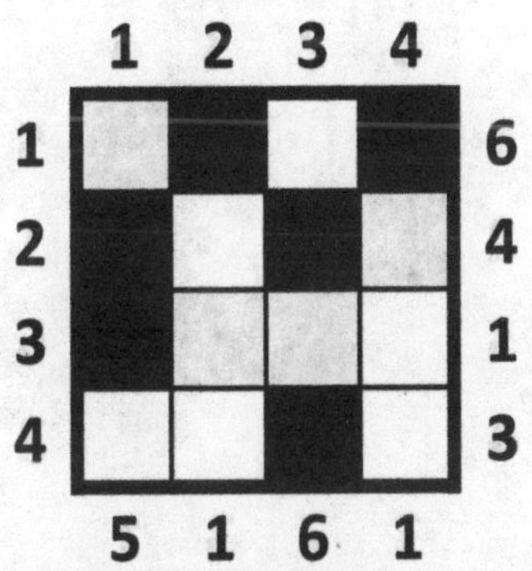

KAKURASU - 10 (Solution)

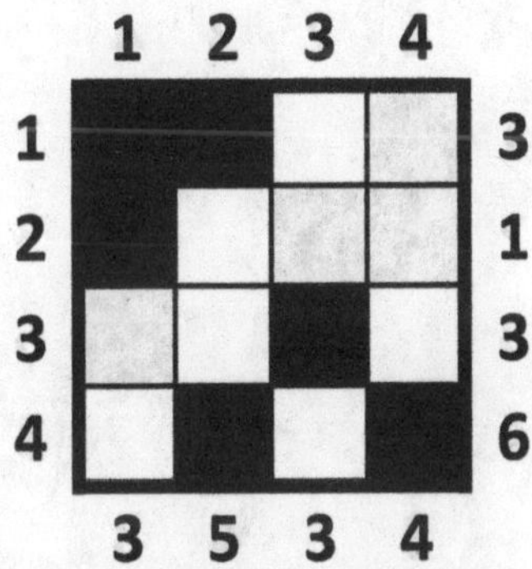

KAKURASU - 11 (Solution)

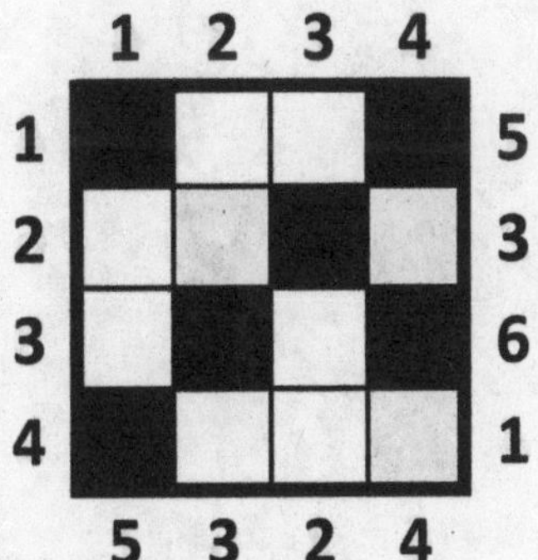

KAKURASU - 12 (Solution)

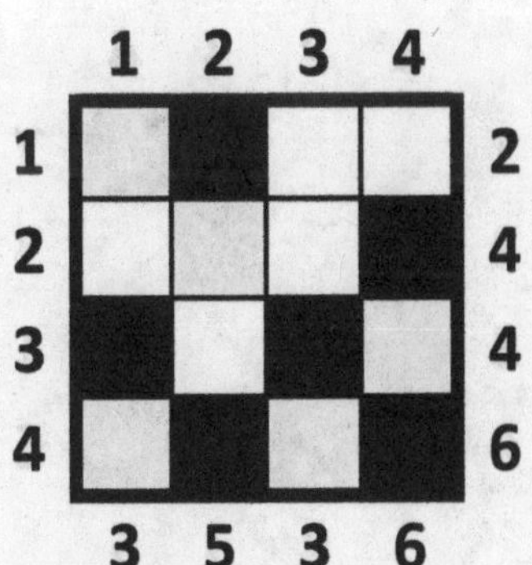

KAKURASU - 13 (Solution)

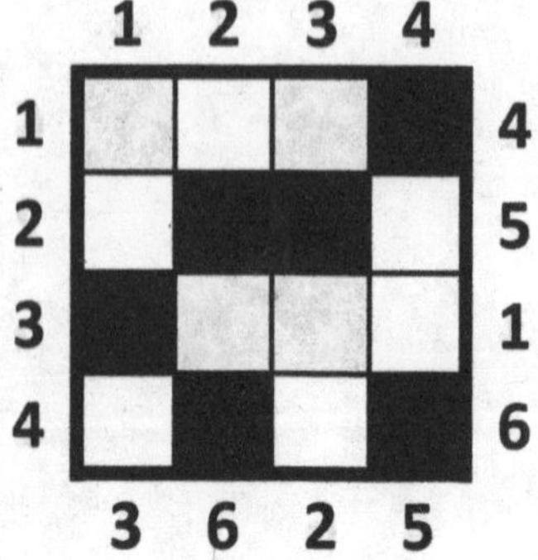

KAKURASU - 14 (Solution)

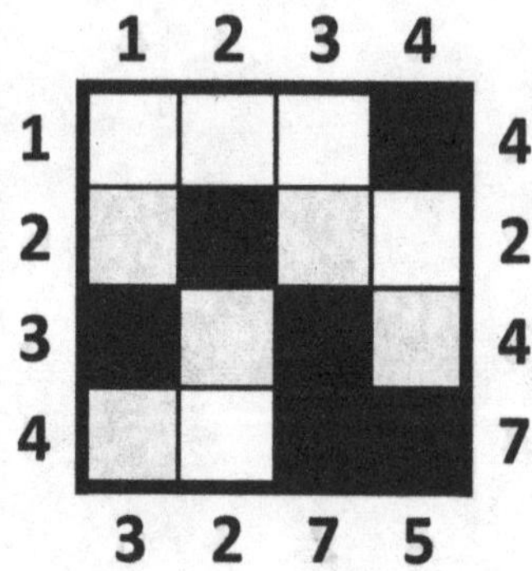

KAKURASU - 15 (Solution)

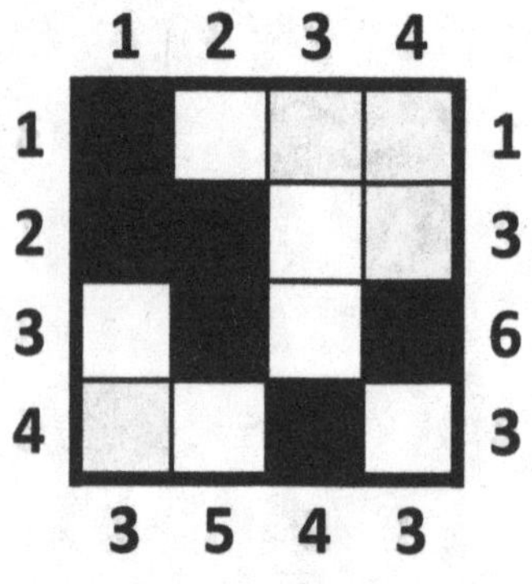

KAKURASU - 16 (Solution)

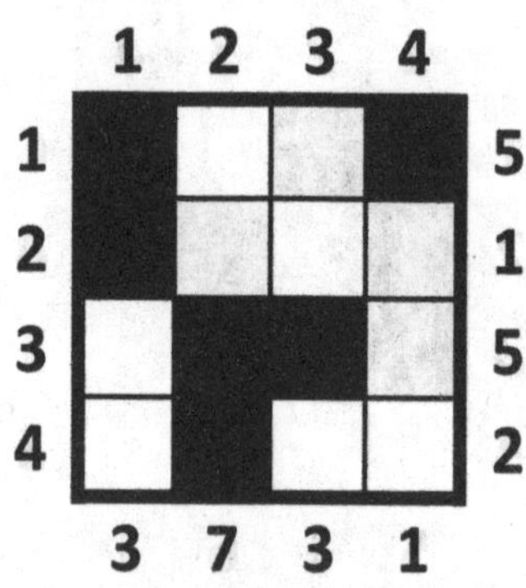

KAKURASU - 17 (Solution)

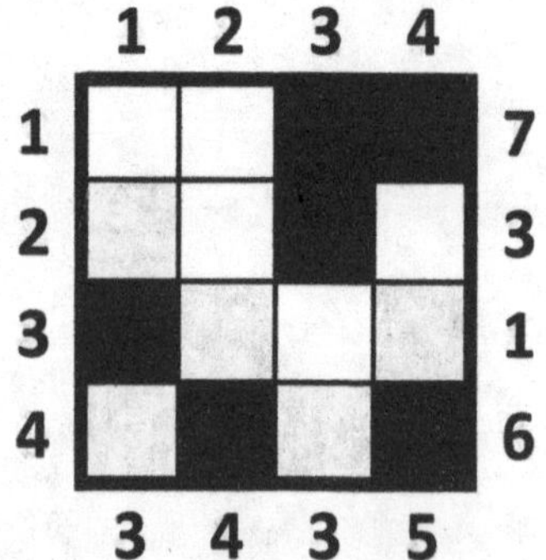

KAKURASU - 18 (Solution)

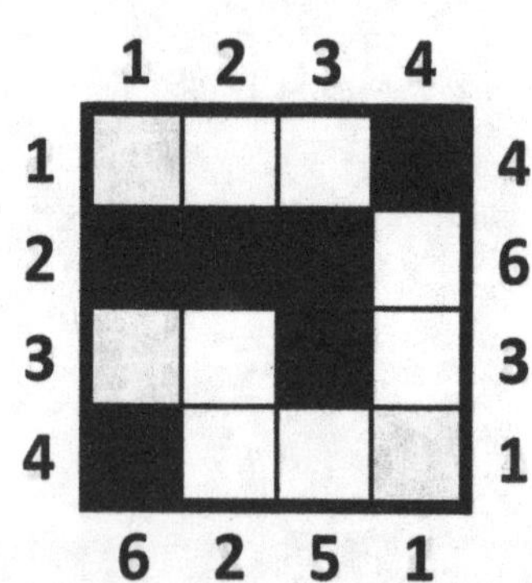

KAKURASU - 19 (Solution)

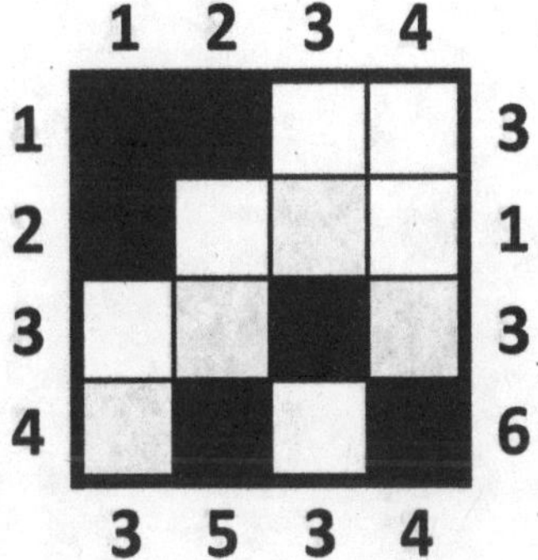

KAKURASU - 20 (Solution)

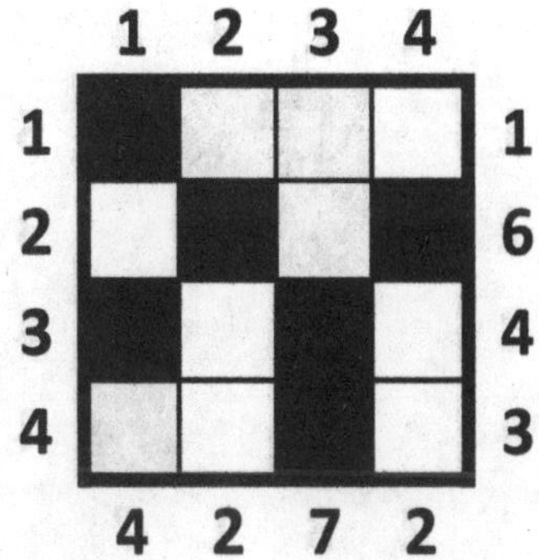

KAKURASU - 21 (Solution)

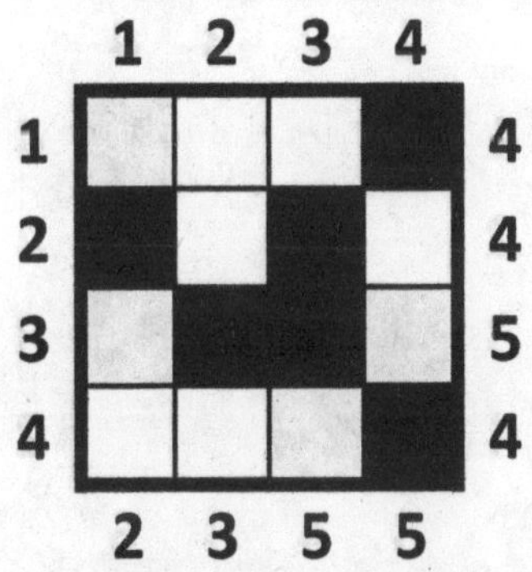

KAKURASU - 22 (Solution)

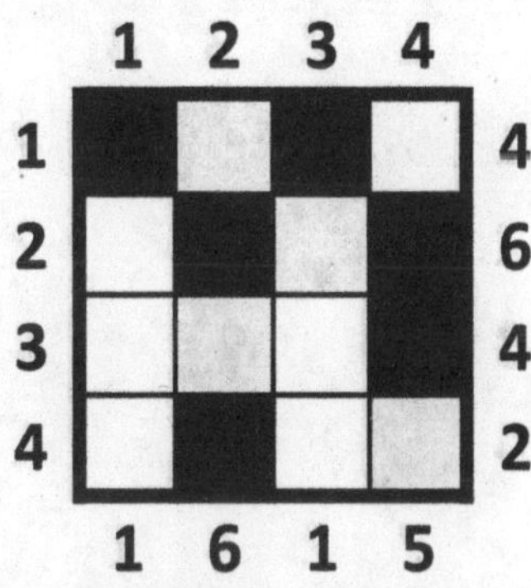

KAKURASU - 23 (Solution)

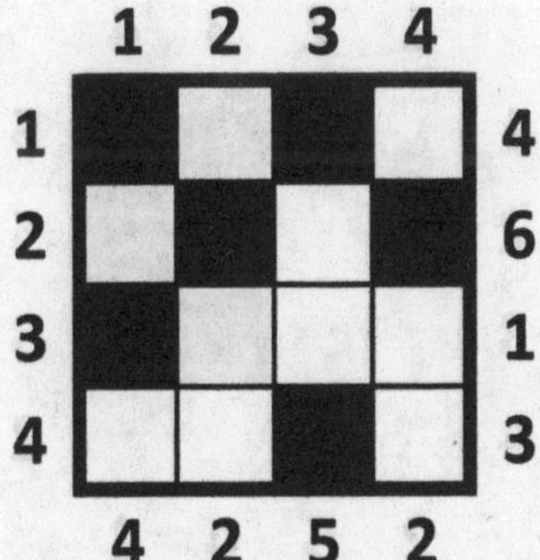

KAKURASU - 24 (Solution)

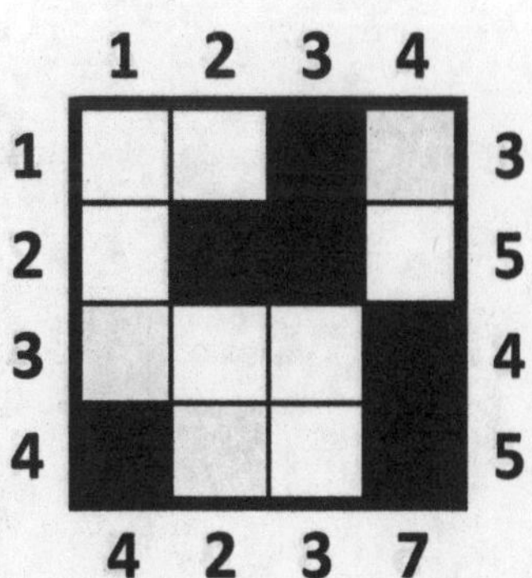

KAKURASU - 25 (Solution)

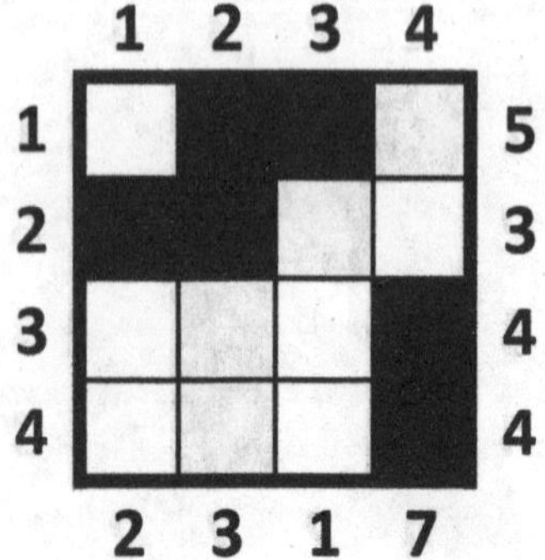

KAKURASU - 26 (Solution)

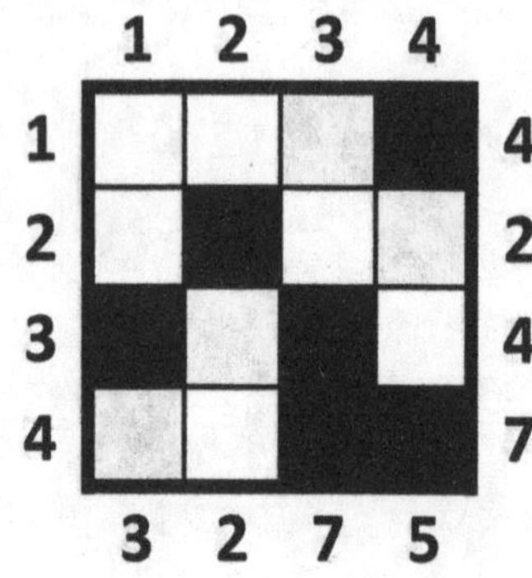

KAKURASU - 27 (Solution)

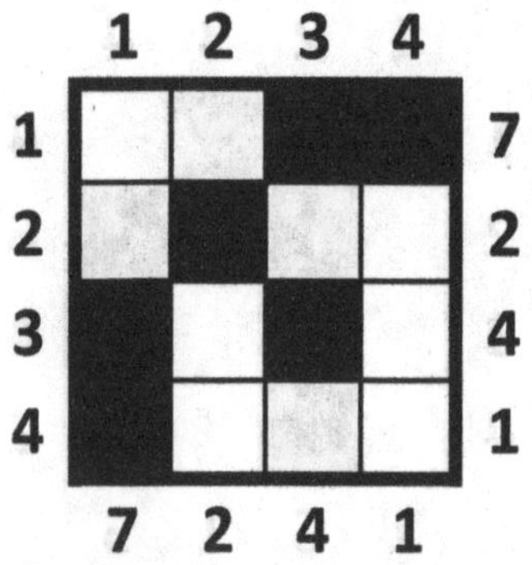

KAKURASU - 28 (Solution)

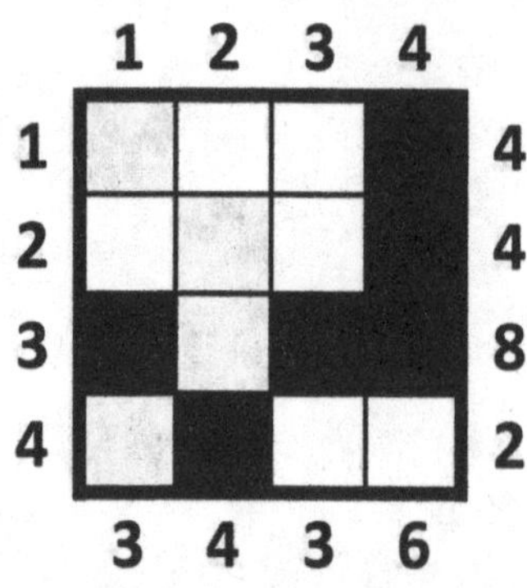

KAKURASU - 29 (Solution)

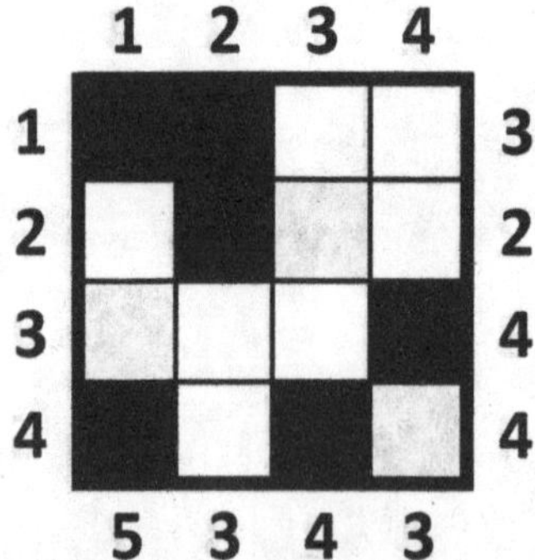

KAKURASU - 30 (Solution)

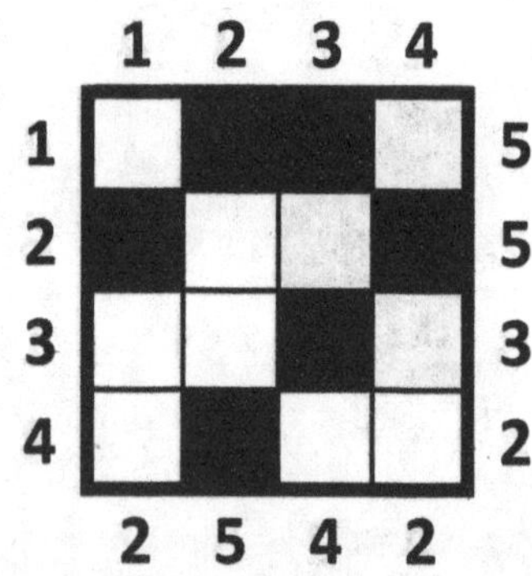

CHALLENGING NUMBER PLACE
HOW TO PLAY

Number Place is played on a rectangular grid, in which some cells of the grid are shaded.

Additionally, external to the grid, several numeric values are given, some denoted as horizontal, and some denoted as vertical.

The puzzle functions as a simple numeric crossword puzzle.

The object is to fill in the empty cells with single digits, such that the given numeric values appear on the grid in the orientation specified.

NUMBER PLACE - 1

ACROSS	DOWN
3122, 332, 22	31, 222, 22

NUMBER PLACE - 2

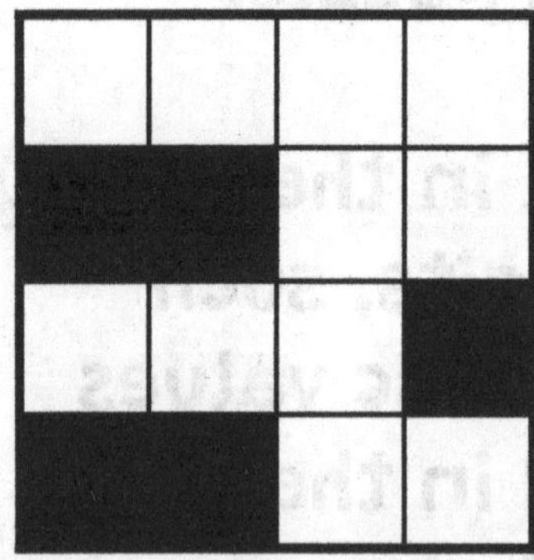

ACROSS	DOWN
32, 22, 122	32, 12, 2221

NUMBER PLACE - 3

ACROSS	DOWN
2132, 212, 11, 33	3321, 23

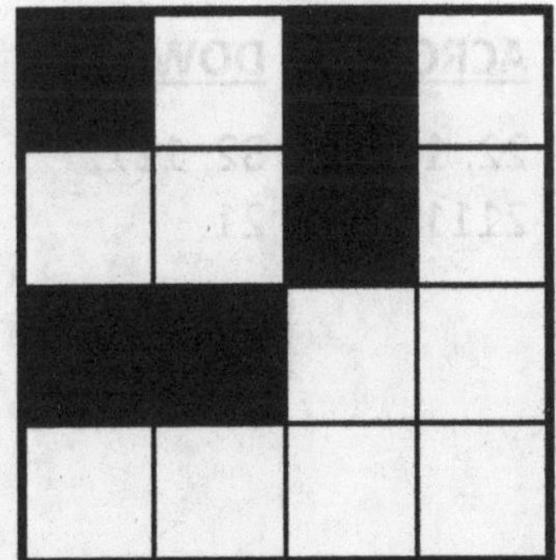

ACROSS

31, 33, 1113

DOWN

133, 1332, 31

NUMBER PLACE - 5

ACROSS

12, 2111, 31, 21

DOWN

3111, 12, 11

NUMBER PLACE - 6

ACROSS

2121, 23, 22

DOWN

32, 1331, 22

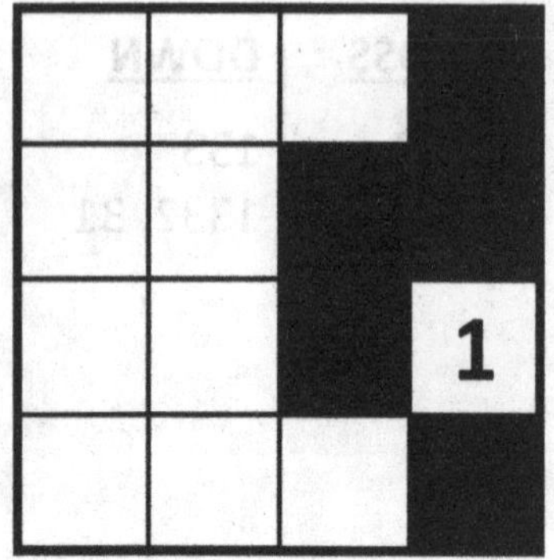

ACROSS	DOWN
33, 13, 121, 123	1131, 2332

ACROSS	DOWN
312, 33, 32, 3221	322, 33, 13, 23

ACROSS	DOWN
22, 12, 2111	32, 121, 21

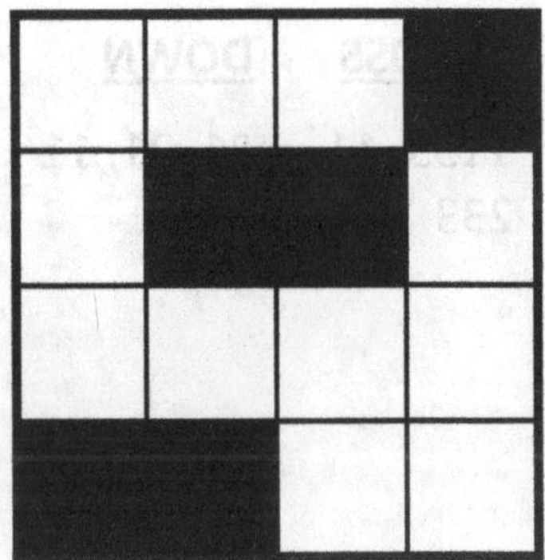

ACROSS

2323, 332, 23

DOWN

312, 233, 22

NUMBER PLACE - 11

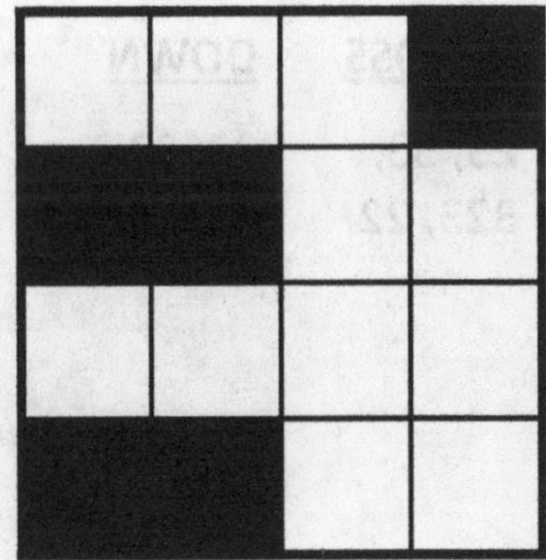

ACROSS

2232, 23, 21

DOWN

21, 2213

NUMBER PLACE - 12

ACROSS

22, 1123, 133, 13

DOWN

3221, 233

NUMBER PLACE - 13

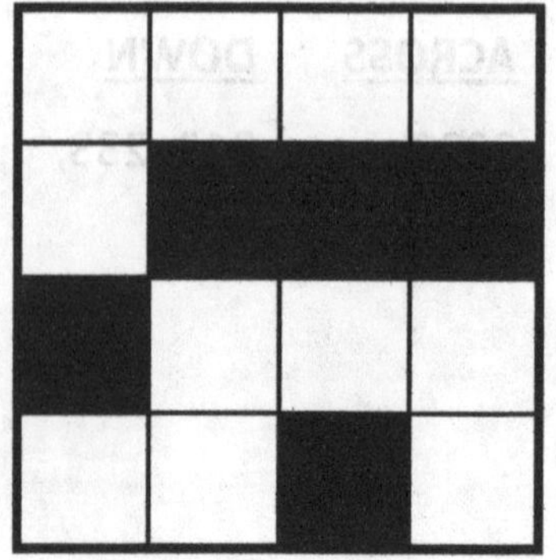

ACROSS	DOWN
1133, 11, 233	31, 21, 11

NUMBER PLACE - 14

ACROSS	DOWN
2333, 112, 31	33, 233, 31, 22

NUMBER PLACE - 15

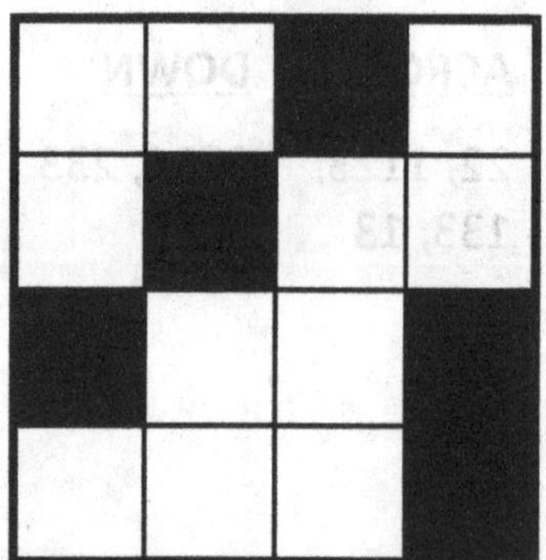

ACROSS	DOWN
23, 33, 323, 22	32, 22, 12, 233

NUMBER PLACE - 1 (Solution)

ACROSS	DOWN
3122, 332, 22	31, 222, 22

NUMBER PLACE - 2 (Solution)

ACROSS	DOWN
32, 22, 122	32, 12, 2221

NUMBER PLACE - 3 (Solution)

ACROSS	DOWN
2132, 212, 11, 33	3321, 23

NUMBER PLACE - 4 (Solution)

ACROSS

31, 33, 1113

DOWN

133, 1332, 31

NUMBER PLACE - 5 (Solution)

ACROSS

12, 2111, 31, 21

DOWN

3111, 12, 11

NUMBER PLACE - 6 (Solution)

ACROSS

2121, 23, 22

DOWN

32, 1331, 22

NUMBER PLACE - 7 (Solution)

1	2	3	
1	3		
3	3		1
1	2	1	

ACROSS

33, 13, 121, 123

DOWN

1131, 2332

NUMBER PLACE - 8 (Solution)

	3	1	2
3	2		
3	2	2	1
		3	3

ACROSS

312, 33, 32, 3221

DOWN

322, 33, 13, 23

NUMBER PLACE - 9 (Solution)

	3		3
3		1	2
	2	2	
2	1	1	1

ACROSS

22, 12, 2111

DOWN

32, 121, 21

NUMBER PLACE - 10 (Solution)

3	3	2	■
1	■	■	2
2	3	2	3
■	■	2	3

ACROSS

2323, 332, 23

DOWN

312, 233, 22

NUMBER PLACE - 11 (Solution)

2	2	3	2
1	■	■	2
■	■	2	1
2	3	■	3

ACROSS

2232, 23, 21

DOWN

21, 2213

NUMBER PLACE - 12 (Solution)

1	3	3	■
■	■	2	2
1	1	2	3
■	■	1	3

ACROSS

22, 1123, 133, 13

DOWN

3221, 233

NUMBER PLACE - 13 (Solution)

1	1	3	3
1	■	■	■
■	2	3	3
1	1	■	1

ACROSS	DOWN
1133, 11, 233	31, 21, 11

NUMBER PLACE - 14 (Solution)

■	1	1	2
2	■	■	3
2	3	3	3
■	3	1	■

ACROSS	DOWN
2333, 112, 31	33, 233, 31, 22

NUMBER PLACE - 15 (Solution)

2	3	■	1
2	■	2	2
■	3	3	■
3	2	3	■

ACROSS	DOWN
23, 33, 323, 22	32, 22, 12, 233

SHIKAKU LOGIC

HOW TO PLAY

The goal is to fill grids cells by numbers in order to accomplish the following

1. Divide the grid into blocks.

2. Each block contains only one number.

3. The number indicates how many cells are contained in the blocks.

SHIKAKU - 1

4		2	2
4		4	

SHIKAKU - 2

4		2	3
3			
2		2	

SHIKAKU - 3

4		4	
2		2	
2		2	

SHIKAKU - 4

4		2	2
4		4	

SHIKAKU - 5

4		4	
2		2	
2		2	

SHIKAKU - 6

4		3	4
2			
3			

SHIKAKU - 7

4			4
4		4	

SHIKAKU - 8

4		4	
2		4	
2			

SHIKAKU - 9

4		4	
4		2	2

SHIKAKU - 10

4		4	
2		2	
2		2	

SHIKAKU - 11

4		2	2
4		2	2

SHIKAKU - 12

4		2	2
4		2	2

SHIKAKU - 13

6		4	
		4	
2			

SHIKAKU - 14

4		2	4
4		2	

SHIKAKU - 15

4		4	
2		2	
2		2	

SHIKAKU - 16

		2	2
8		2	2

SHIKAKU - 17

6			2
4		2	2

SHIKAKU - 18

4		6	
2			
2		2	

SHIKAKU - 19

4		2	
			4
4		2	

SHIKAKU - 20

		3	
6			4
3			

SHIKAKU - 21

4		2	2
4		2	2

SHIKAKU - 22

4		4	
4		2	2

SHIKAKU - 23

4		4	
4		2	
		2	

SHIKAKU - 24

4		8	
2			
2			

SHIKAKU - 25

4		2	4
3			
3			

SHIKAKU - 26

4		4	
4		4	

SHIKAKU - 27

4		4	
2		2	
2		2	

SHIKAKU - 28

4		2	2
2		2	2
2			

SHIKAKU - 29

6		4	
		2	
2		2	

SHIKAKU - 30

4		4	
4		2	
		2	

SHIKAKU - 1 (Solution)

4	4	2	2
4	4	2	2
4	4	4	4
4	4	4	4

SHIKAKU - 2 (Solution)

4	4	2	3
4	4	2	3
3	3	3	3
2	2	2	2

SHIKAKU - 3 (Solution)

4	4	4	4
4	4	4	4
2	2	2	2
2	2	2	2

SHIKAKU - 4 (Solution)

4	4	2	2
4	4	2	2
4	4	4	4
4	4	4	4

SHIKAKU - 5 (Solution)

4	4	4	4
4	4	4	4
2	2	2	2
2	2	2	2

SHIKAKU - 6 (Solution)

4	4	3	4
4	4	3	4
2	2	3	4
3	3	3	4

SHIKAKU - 7 (Solution)

4	4	4	4
4	4	4	4
4	4	4	4
4	4	4	4

SHIKAKU - 8 (Solution)

4	4	4	4
4	4	4	4
2	2	4	4
2	2	4	4

SHIKAKU - 9 (Solution)

4	4	4	4
4	4	4	4
4	4	2	2
4	4	2	2

SHIKAKU - 10 (Solution)

4	4	4	4
4	4	4	4
2	2	2	2
2	2	2	2

SHIKAKU - 11 (Solution)

4	4	2	2
4	4	2	2
4	4	2	2
4	4	2	2

SHIKAKU - 12 (Solution)

4	4	2	2
4	4	2	2
4	4	2	2
4	4	2	2

SHIKAKU - 13 (Solution)

6	6	4	4
6	6	4	4
6	6	4	4
2	2	4	4

SHIKAKU - 14 (Solution)

4	4	2	4
4	4	2	4
4	4	2	4
4	4	2	4

SHIKAKU - 15 (Solution)

4	4	4	4
4	4	4	4
2	2	2	2
2	2	2	2

SHIKAKU - 16 (Solution)

8	8	2	2
8	8	2	2
8	8	2	2
8	8	2	2

SHIKAKU - 17 (Solution)

6	6	6	2
6	6	6	2
4	4	2	2
4	4	2	2

SHIKAKU - 18 (Solution)

4	4	6	6
4	4	6	6
2	2	6	6
2	2	2	2

SHIKAKU - 19 (Solution)

4	4	2	4
4	4	2	4
4	4	2	4
4	4	2	4

SHIKAKU - 20 (Solution)

6	6	3	4
6	6	3	4
6	6	3	4
3	3	3	4

SHIKAKU - 21 (Solution)

4	4	2	2
4	4	2	2
4	4	2	2
4	4	2	2

SHIKAKU - 22 (Solution)

4	4	4	4
4	4	4	4
4	4	2	2
4	4	2	2

SHIKAKU - 23 (Solution)

4	4	4	4
4	4	4	4
4	4	2	2
4	4	2	2

SHIKAKU - 24 (Solution)

4	4	8	8
4	4	8	8
2	2	8	8
2	2	8	8

SHIKAKU - 25 (Solution)

4	4	2	4
4	4	2	4
3	3	3	4
3	3	3	4

SHIKAKU - 26 (Solution)

4	4	4	4
4	4	4	4
4	4	4	4
4	4	4	4

SHIKAKU - 27 (Solution)

4	4	4	4
4	4	4	4
2	2	2	2
2	2	2	2

SHIKAKU - 28 (Solution)

4	4	2	2
4	4	2	2
2	2	2	2
2	2	2	2

SHIKAKU - 29 (Solution)

6	6	4	4
6	6	4	4
6	6	2	2
2	2	2	2

SHIKAKU - 30 (Solution)

4	4	4	4
4	4	4	4
4	4	2	2
4	4	2	2

2-PLAYERS BRAIN TEASER

HOW TO PLAY

The game is a two-player game, in which the players choose a color pen or pencil and then take turns 'dropping' colored discs by highlighting a circle on the game.

The two players alternate turns dropping one of their discs at a time into a column, until one of the player achieves a column, row or diagonal four in a row, and wins the game.

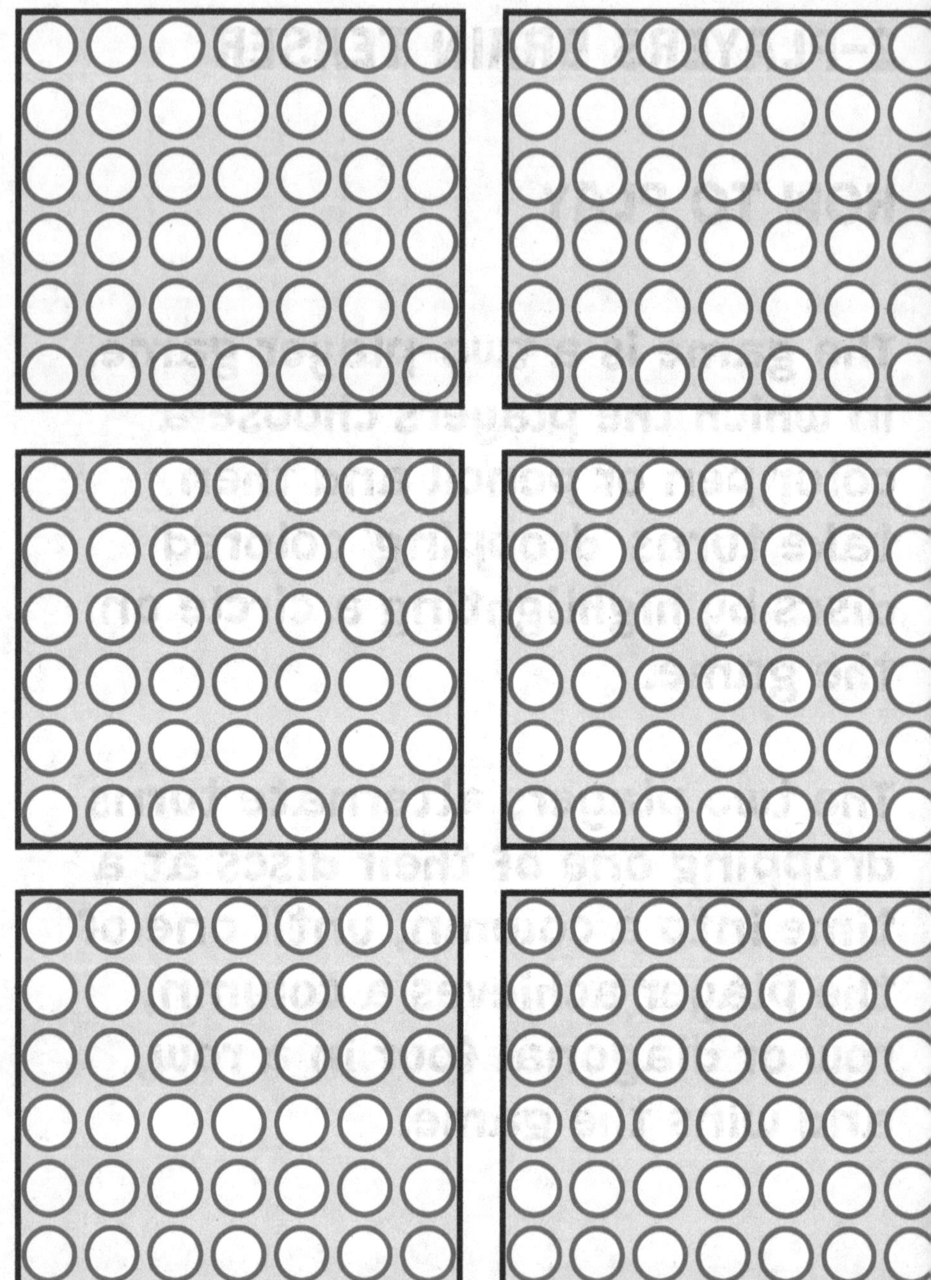

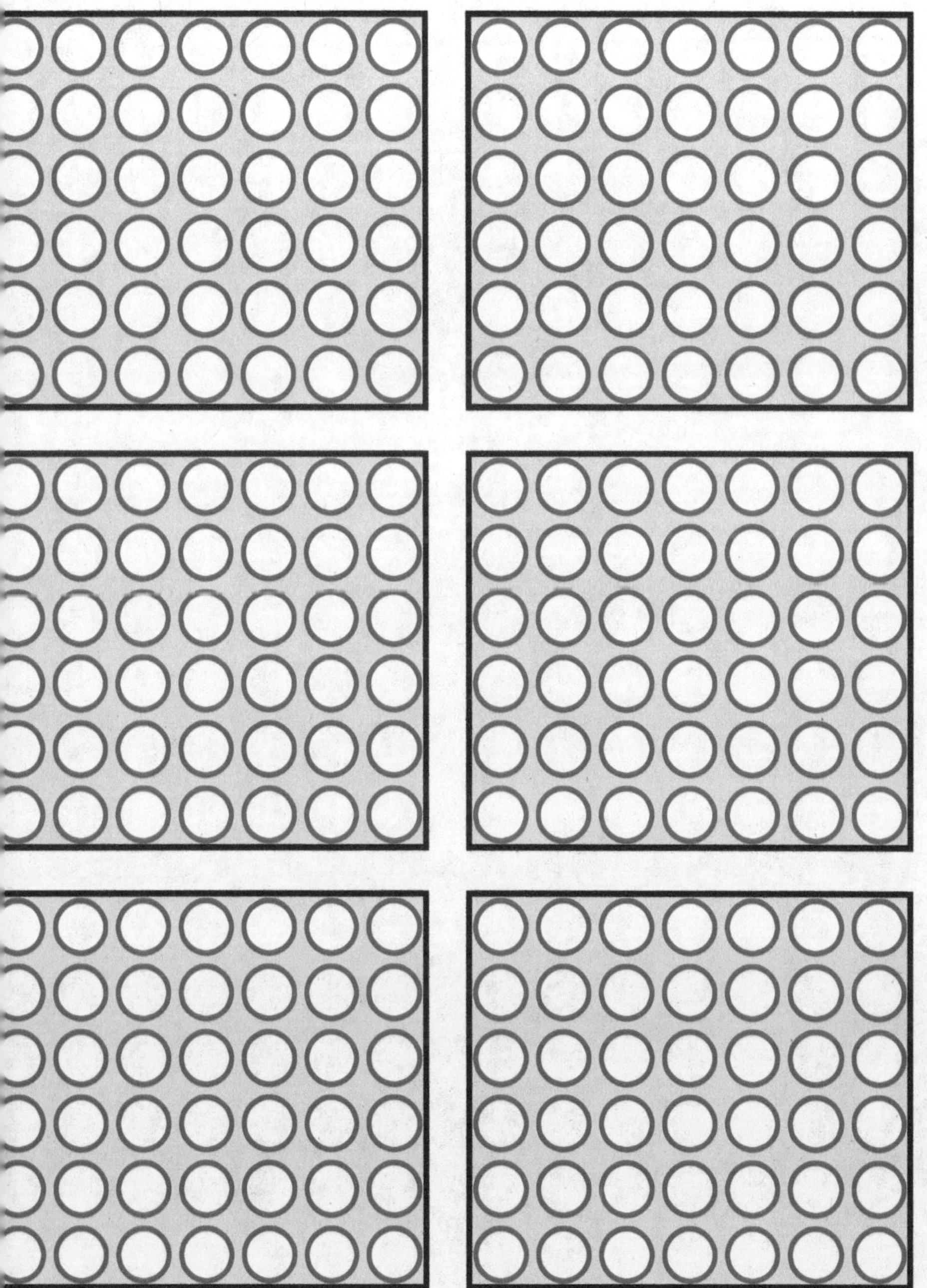

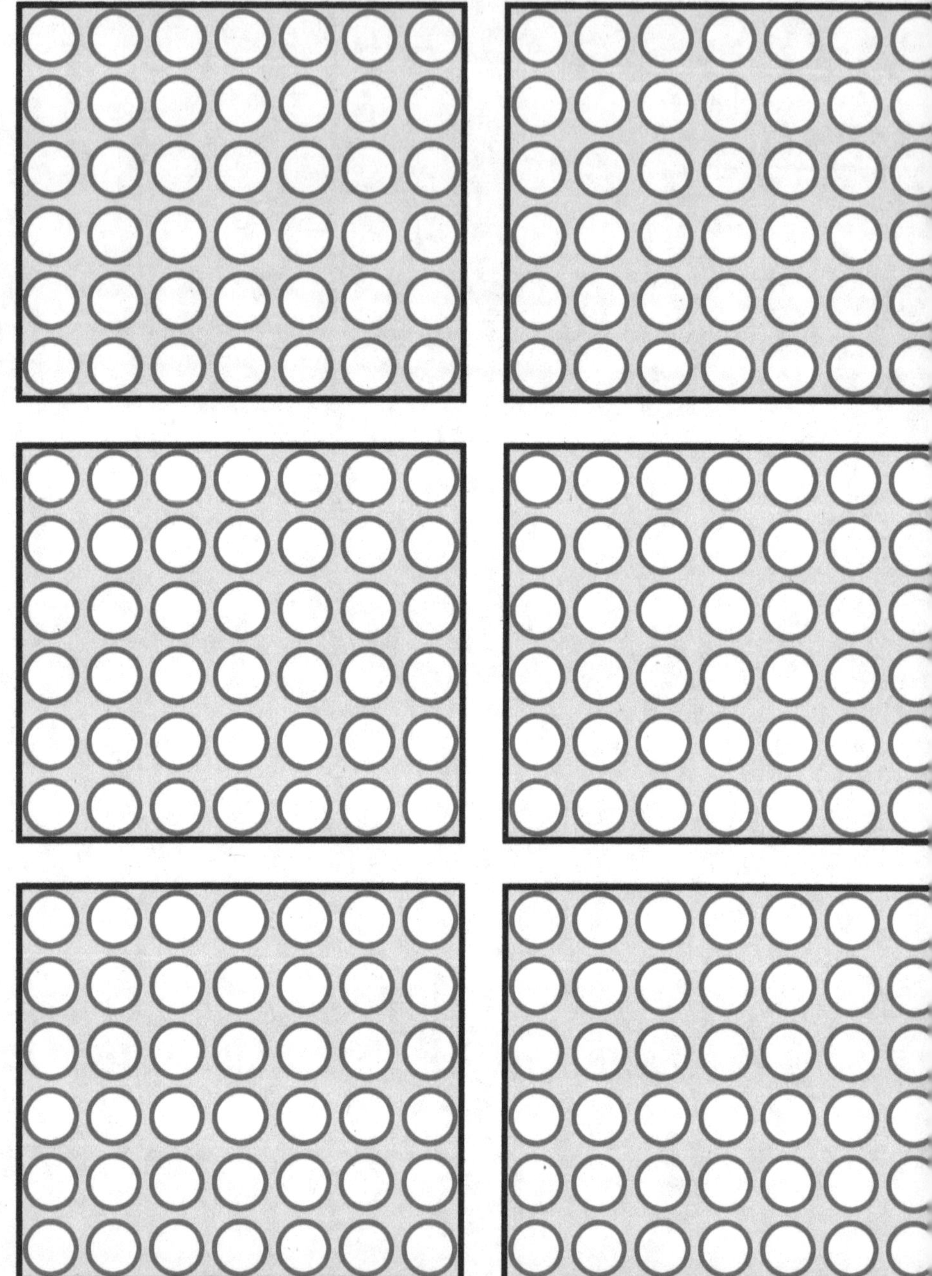

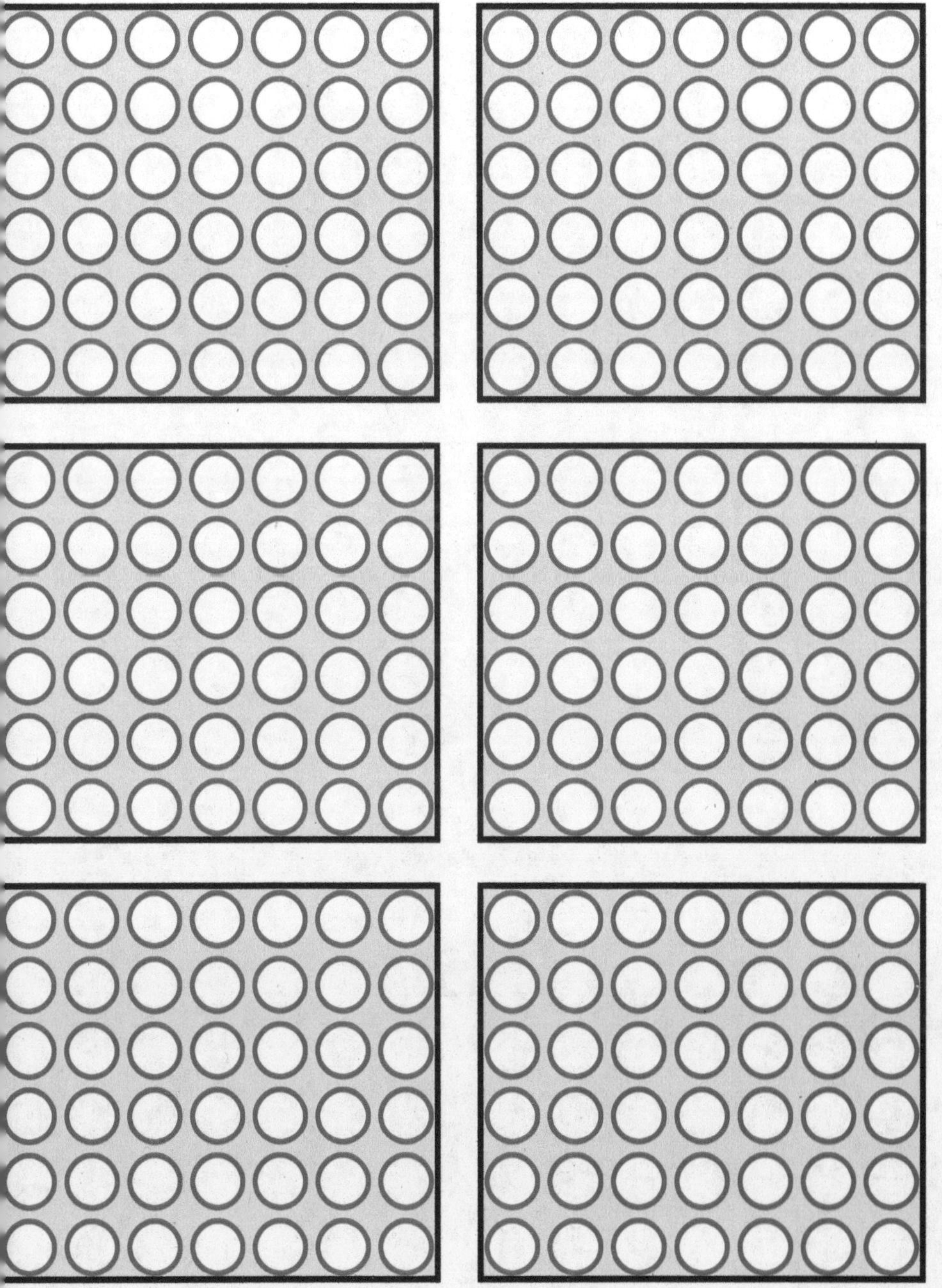

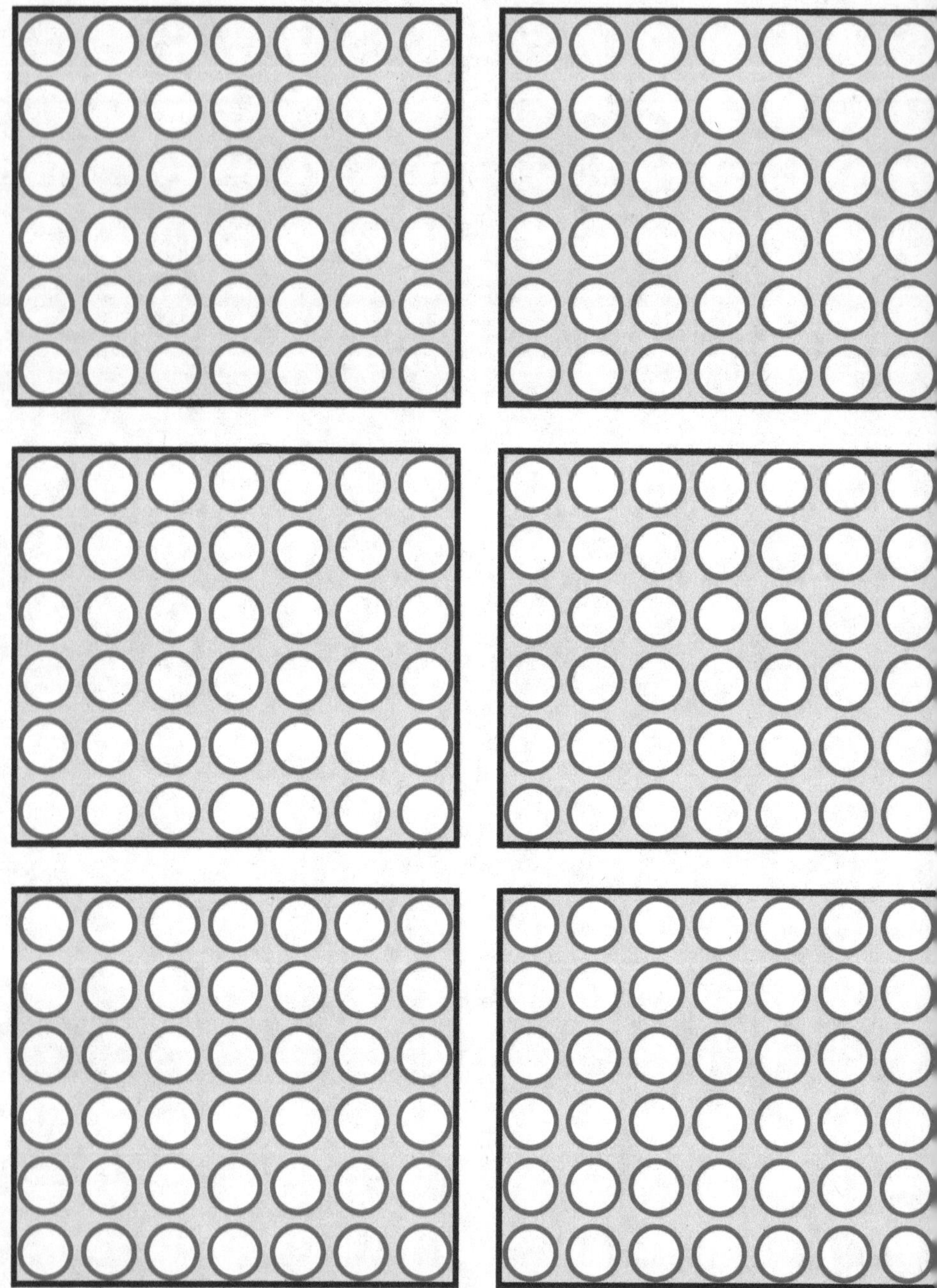

CHALLENGING ABC PATH GAME

HOW TO PLAY

ABC Path consists of a 5x5 grid. Around the edges of the grid are the letters B to Y. The letter A has been placed.

- The goal is to fill in all the cells so that all letters A to Y appear exactly once.
- Each letter must appear in the row, column, or diagonal corresponding to its clue.

- Each letter must be a neighbor to the letter that comes before and after it.

ABC PATH - 1

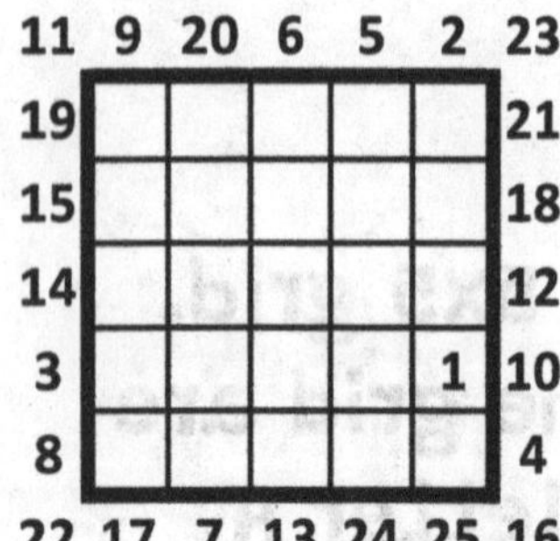

ABC PATH - 2

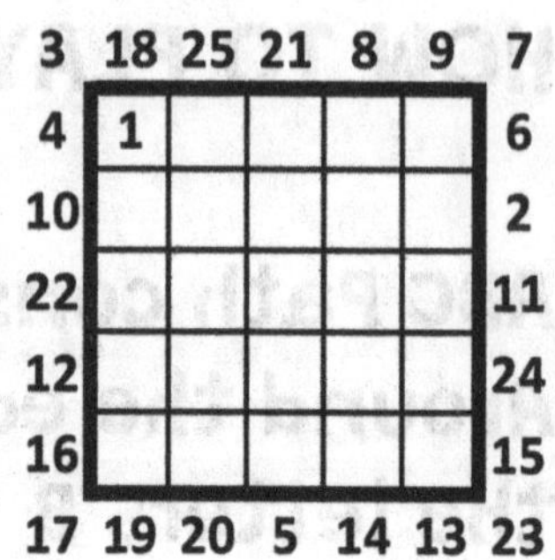

ABC PATH - 3

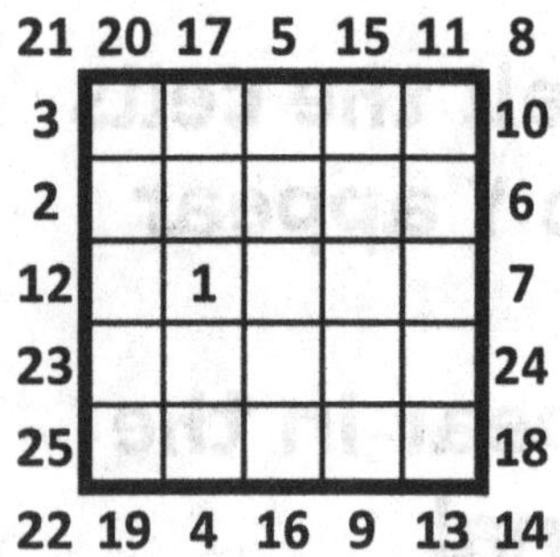

ABC PATH - 4

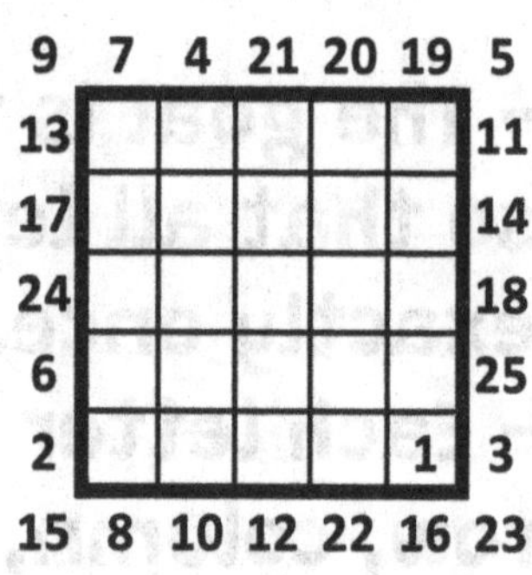

ABC PATH - 5

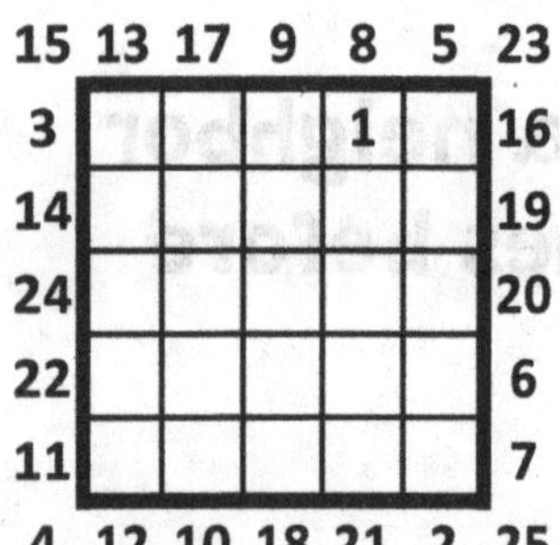

ABC PATH - 6

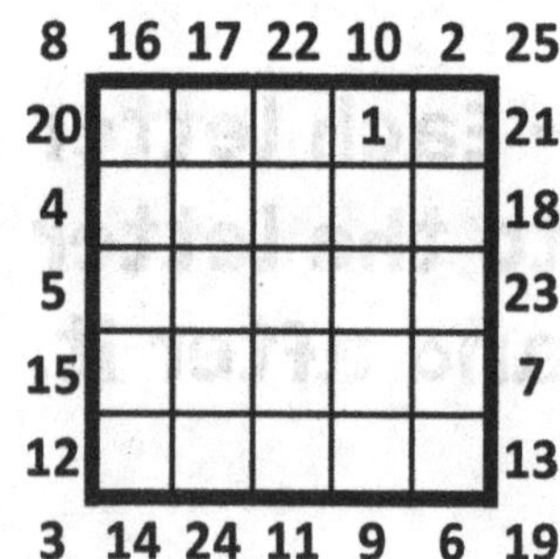

ABC PATH - 7

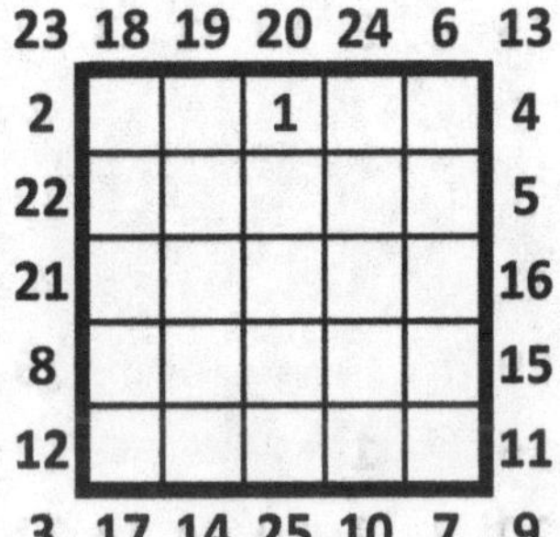

ABC PATH - 8

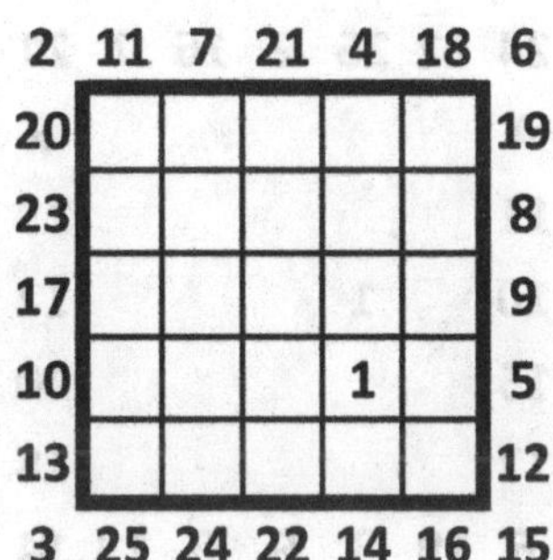

ABC PATH - 9

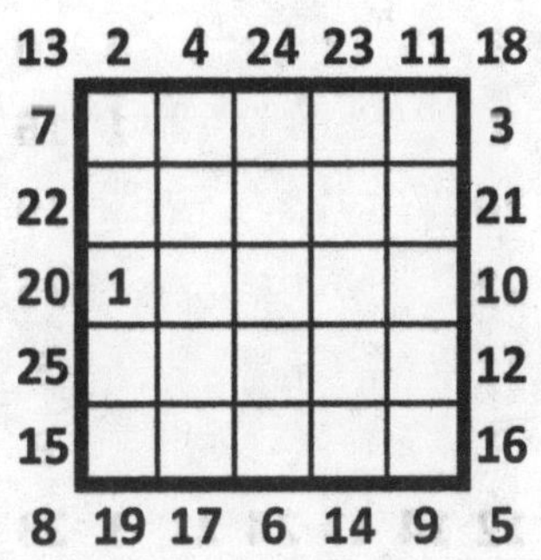

ABC PATH - 10

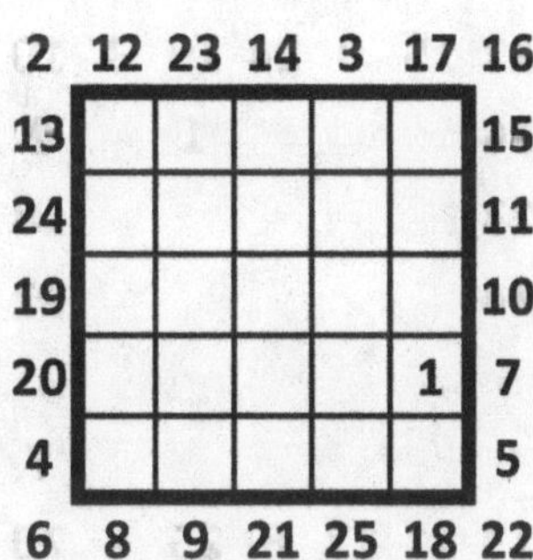

ABC PATH - 11

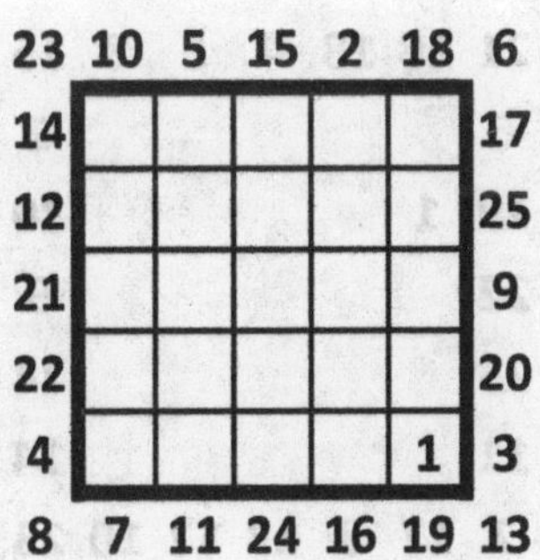

ABC PATH - 12

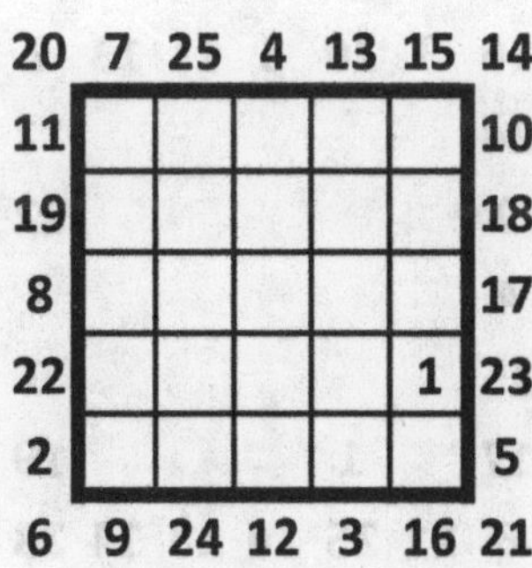

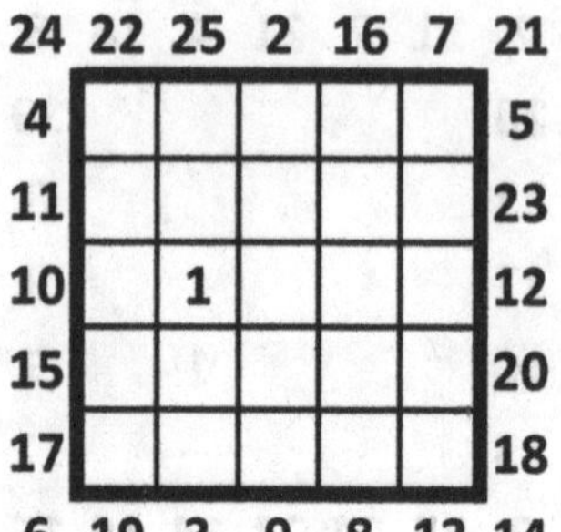

ABC PATH - 13

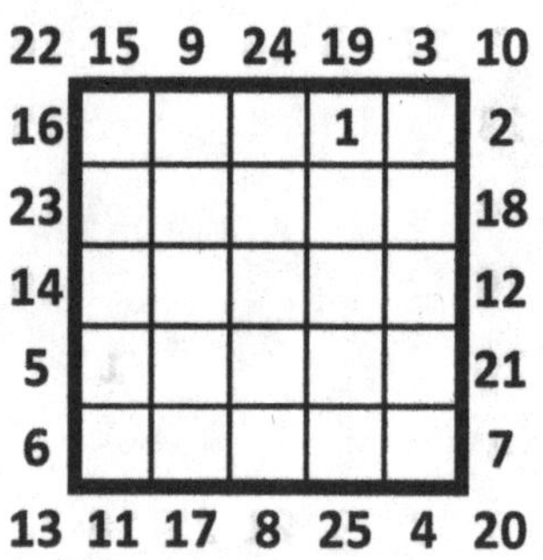

ABC PATH - 15

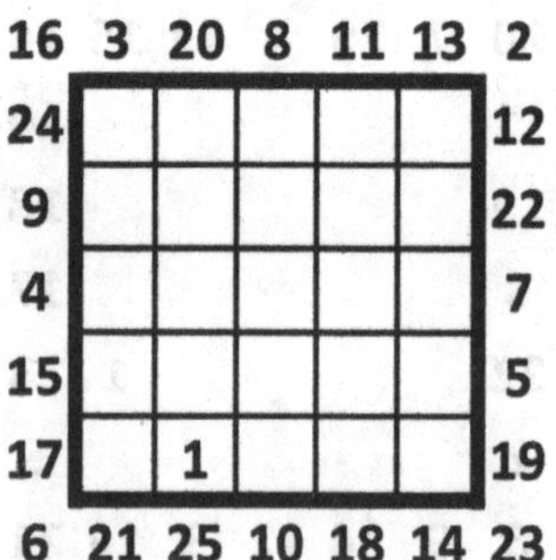

ABC PATH - 17

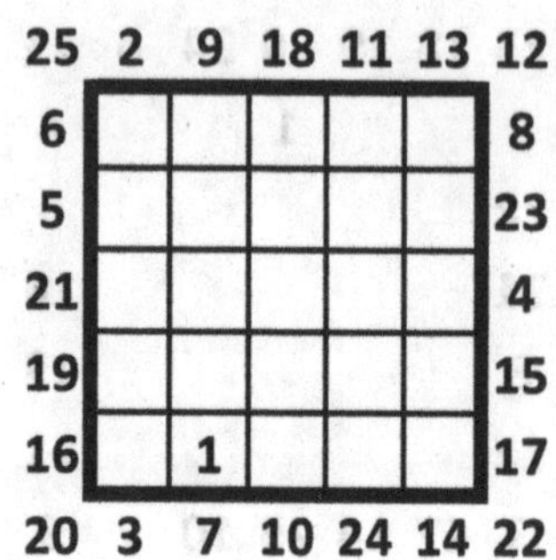

ABC PATH - 14

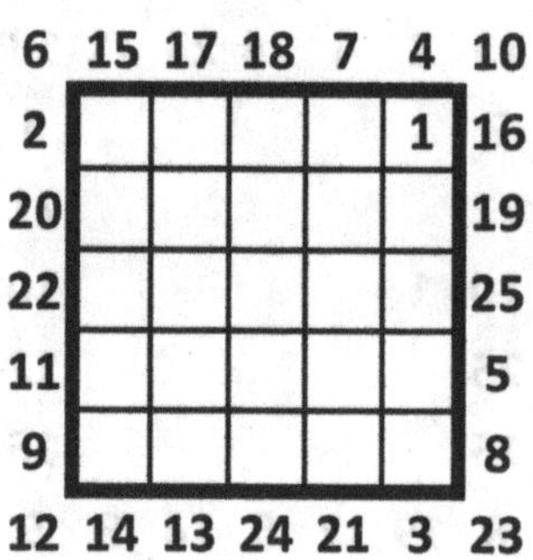

ABC PATH - 16

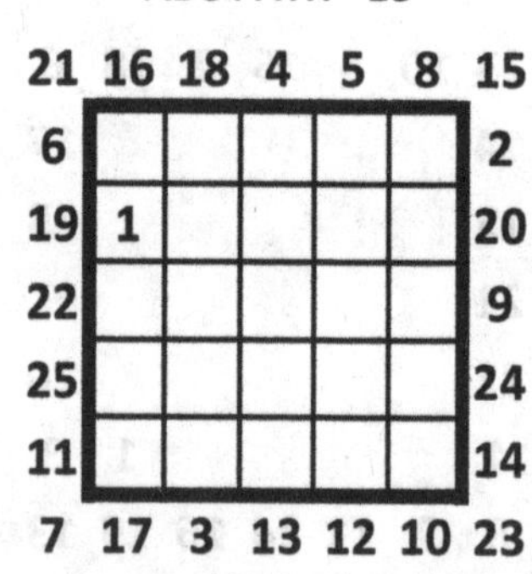

ABC PATH - 18

ABC PATH - 19

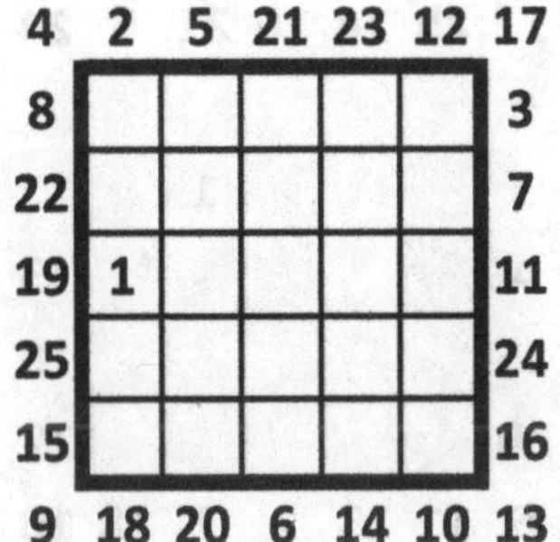

ABC PATH - 20

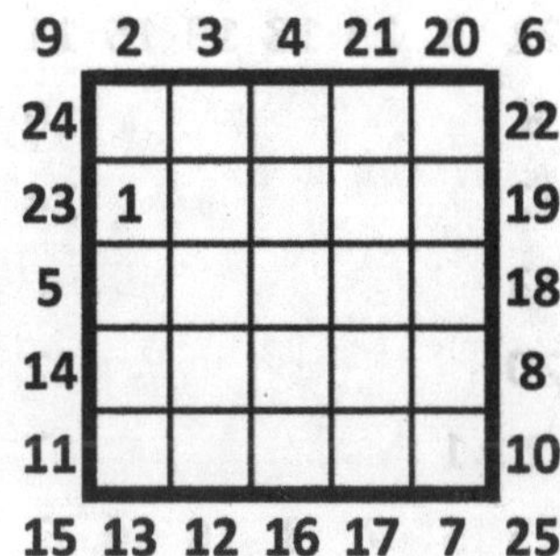

ABC PATH - 21

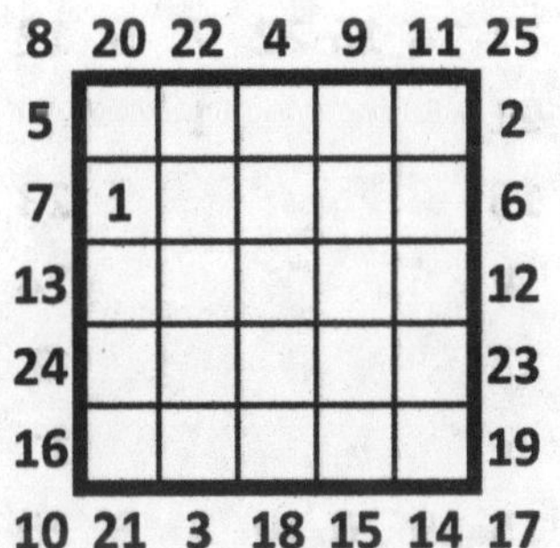

ABC PATH - 22

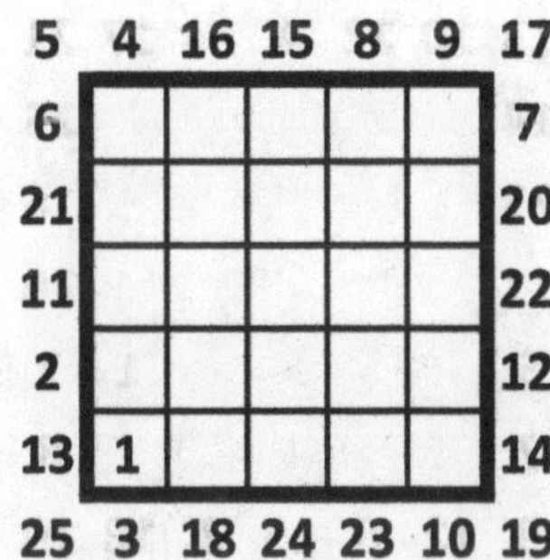

ABC PATH - 23

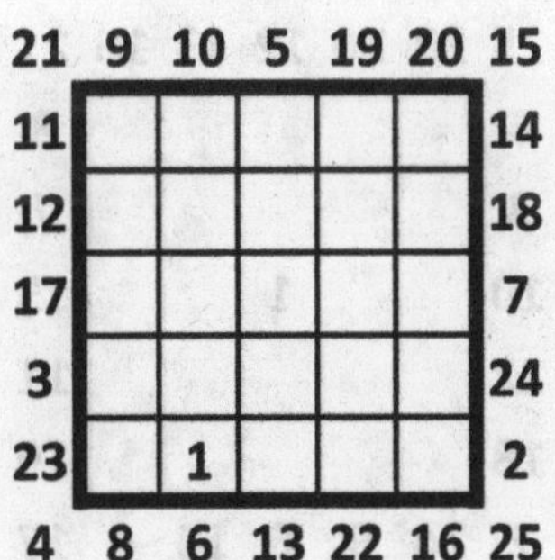

ABC PATH - 24

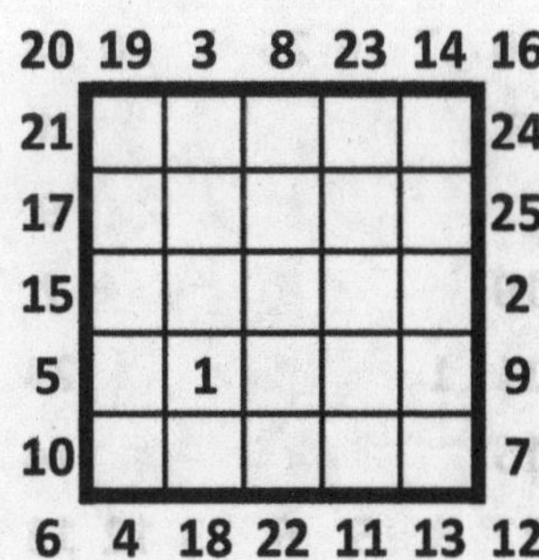

ABC PATH - 25

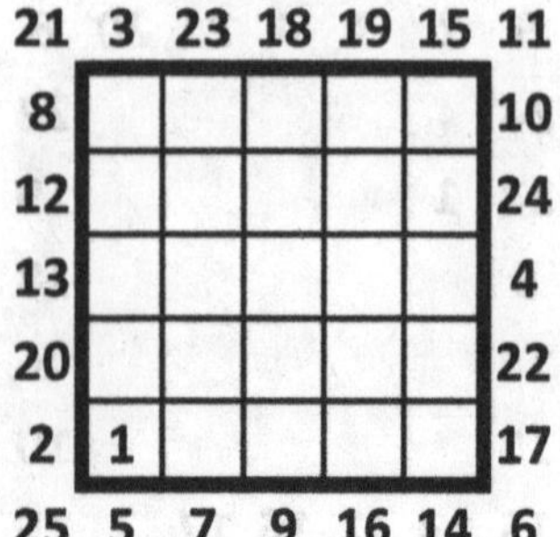

ABC PATH - 26

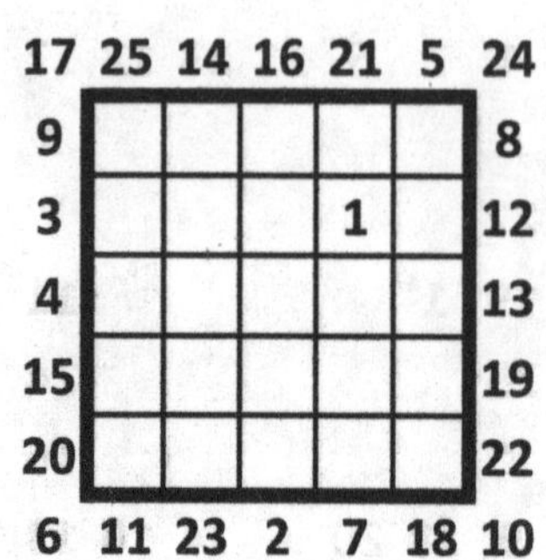

ABC PATH - 27

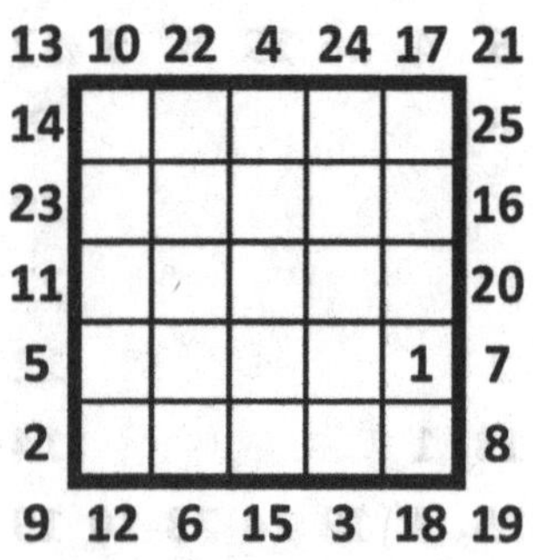

ABC PATH - 28

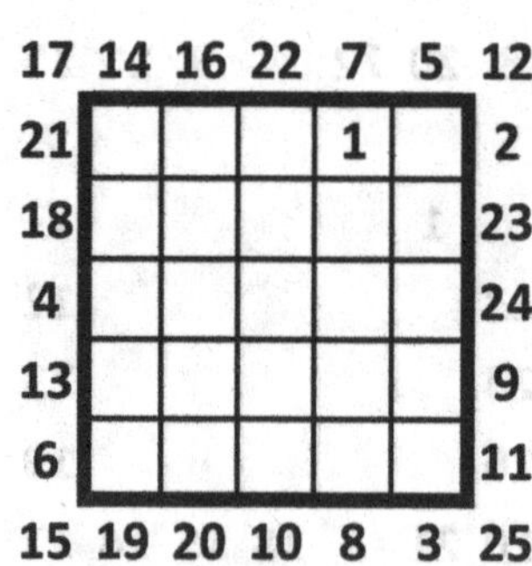

ABC PATH - 29

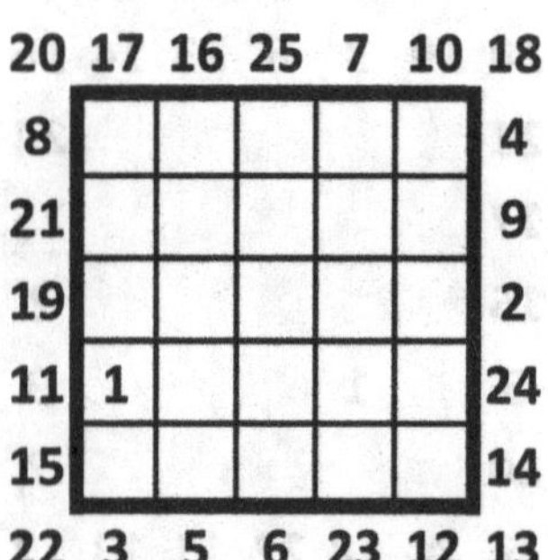

ABC PATH - 30

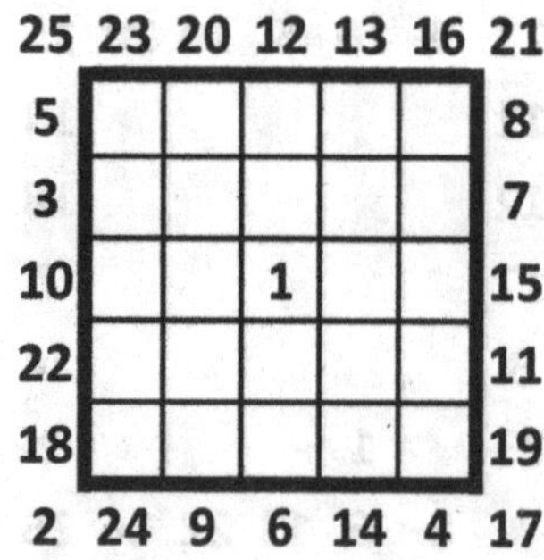

ABC PATH - 1 (Solution)

11	9	20	6	5	2	23
19	19	20	21	24	23	21
15	18	16	15	22	25	18
14	17	12	11	14	2	12
3	9	10	13	3	1	10
8	8	7	6	5	4	4
22	17	7	13	24	25	16

ABC PATH - 2 (Solution)

3	18	25	21	8	9	7
4	1	4	6	8	9	6
10	2	3	5	7	10	2
22	19	20	21	22	11	11
12	18	25	24	23	12	24
16	17	16	15	14	13	15
17	19	20	5	14	13	23

ABC PATH - 3 (Solution)

21	20	17	5	15	11	8
3	3	4	5	9	10	10
2	2	21	6	8	11	6
12	20	1	22	7	12	7
23	19	17	24	23	13	24
25	18	25	16	15	14	18
22	19	4	16	9	13	14

ABC PATH - 4 (Solution)

9	7	4	21	20	19	5
13	9	11	12	13	16	11
17	8	10	14	15	17	14
24	7	24	23	22	18	18
6	6	25	21	20	19	25
2	5	4	3	2	1	3
15	8	10	12	22	16	23

ABC PATH - 5 (Solution)

15	13	17	9	8	5	23
3	16	17	18	1	3	16
14	14	15	19	4	2	19
24	13	24	25	20	5	20
22	12	23	22	21	6	6
11	11	10	9	8	7	7
4	12	10	18	21	2	25

ABC PATH - 6 (Solution)

8	16	17	22	10	2	25
20	19	20	21	1	3	21
4	18	17	22	4	2	18
5	16	24	23	5	6	23
15	15	25	11	10	7	7
12	14	13	12	9	8	13
3	14	24	11	9	6	19

ABC PATH - 7 (Solution)

	18	19	20	24	6	
23						13
2	18	19	1	2	4	4
22	17	22	20	3	5	5
21	16	21	23	24	6	16
8	15	14	25	8	7	15
12	13	12	11	10	9	11
3	17	14	25	10	7	9

ABC PATH - 8 (Solution)

	11	7	21	4	18	
2						6
20	25	24	21	20	19	19
23	8	23	22	3	18	8
17	9	7	2	4	17	9
10	10	6	5	1	16	5
13	11	12	13	14	15	12
3	25	24	22	14	16	15

ABC PATH - 9 (Solution)

	2	4	24	23	11	
13						18
7	3	4	6	7	8	3
22	2	5	21	22	9	21
20	1	20	24	23	10	10
25	19	17	25	12	11	12
15	18	16	15	14	13	16
8	19	17	6	14	9	5

ABC PATH - 10 (Solution)

	12	23	14	3	17	
2						16
13	12	13	14	15	16	15
24	11	23	24	25	17	11
19	8	10	22	19	18	10
20	7	9	21	20	1	7
4	6	5	4	3	2	5
6	8	9	21	25	18	22

ABC PATH - 11 (Solution)

	10	5	15	2	18	
23						6
14	13	14	15	16	17	17
12	10	12	24	25	18	25
21	9	11	23	21	19	9
22	7	8	22	2	20	20
4	6	5	4	3	1	3
8	7	11	24	16	19	13

ABC PATH - 12 (Solution)

	7	25	4	13	15	
20						14
11	10	11	12	13	14	10
19	9	25	19	18	15	18
8	8	24	20	17	16	17
22	7	23	22	21	1	23
2	6	5	4	3	2	5
6	9	24	12	3	16	21

ABC PATH - 13 (Solution)

24	22	25	2	16	7	21
4	24	3	4	5	6	5
11	23	25	2	11	7	23
10	22	1	10	8	12	12
15	20	21	9	15	13	20
17	19	18	17	16	14	18
6	19	3	9	8	13	14

ABC PATH - 14 (Solution)

25	2	9	18	11	13	12
6	6	7	8	11	12	8
5	5	9	10	23	13	23
21	4	21	22	24	14	4
19	3	20	19	25	15	15
16	2	1	18	17	16	17
20	3	7	10	24	14	22

ABC PATH - 15 (Solution)

22	15	9	24	19	3	10
16	16	17	24	1	2	2
23	15	23	18	25	3	18
14	14	12	22	19	4	12
5	11	13	21	20	5	21
6	10	9	8	7	6	7
13	11	17	8	25	4	20

ABC PATH - 16 (Solution)

6	15	17	18	7	4	10
2	16	17	18	2	1	16
20	15	19	20	21	3	19
22	14	13	25	22	4	25
11	11	12	24	23	5	5
9	10	9	8	7	6	8
12	14	13	24	21	3	23

ABC PATH - 17 (Solution)

16	3	20	8	11	13	2
24	23	24	10	11	12	12
9	22	25	8	9	13	22
4	21	4	6	7	14	7
15	3	20	5	16	15	5
17	2	1	19	18	17	19
6	21	25	10	18	14	23

ABC PATH - 18 (Solution)

21	16	18	4	5	8	15
6	2	3	4	6	7	2
19	1	19	20	5	8	20
22	17	18	21	22	9	9
25	16	25	24	23	10	24
11	15	14	13	12	11	14
7	17	3	13	12	10	23

ABC PATH - 19 (Solution)

4	2	5	21	23	12	17
8	3	5	6	8	9	3
22	2	4	7	22	10	7
19	1	19	21	23	11	11
25	18	20	25	24	12	24
15	17	16	15	14	13	16
9	18	20	6	14	10	13

ABC PATH - 20 (Solution)

9	2	3	4	21	20	6
24	25	24	22	21	20	22
23	1	23	4	6	19	19
5	2	3	5	18	7	18
14	14	15	16	17	8	8
11	13	12	11	10	9	10
15	13	12	16	17	7	25

ABC PATH - 21 (Solution)

8	20	22	4	9	11	25
5	2	3	4	5	10	2
7	1	7	6	9	11	6
13	21	22	8	13	12	12
24	20	24	23	17	14	23
16	25	19	18	15	16	19
10	21	3	18	15	14	17

ABC PATH - 22 (Solution)

5	4	16	15	8	9	17
6	5	6	7	8	9	7
21	4	19	20	21	10	20
11	3	18	25	22	11	22
2	2	17	24	23	12	12
13	1	16	15	14	13	14
25	3	18	24	23	10	19

ABC PATH - 23 (Solution)

21	9	10	5	19	20	15
11	9	10	11	14	15	14
12	8	12	13	18	16	18
17	7	6	25	19	17	7
3	3	4	5	24	20	24
23	2	1	23	22	21	2
4	8	6	13	22	16	25

ABC PATH - 24 (Solution)

20	19	3	8	23	14	16
21	20	21	22	23	24	24
17	19	18	17	16	25	25
15	4	3	2	15	14	2
5	5	1	9	11	13	9
10	6	7	8	10	12	7
6	4	18	22	11	13	12

ABC PATH - 25 (Solution)

21	3	23	18	19	15	11
8	6	8	9	10	11	10
12	5	7	24	25	12	24
13	4	23	21	19	13	4
20	3	22	18	20	14	22
2	1	2	17	16	15	17
25	5	7	9	16	14	6

ABC PATH - 26 (Solution)

17	25	14	16	21	5	24
9	11	9	8	7	6	8
3	12	10	3	1	5	12
4	13	14	2	4	18	13
15	25	15	16	17	19	19
20	24	23	22	21	20	22
6	11	23	2	7	18	10

ABC PATH - 27 (Solution)

13	10	22	4	24	17	21
14	13	14	15	24	25	25
23	12	22	23	16	17	16
11	11	6	21	20	18	20
5	10	7	5	19	1	7
2	9	8	4	3	2	8
9	12	6	15	3	18	19

ABC PATH - 28 (Solution)

17	14	16	22	7	5	12
21	19	20	21	1	2	2
18	18	17	22	23	3	23
4	14	16	25	24	4	24
13	13	15	9	8	5	9
6	12	11	10	7	6	11
15	19	20	10	8	3	25

ABC PATH - 29 (Solution)

20	17	16	25	7	10	18
8	4	5	6	7	8	4
21	3	20	21	22	9	9
19	2	19	25	23	10	2
11	1	18	24	13	11	24
15	17	16	15	14	12	14
22	3	5	6	23	12	13

ABC PATH - 30 (Solution)

25	23	20	12	13	16	21
5	25	8	6	5	4	8
3	24	9	7	2	3	7
10	23	10	1	14	15	15
22	22	11	12	13	16	11
18	21	20	19	18	17	19
2	24	9	6	14	4	17

CHALLENGING HANGMAN GAME

HOW TO PLAY

The game is typically played between two people.
- One person, the 'host' chooses a word and marks the length of the word on the grid.

- The other player has to guess the letters in this word/phrase before all the parts of the hangman are drawn,
- If the player guesses correctly the letter is marked in the correct place, if the player guesses incorrectly the host draws another
part of the hangman,
- The game continues until
  - the word/phrase is guessed (all letters are revealed) in this case the second person has won

  - all the parts of the hangman are displayed in which case the second person has lost.

Word: _______________________

A B C D E F G H I J K L M
N O P Q R S T U V W X Y Z

Word: _______________________

A B C D E F G H I J K L M
N O P Q R S T U V W X Y Z

Word: _______________________

A B C D E F G H I J K L M
N O P Q R S T U V W X Y Z

Word: _______________________

A B C D E F G H I J K L M
N O P Q R S T U V W X Y Z

Word: _______________________

A B C D E F G H I J K L M
N O P Q R S T U V W X Y Z

Word: _______________________

A B C D E F G H I J K L M
N O P Q R S T U V W X Y Z

Word: ___________________________

A B C D E F G H I J K L M
N O P Q R S T U V W X Y Z

Word: ___________________________

A B C D E F G H I J K L M
N O P Q R S T U V W X Y Z

Word: ___________________________

A B C D E F G H I J K L M
N O P Q R S T U V W X Y Z

Word: ___________________________

A B C D E F G H I J K L M
N O P Q R S T U V W X Y Z

Word: ___________________________

A B C D E F G H I J K L M
N O P Q R S T U V W X Y Z

Word: ___________________________

A B C D E F G H I J K L M
N O P Q R S T U V W X Y Z

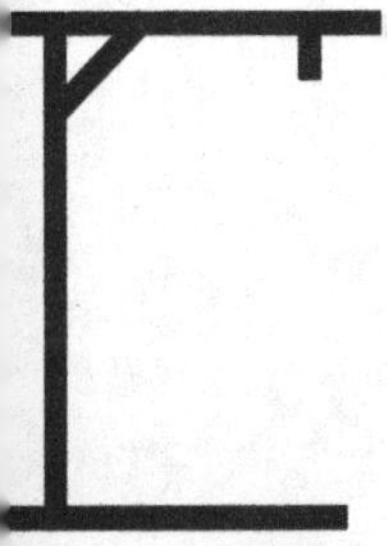

Word: _______________________

A B C D E F G H I J K L M
N O P Q R S T U V W X Y Z

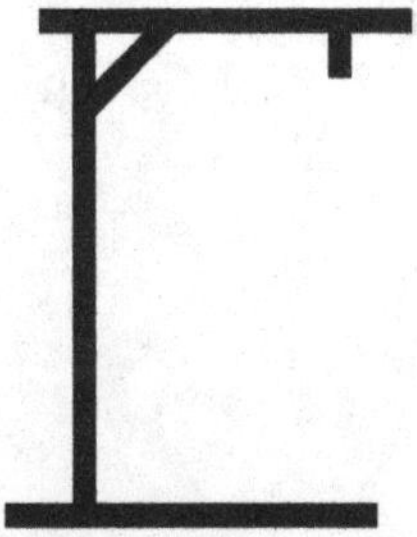

Word: _______________________

A B C D E F G H I J K L M
N O P Q R S T U V W X Y Z

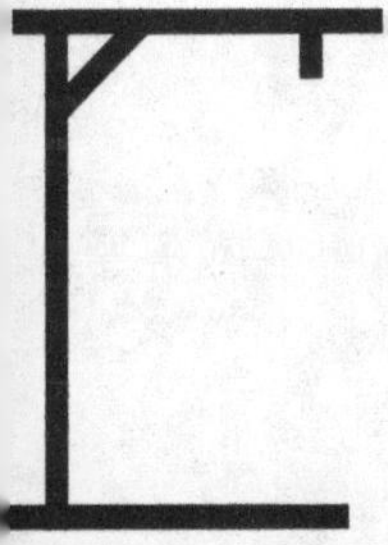

Word: _______________________

A B C D E F G H I J K L M
N O P Q R S T U V W X Y Z

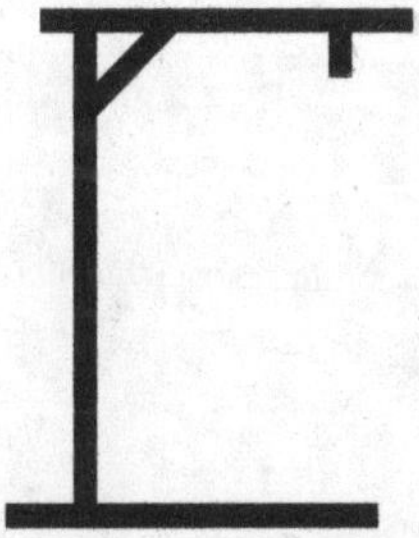

Word: _______________________

A B C D E F G H I J K L M
N O P Q R S T U V W X Y Z

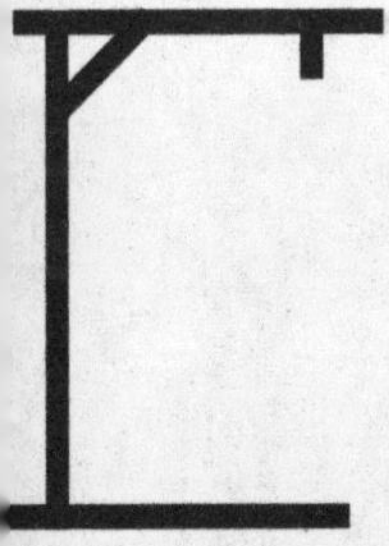

Word: _______________________

A B C D E F G H I J K L M
N O P Q R S T U V W X Y Z

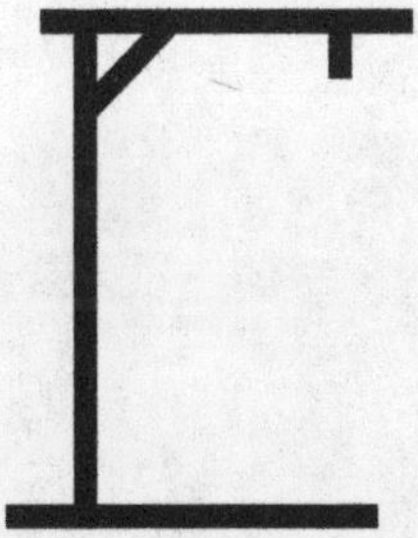

Word: _______________________

A B C D E F G H I J K L M
N O P Q R S T U V W X Y Z

Word: ___________________________

A B C D E F G H I J K L M
N O P Q R S T U V W X Y Z

Word: ___________________________

A B C D E F G H I J K L M
N O P Q R S T U V W X Y Z

Word: ___________________________

A B C D E F G H I J K L M
N O P Q R S T U V W X Y Z

Word: ___________________________

A B C D E F G H I J K L M
N O P Q R S T U V W X Y Z

Word: ___________________________

A B C D E F G H I J K L M
N O P Q R S T U V W X Y Z

Word: ___________________________

A B C D E F G H I J K L M
N O P Q R S T U V W X Y Z

Word: _______________

A B C D E F G H I J K L M
N O P Q R S T U V W X Y Z

Word: _______________

A B C D E F G H I J K L M
N O P Q R S T U V W X Y Z

Word: _______________

A B C D E F G H I J K L M
N O P Q R S T U V W X Y Z

Word: _______________

A B C D E F G H I J K L M
N O P Q R S T U V W X Y Z

Word: _______________

A B C D E F G H I J K L M
N O P Q R S T U V W X Y Z

Word: _______________

A B C D E F G H I J K L M
N O P Q R S T U V W X Y Z

SUDOKU

HOW TO PLAY

Sudoku is 9×9 (classic, adult version), or 4x4 and 6x6 (kids versions) grid puzzle game.

In the adult version, the objective is to fill the 9×9 grid with digits so that each column, each row, and each of the nine 3×3 subgrids that compose the grid (also called "boxes", "blocks", or "regions") contain all of the digits from 1 to 9.

You are provided a partially completed puzzle to complete, with a single solution.

In the adult version, 4 difficulty levels can be found, Easy, Intermediate, Hard and Insane.

SUDOKU - 1

	1	3	
3			1
4			3
	3	4	

SUDOKU - 2

2			1
	3	4	
	1		4
4		1	

SUDOKU - 3

2		3	
	1		4
	2		3
1		4	

SUDOKU - 4

1			2
		1	4
4	1		
	2	4	

SUDOKU - 5

	2	1	
	3		2
2			4
3		2	

SUDOKU - 6

	3	1	
1			3
2			4
	4	2	

SUDOKU - 7

2		1	
	4		2
	2		1
4		2	

SUDOKU - 8

2	4		
		4	2
4			3
	2	1	

SUDOKU - 9

	1		2
3		1	
	4	2	
2			1

SUDOKU - 10

4	3		
2		4	
		1	2
	2		4

SUDOKU - 11

	1		4
4		1	
	2	4	
3			1

SUDOKU - 12

2		4	
1	4		
	1		4
		1	3

SUDOKU - 13

1	3		
2			3
	1	3	
		4	1

SUDOKU - 14

	1		3
2		4	
1		3	
	4		2

SUDOKU - 15

1	4		
	3		1
		1	4
4		3	

SUDOKU - 16

1			3
	2		4
4		3	
	3	4	

SUDOKU - 17

		4	1
4		2	
3	2		
	4		2

SUDOKU - 18

	4		1
3		2	
4			2
	2	4	

SUDOKU - 19

	1		4
2	4		
		3	1
1		4	

SUDOKU - 20

		2	1
2		4	
	3		2
1	2		

SUDOKU - 21

1		4	
	2		1
		2	4
2	4		

SUDOKU - 22

		1	4
1	4		
3		4	
	1		3

SUDOKU - 23

		3	4
	3		1
3	1		
2		1	

SUDOKU - 24

1			2
	3		1
	1	2	
3		1	

SUDOKU - 25

		4	1
	4	2	
2			4
4	3		

SUDOKU - 26

3			1
1	4		
	3	1	
		3	4

SUDOKU - 27

	1		2
4		3	
1		2	
	4		3

SUDOKU - 28

	4		1
	2	4	
4		3	
2			4

SUDOKU - 29

	4		2
2		4	
3			4
	2	1	

SUDOKU - 30

	1	4	
		1	3
1			4
4	2		

SUDOKU - 1 (Solution)

2	1	3	4
3	4	2	1
4	2	1	3
1	3	4	2

SUDOKU - 2 (Solution)

2	4	3	1
1	3	4	2
3	1	2	4
4	2	1	3

SUDOKU - 3 (Solution)

2	4	3	1
3	1	2	4
4	2	1	3
1	3	4	2

SUDOKU - 4 (Solution)

1	4	3	2
2	3	1	4
4	1	2	3
3	2	4	1

SUDOKU - 5 (Solution)

4	2	1	3
1	3	4	2
2	1	3	4
3	4	2	1

SUDOKU - 6 (Solution)

4	3	1	2
1	2	4	3
2	1	3	4
3	4	2	1

SUDOKU - 7 (Solution)

2	3	1	4
1	4	3	2
3	2	4	1
4	1	2	3

SUDOKU - 8 (Solution)

2	4	3	1
1	3	4	2
4	1	2	3
3	2	1	4

SUDOKU - 9 (Solution)

4	1	3	2
3	2	1	4
1	4	2	3
2	3	4	1

SUDOKU - 10 (Solution)

4	3	2	1
2	1	4	3
3	4	1	2
1	2	3	4

SUDOKU - 11 (Solution)

2	1	3	4
4	3	1	2
1	2	4	3
3	4	2	1

SUDOKU - 12 (Solution)

2	3	4	1
1	4	3	2
3	1	2	4
4	2	1	3

SUDOKU - 13 (Solution)

1	3	2	4
2	4	1	3
4	1	3	2
3	2	4	1

SUDOKU - 14 (Solution)

4	1	2	3
2	3	4	1
1	2	3	4
3	4	1	2

SUDOKU - 15 (Solution)

1	4	2	3
2	3	4	1
3	2	1	4
4	1	3	2

SUDOKU - 16 (Solution)

1	4	2	3
3	2	1	4
4	1	3	2
2	3	4	1

SUDOKU - 17 (Solution)

2	3	4	1
4	1	2	3
3	2	1	4
1	4	3	2

SUDOKU - 18 (Solution)

2	4	3	1
3	1	2	4
4	3	1	2
1	2	4	3

SUDOKU - 19 (Solution)

3	1	2	4
2	4	1	3
4	2	3	1
1	3	4	2

SUDOKU - 20 (Solution)

3	4	2	1
2	1	4	3
4	3	1	2
1	2	3	4

SUDOKU - 21 (Solution)

1	3	4	2
4	2	3	1
3	1	2	4
2	4	1	3

SUDOKU - 22 (Solution)

2	3	1	4
1	4	3	2
3	2	4	1
4	1	2	3

SUDOKU - 23 (Solution)

1	2	3	4
4	3	2	1
3	1	4	2
2	4	1	3

SUDOKU - 24 (Solution)

1	4	3	2
2	3	4	1
4	1	2	3
3	2	1	4

SUDOKU - 25 (Solution)

3	2	4	1
1	4	2	3
2	1	3	4
4	3	1	2

SUDOKU - 26 (Solution)

3	2	4	1
1	4	2	3
4	3	1	2
2	1	3	4

SUDOKU - 27 (Solution)

3	1	4	2
4	2	3	1
1	3	2	4
2	4	1	3

SUDOKU - 28 (Solution)

3	4	2	1
1	2	4	3
4	1	3	2
2	3	1	4

SUDOKU - 29 (Solution)

1	4	3	2
2	3	4	1
3	1	2	4
4	2	1	3

SUDOKU - 30 (Solution)

3	1	4	2
2	4	1	3
1	3	2	4
4	2	3	1

CALCUDOKU

HOW TO PLAY

Each puzzle consists of a grid containing blocks surrounded by bold lines.

The object is to fill all empty squares so that the numbers 1 to N (where N is the number of rows or columns in the grid) appear exactly once in each row and column and the numbers in each block produce the result shown in the top-left corner of the block according to the math operation appearing on the top of the grid.

In CalcuDoku a number may be used more than once in the same block. Single, double or multi-operator can be used.

In multi-operator option, all operators could not be used in a grid.

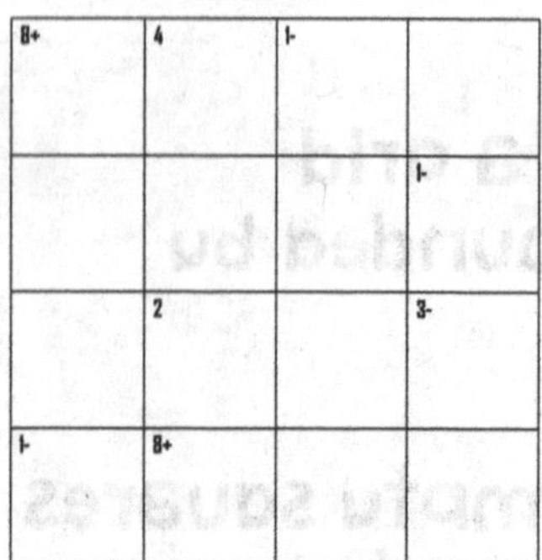

CALCUDUKO - 1

CALCUDUKO - 2

CALCUDUKO - 3

CALCUDUKO - 4

CALCUDUKO - 5

CALCUDUKO - 6

CALCUDUKO - 7

CALCUDUKO - 8

CALCUDUKO - 9

CALCUDUKO - 10

CALCUDUKO - 11

CALCUDUKO - 12

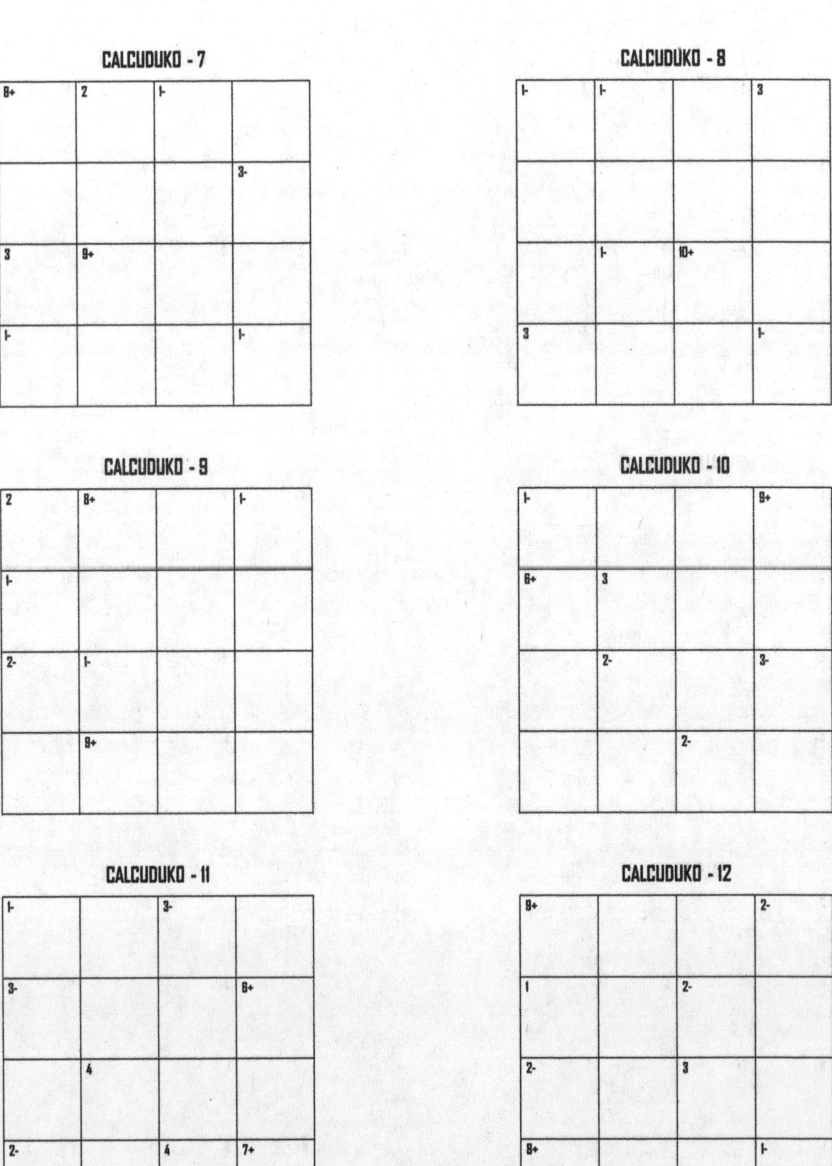

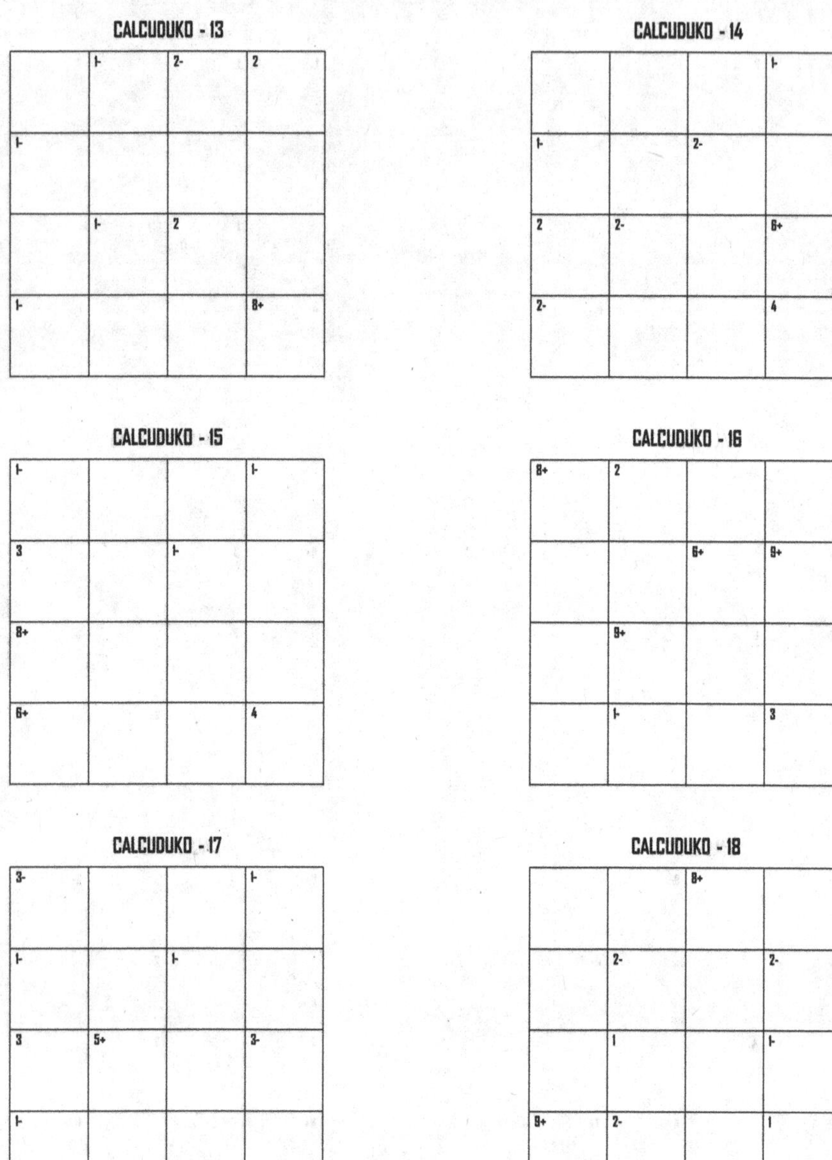

CALCUDUKO - 13

CALCUDUKO - 14

CALCUDUKO - 15

CALCUDUKO - 16

CALCUDUKO - 17

CALCUDUKO - 18

CALCUDUKO - 19   ## CALCUDUKO - 20

CALCUDUKO - 21   ## CALCUDUKO - 22

CALCUDUKO - 23   ## CALCUDUKO - 24

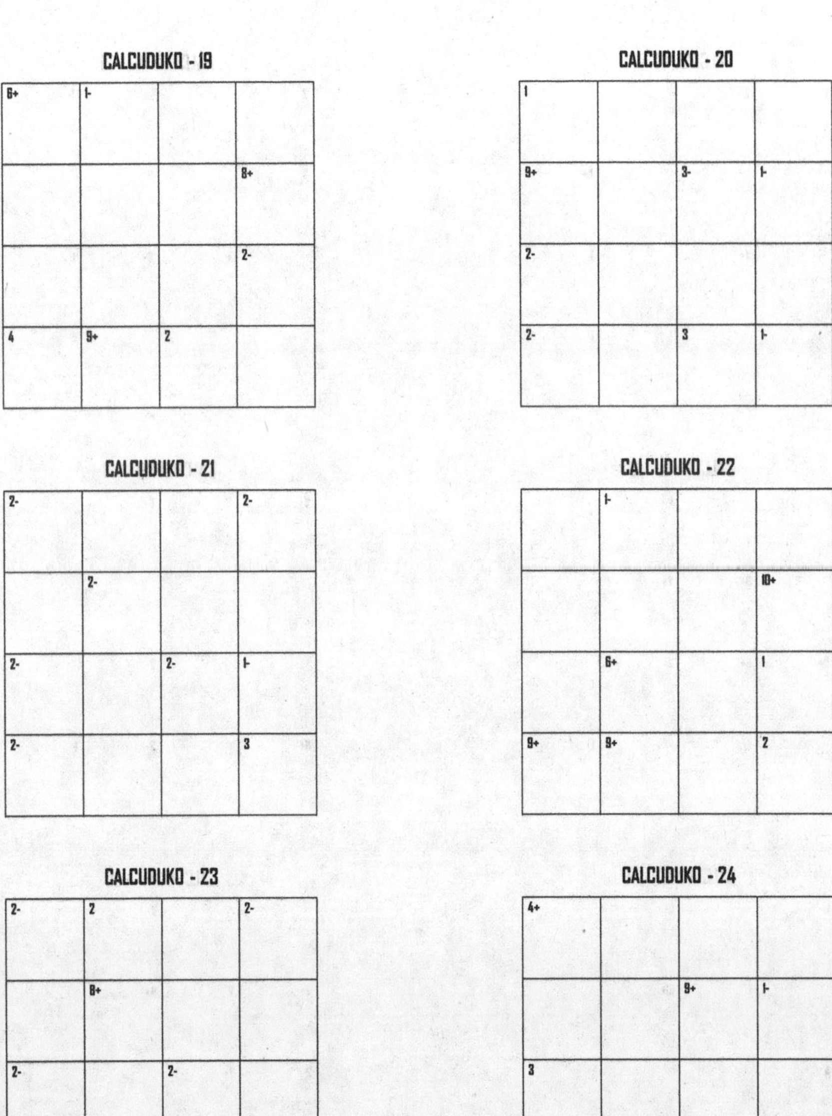

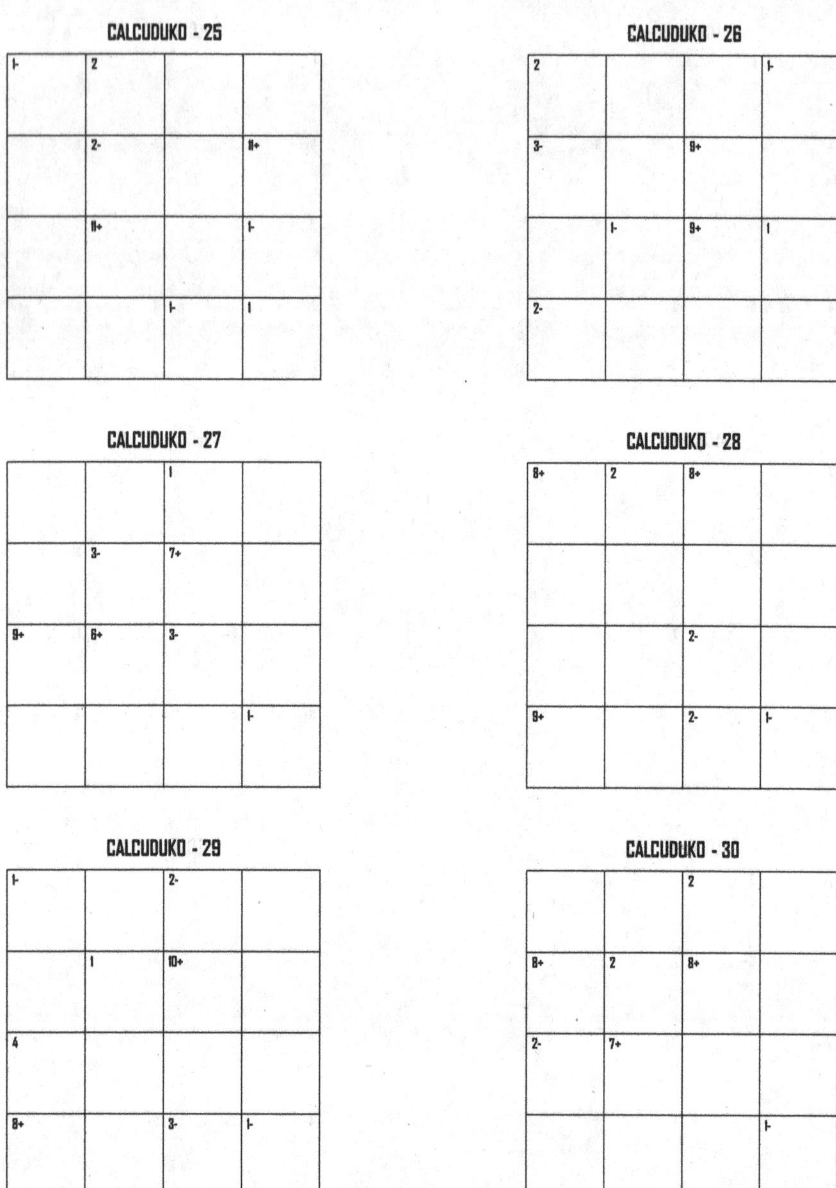

CALCUDUKO - 25
CALCUDUKO - 26
CALCUDUKO - 27
CALCUDUKO - 28
CALCUDUKO - 29
CALCUDUKO - 30

CALCUDUKO - 1 (Solution)

1	4	2	3
4	3	1	2
3	2	4	1
2	1	3	4

CALCUDUKO - 2 (Solution)

2	3	4	1
1	4	2	3
3	2	1	4
4	1	3	2

CALCUDUKO - 3 (Solution)

4	2	3	1
3	1	2	4
2	4	1	3
1	3	4	2

CALCUDUKO - 4 (Solution)

3	1	4	2
2	4	1	3
1	3	2	4
4	2	3	1

CALCUDUKO - 5 (Solution)

3	1	4	2
1	3	2	4
4	2	3	1
2	4	1	3

CALCUDUKO - 6 (Solution)

4	3	2	1
2	1	3	4
1	2	4	3
3	4	1	2

CALCUDUKO - 7 (Solution)

4	2	3	1
1	3	2	4
3	4	1	2
2	1	4	3

CALCUDUKO - 8 (Solution)

4	2	1	3
2	3	4	1
1	4	3	2
3	1	2	4

CALCUDUKO - 9 (Solution)

2	4	3	1
4	3	1	2
3	1	2	4
1	2	4	3

CALCUDUKO - 10 (Solution)

4	2	1	3
1	3	4	2
3	4	2	1
2	1	3	4

CALCUDUKO - 11 (Solution)

2	3	1	4
4	2	3	1
1	4	2	3
3	1	4	2

CALCUDUKO - 12 (Solution)

2	4	1	3
1	3	2	4
4	2	3	1
3	1	4	2

CALCUDUKO - 13 (Solution)

1	4	3	2
2	3	1	4
4	1	2	3
3	2	4	1

CALCUDUKO - 14 (Solution)

3	1	4	2
4	2	1	3
2	4	3	1
1	3	2	4

CALCUDUKO - 15 (Solution)

4	1	2	3
3	2	4	1
1	4	3	2
2	3	1	4

CALCUDUKO - 16 (Solution)

3	2	4	1
2	3	1	4
1	4	3	2
4	1	2	3

CALCUDUKO - 17 (Solution)

1	4	3	2
2	1	4	3
3	2	1	4
4	3	2	1

CALCUDUKO - 18 (Solution)

1	4	3	2
2	3	1	4
4	1	2	3
3	2	4	1

CALCUDUKO - 19 (Solution)

6+	1-		
3	1	4	2
1	2	3	4 (8+)
2	4	1	3 (2-)
4 (4)	3 (9+)	2 (2)	1

CALCUDUKO - 20 (Solution)

1			
1	3	4	2
4 (9+)	2	1 (3-)	3 (1-)
3 (2-)	1	2	4
2 (2-)	4	3 (3)	1 (1-)

CALCUDUKO - 21 (Solution)

2-			2-
1	3	4	2
3	1 (2-)	2	4
4 (2-)	2	3 (2-)	1 (1-)
2 (2-)	4	1	3 (3)

CALCUDUKO - 22 (Solution)

	1-		
1	2	3	4
4	1	2	3 (10+)
2	3 (6+)	4	1 (1)
3 (9+)	4 (9+)	1	2 (2)

CALCUDUKO - 23 (Solution)

2-	2		2-
4	2	3	1
2	3 (8+)	1	4
3 (2-)	1	4 (2-)	2
1	4	2 (1-)	3 (3)

CALCUDUKO - 24 (Solution)

4+			
1	2	4	3
2	1	3 (9+)	4 (1-)
3 (3)	4	1	2
4 (4)	3 (8+)	2 (5+)	1

CALCUDUKO - 25 (Solution)

1	2	4	3
2	1	3	4
3	4	1	2
4	3	2	1

CALCUDUKO - 26 (Solution)

2	4	1	3
1	3	4	2
4	2	3	1
3	1	2	4

CALCUDUKO - 27 (Solution)

3	4	1	2
4	1	2	3
2	3	4	1
1	2	3	4

CALCUDUKO - 28 (Solution)

3	2	1	4
1	4	2	3
2	3	4	1
4	1	3	2

CALCUDUKO - 29 (Solution)

1	4	2	3
2	1	3	4
4	3	1	2
3	2	4	1

CALCUDUKO - 30 (Solution)

1	4	2	3
3	2	4	1
4	3	1	2
2	1	3	4

SKYSCRAPER

HOW TO PLAY

A Skyscraper puzzle consists of a square grid with some exterior 'skyscraper' clues.

Every square in the grid must be filled with a digit from 1 to n (n is the size of the grid) so that every row and column contains one of each digit.

In Skyscraper each digit placed in the grid can be visualised as a building of that many storeys. A '5' is a 5 storey building, for example.

Each number outside the grid reveals the number of 'buildings' that can be seen from that point, looking along the adjacent row or column.

Every building blocks all buildings of a lower height from view, while taller buildings are still visible beyond it.

SKYSCRAPER - 1
Intermediate

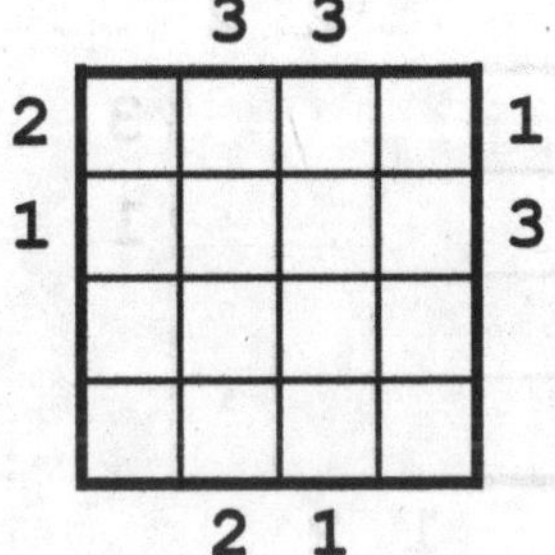

SKYSCRAPER - 2
Intermediate

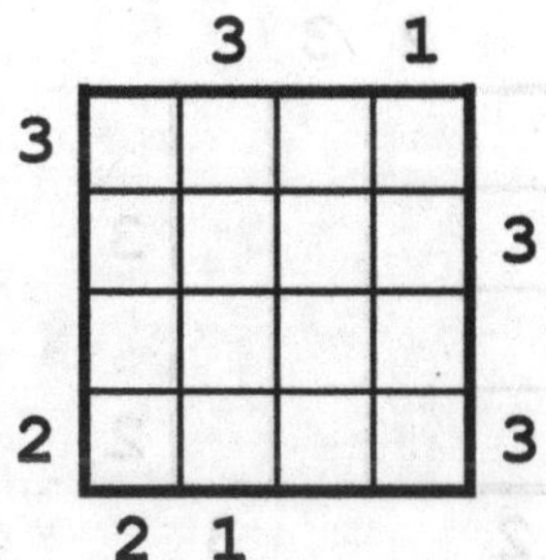

SKYSCRAPER - 3
Intermediate

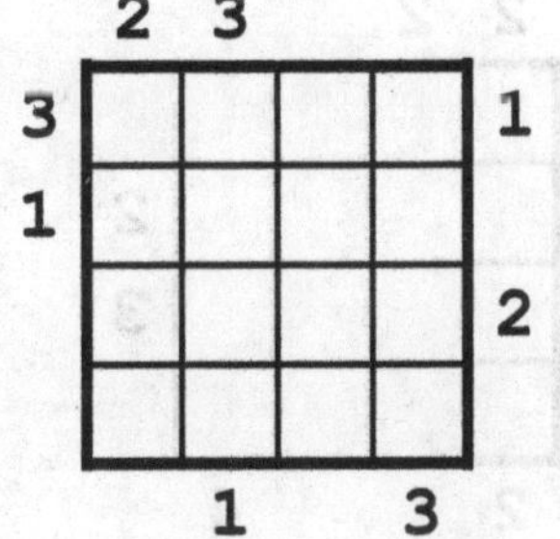

SKYSCRAPER - 4
Intermediate

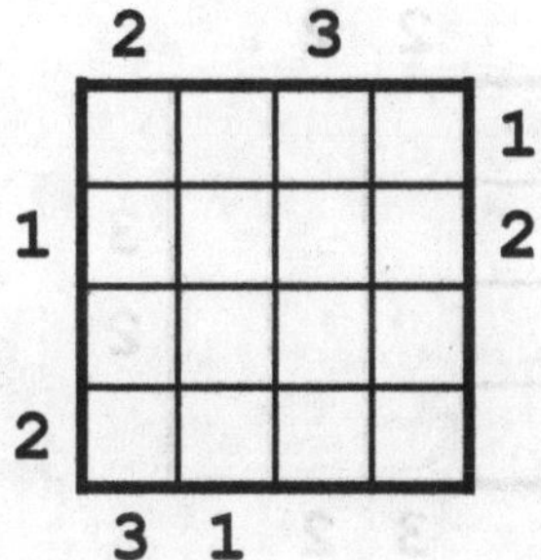

SKYSCRAPER - 5
Intermediate

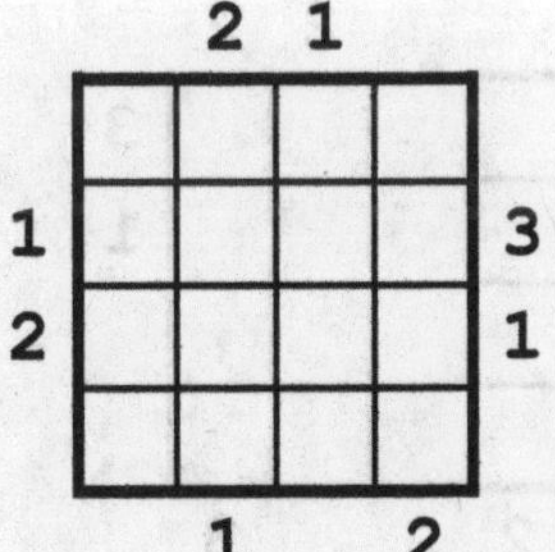

SKYSCRAPER - 6
Intermediate

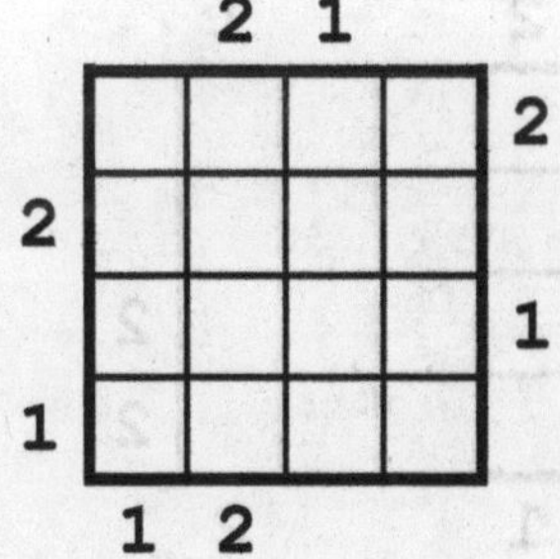

SKYSCRAPER - 7
Intermediate

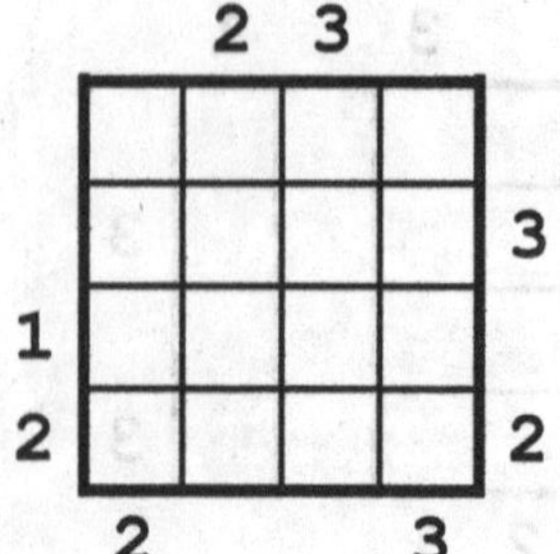

SKYSCRAPER - 8
Intermediate

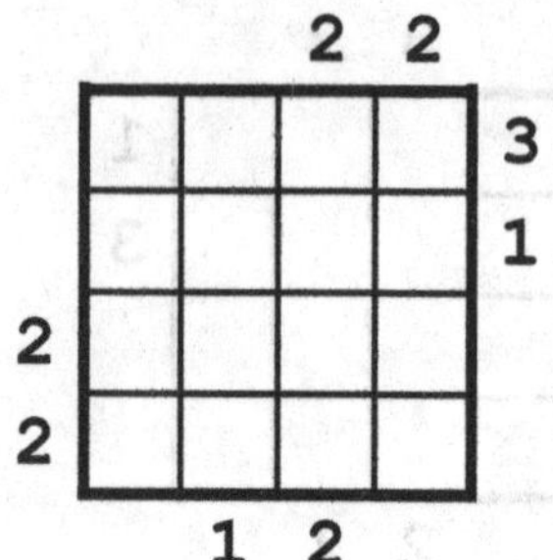

SKYSCRAPER - 9
Intermediate

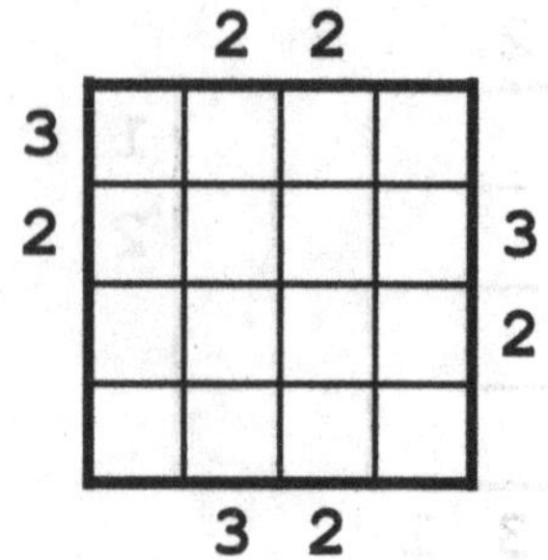

SKYSCRAPER - 10
Intermediate

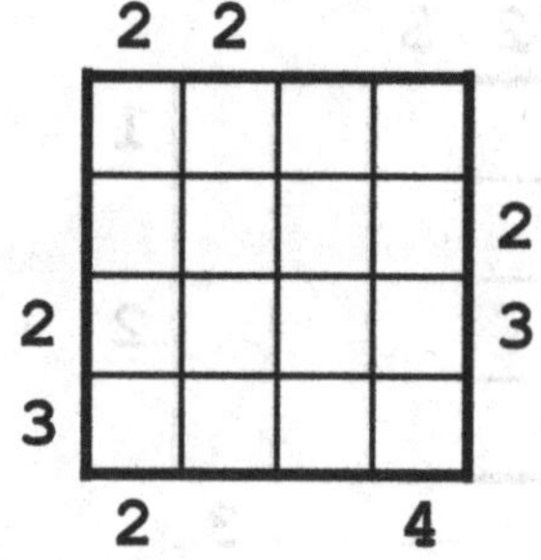

SKYSCRAPER - 11
Intermediate

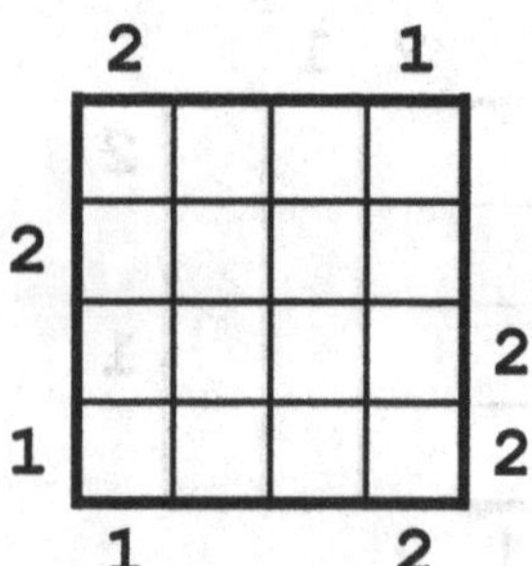

SKYSCRAPER - 12
Intermediate

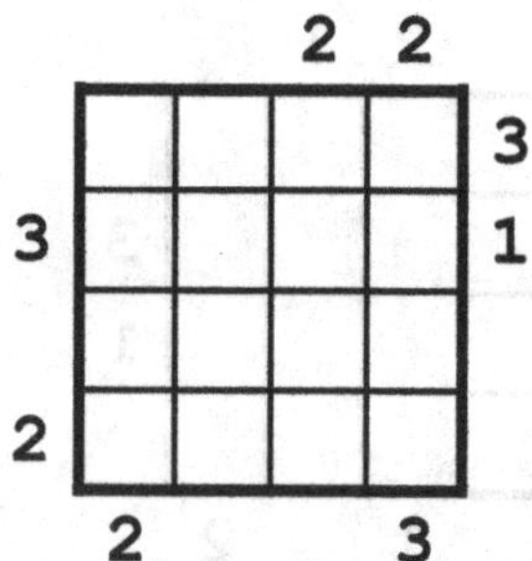

SKYSCRAPER - 13
Intermediate

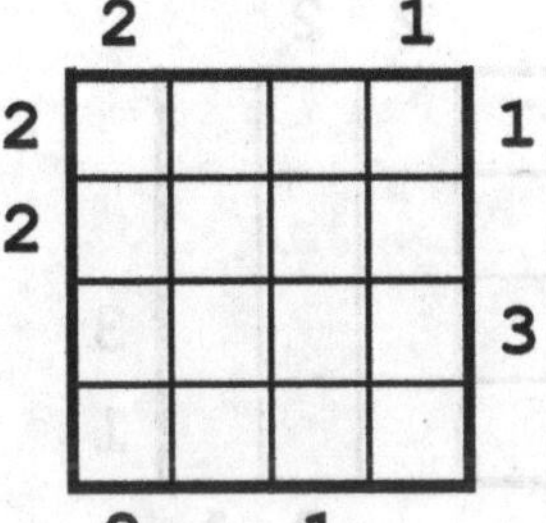

SKYSCRAPER - 14
Intermediate

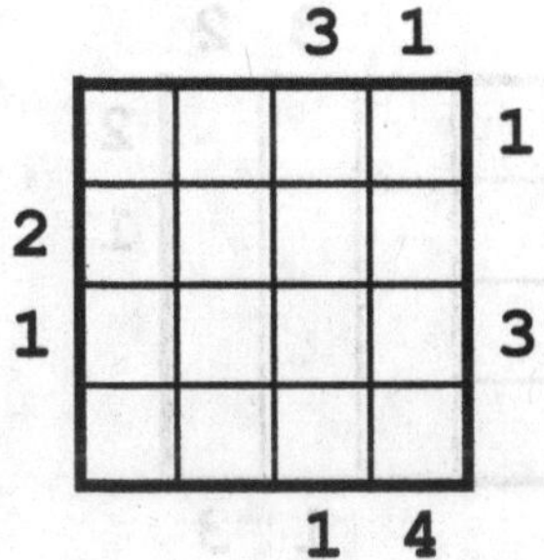

SKYSCRAPER - 15
Intermediate

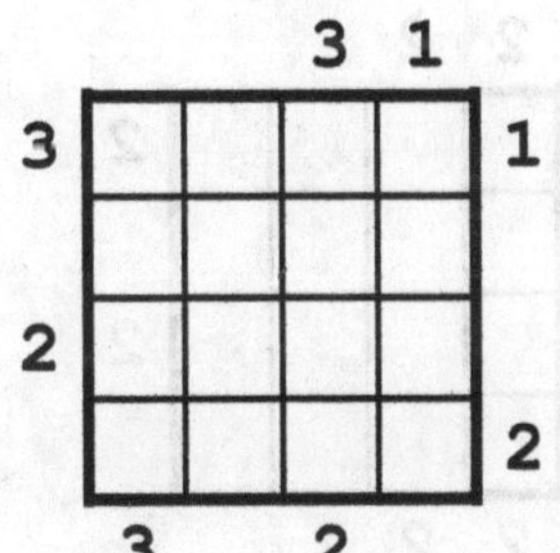

SKYSCRAPER - 16
Intermediate

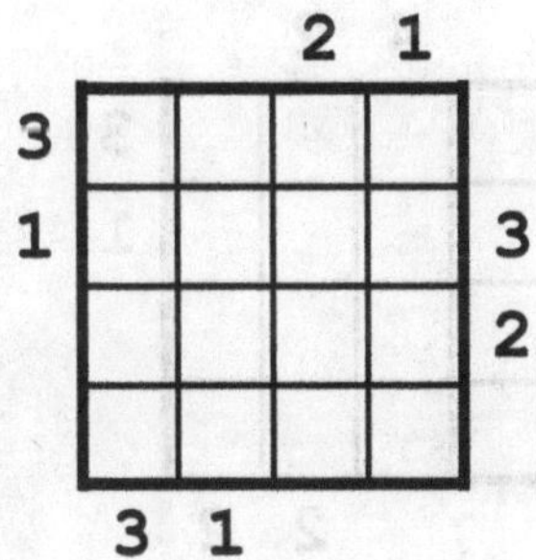

SKYSCRAPER - 17
Intermediate

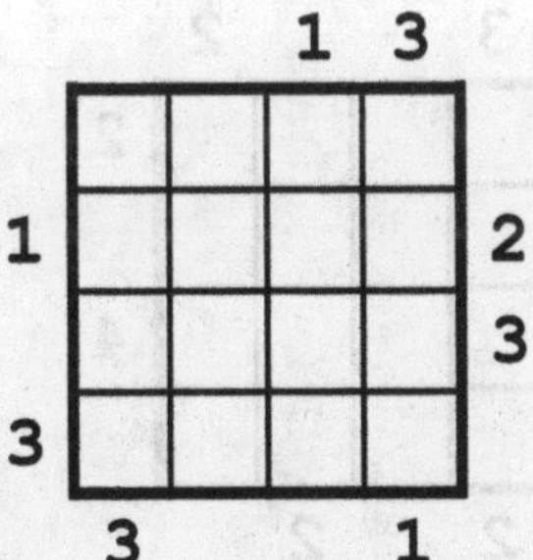

SKYSCRAPER - 18
Intermediate

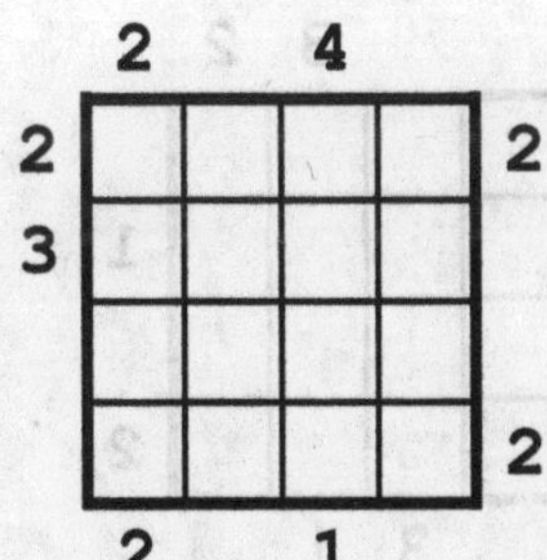

SKYSCRAPER - 19
Intermediate

Top clues: 3 2 · Right clues: 2, 1 · Left clues: 2, 3 · Bottom clues: 1 3

SKYSCRAPER - 20
Intermediate

Top clues: 2 2 · Left clues: 1, 2 · Right clues: 3, 1 · Bottom clues: 3 1

SKYSCRAPER - 21
Intermediate

Top clues: 4 2 · Left clues: 1, 3 · Right clues: 3, 1 · Bottom clues: 2 2

SKYSCRAPER - 22
Intermediate

Top clues: 2 2 · Left clues: 3, 2 · Right clues: 2, 2 · Bottom clues: 2 2

SKYSCRAPER - 23
Intermediate

Top clues: 3 2 · Left clues: 2, 1 · Right clues: 1, 2 · Bottom clues: 3 1

SKYSCRAPER - 24
Intermediate

Top clues: 3 2 · Left clues: 2, 2 · Right clues: 2, 4 · Bottom clues: 2 2

SKYSCRAPER - 25
Intermediate

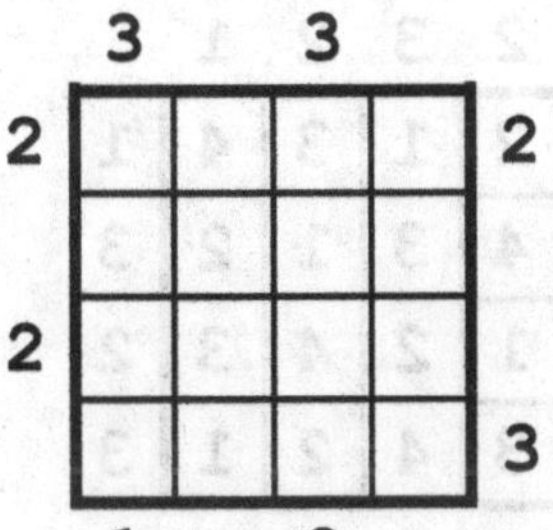

SKYSCRAPER - 26
Intermediate

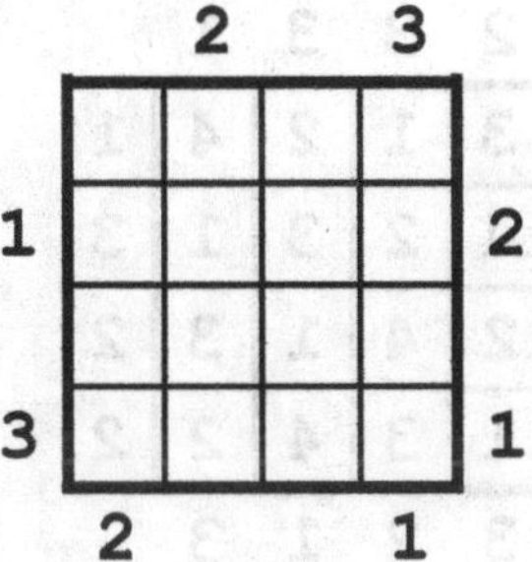

SKYSCRAPER - 27
Intermediate

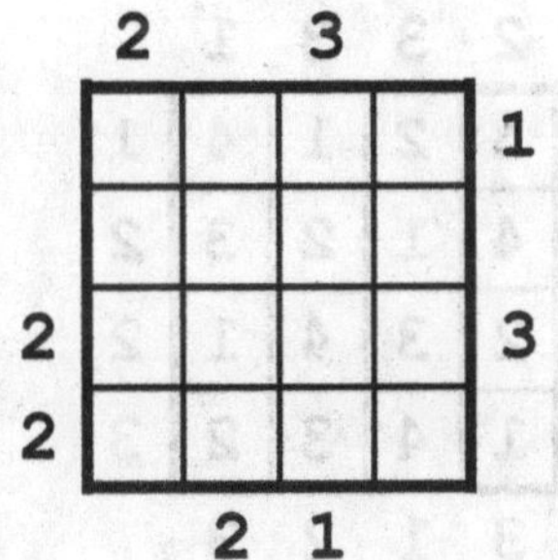

SKYSCRAPER - 28
Intermediate

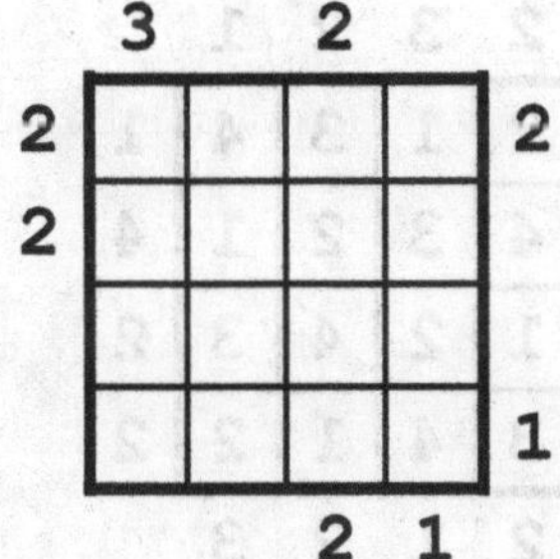

SKYSCRAPER - 29
Intermediate

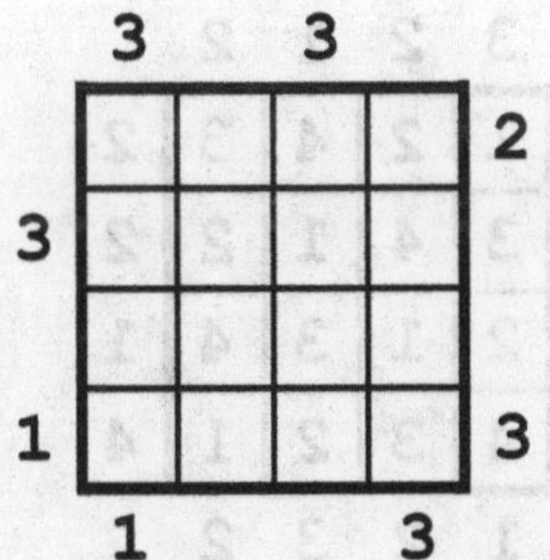

SKYSCRAPER - 30
Intermediate

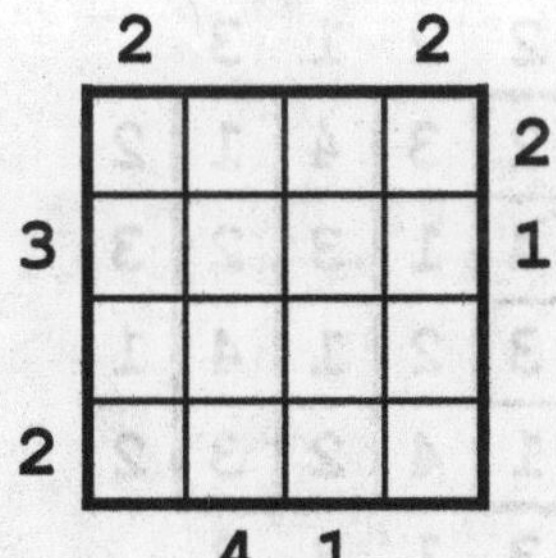

SKYSCRAPER - 1 (Solution)

Intermediate

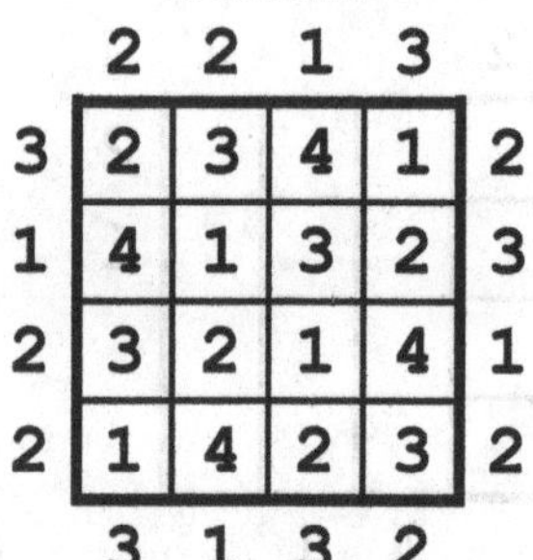

SKYSCRAPER - 2 (Solution)

Intermediate

SKYSCRAPER - 3 (Solution)

Intermediate

SKYSCRAPER - 4 (Solution)

Intermediate

SKYSCRAPER - 5 (Solution)

Intermediate

SKYSCRAPER - 6 (Solution)

Intermediate

SKYSCRAPER - 7 (Solution)
Intermediate

```
      2  2  3  1
   3 [ 2  3  1  4 ] 1
   2 [ 1  4  3  2 ] 3
   1 [ 4  1  2  3 ] 2
   2 [ 3  2  4  1 ] 2
      2  2  1  3
```

SKYSCRAPER - 8 (Solution)
Intermediate

```
      1  3  2  2
   1 [ 4  2  3  1 ] 3
   3 [ 1  3  2  4 ] 1
   2 [ 2  1  4  3 ] 2
   2 [ 3  4  1  2 ] 2
      2  1  2  3
```

SKYSCRAPER - 9 (Solution)
Intermediate

```
      3  2  2  1
   3 [ 2  1  3  4 ] 1
   2 [ 3  4  2  1 ] 3
   3 [ 1  3  4  2 ] 2
   1 [ 4  2  1  3 ] 2
      1  3  2  2
```

SKYSCRAPER - 10 (Solution)
Intermediate

```
      2  2  4  1
   2 [ 3  2  1  4 ] 1
   1 [ 4  1  2  3 ] 2
   2 [ 1  4  3  2 ] 3
   3 [ 2  3  4  1 ] 2
      2  2  1  4
```

SKYSCRAPER - 11 (Solution)
Intermediate

```
      2  2  3  1
   2 [ 3  1  2  4 ] 1
   2 [ 2  4  3  1 ] 3
   3 [ 1  3  4  2 ] 2
   1 [ 4  2  1  3 ] 2
      1  3  2  2
```

SKYSCRAPER - 12 (Solution)
Intermediate

```
      1  3  2  2
   1 [ 4  2  3  1 ] 3
   3 [ 1  3  2  4 ] 1
   2 [ 2  4  1  3 ] 2
   2 [ 3  1  4  2 ] 2
      2  2  1  3
```

SKYSCRAPER - 13 (Solution)
Intermediate

	2	2	3	1	
2	3	1	2	4	1
2	2	4	3	1	3
1	4	3	1	2	3
3	1	2	4	3	2
	2	3	1	2	

SKYSCRAPER - 14 (Solution)
Intermediate

	3	2	3	1	
3	1	3	2	4	1
2	2	4	1	3	2
1	4	1	3	2	3
2	3	2	4	1	2
	2	2	1	4	

SKYSCRAPER - 15 (Solution)
Intermediate

	2	2	3	1	
3	2	3	1	4	1
1	4	1	3	2	3
2	3	2	4	1	2
2	1	4	2	3	2
	3	1	2	2	

SKYSCRAPER - 16 (Solution)
Intermediate

	2	3	2	1	
3	2	1	3	4	1
1	4	3	1	2	3
2	3	2	4	1	2
2	1	4	2	3	2
	3	1	2	2	

SKYSCRAPER - 17 (Solution)
Intermediate

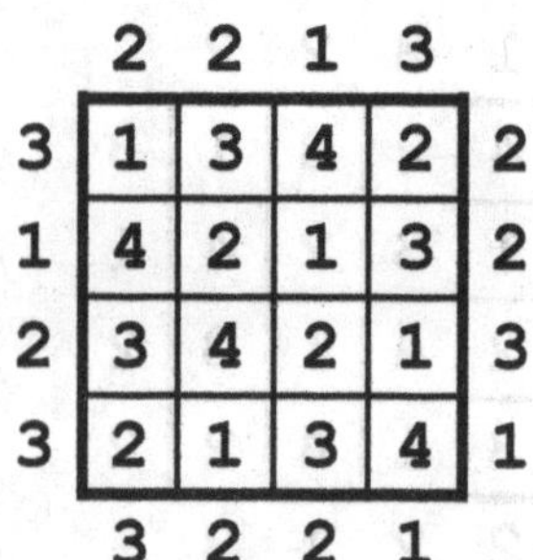

	2	2	1	3	
3	1	3	4	2	2
1	4	2	1	3	2
2	3	4	2	1	3
3	2	1	3	4	1
	3	2	2	1	

SKYSCRAPER - 18 (Solution)
Intermediate

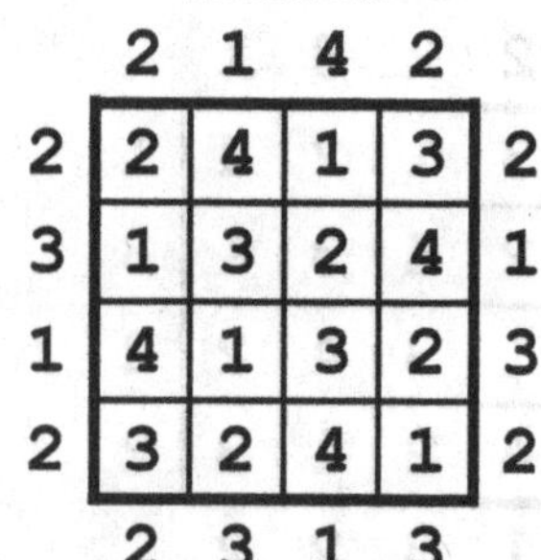

	2	1	4	2	
2	2	4	1	3	2
3	1	3	2	4	1
1	4	1	3	2	3
2	3	2	4	1	2
	2	3	1	3	

SKYSCRAPER - 19 (Solution)

Intermediate

	1	3	3	2	
1	4	1	2	3	2
2	3	2	1	4	1
2	1	4	3	2	3
3	2	3	4	1	2
	3	2	1	3	

SKYSCRAPER - 20 (Solution)

Intermediate

	1	2	2	3	
1	4	3	2	1	4
2	2	1	4	3	2
2	1	4	3	2	3
2	3	2	1	4	1
	2	2	3	1	

SKYSCRAPER - 21 (Solution)

Intermediate

	1	4	2	2	
1	4	1	3	2	3
2	3	2	1	4	1
3	2	3	4	1	2
2	1	4	2	3	2
	4	1	2	2	

SKYSCRAPER - 22 (Solution)

Intermediate

	2	2	1	4	
3	2	3	4	1	2
1	4	1	3	2	3
2	1	4	2	3	2
2	3	2	1	4	1
	2	2	4	1	

SKYSCRAPER - 23 (Solution)

Intermediate

	2	1	3	2	
2	3	4	2	1	3
4	1	2	3	4	1
1	4	3	1	2	3
2	2	1	4	3	2
	2	3	1	2	

SKYSCRAPER - 24 (Solution)

Intermediate

	3	1	2	2	
2	2	4	1	3	2
2	3	1	4	2	2
1	4	3	2	1	4
4	1	2	3	4	1
	2	3	2	1	

SKYSCRAPER - 25 (Solution)
Intermediate

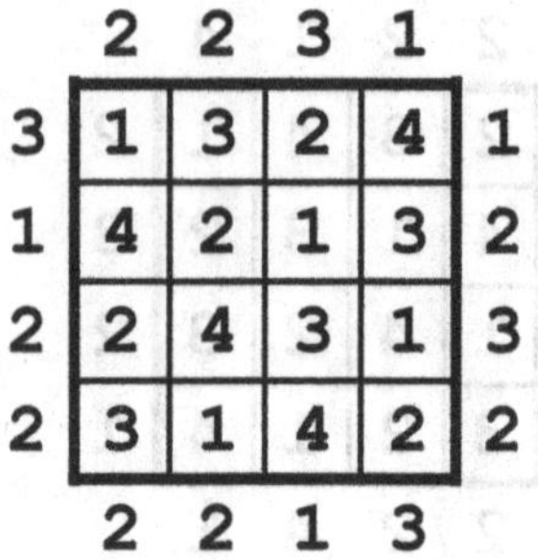

<table>
<tr><td></td><td>3</td><td>1</td><td>3</td><td>2</td><td></td></tr>
<tr><td>2</td><td>2</td><td>4</td><td>1</td><td>3</td><td>2</td></tr>
<tr><td>3</td><td>1</td><td>3</td><td>2</td><td>4</td><td>1</td></tr>
<tr><td>2</td><td>3</td><td>1</td><td>4</td><td>2</td><td>2</td></tr>
<tr><td>1</td><td>4</td><td>2</td><td>3</td><td>1</td><td>3</td></tr>
<tr><td></td><td>1</td><td>3</td><td>2</td><td>3</td><td></td></tr>
</table>

SKYSCRAPER - 26 (Solution)
Intermediate

<table>
<tr><td></td><td>2</td><td>2</td><td>1</td><td>3</td><td></td></tr>
<tr><td>2</td><td>3</td><td>2</td><td>4</td><td>1</td><td>2</td></tr>
<tr><td>1</td><td>4</td><td>1</td><td>2</td><td>3</td><td>2</td></tr>
<tr><td>2</td><td>1</td><td>4</td><td>3</td><td>2</td><td>3</td></tr>
<tr><td>3</td><td>2</td><td>3</td><td>1</td><td>4</td><td>1</td></tr>
<tr><td></td><td>2</td><td>2</td><td>3</td><td>1</td><td></td></tr>
</table>

SKYSCRAPER - 27 (Solution)
Intermediate

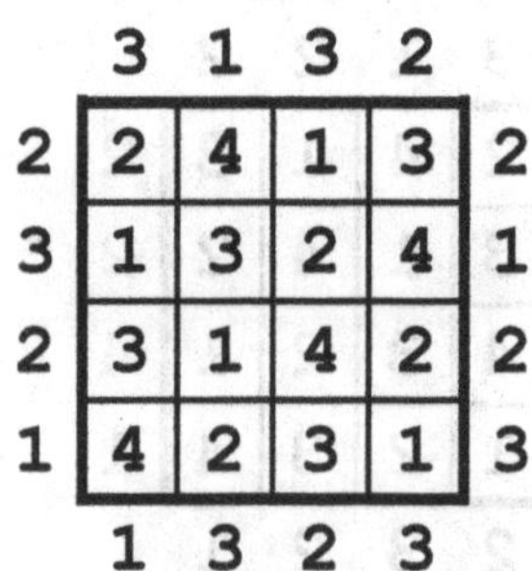

<table>
<tr><td></td><td>2</td><td>2</td><td>3</td><td>1</td><td></td></tr>
<tr><td>3</td><td>1</td><td>3</td><td>2</td><td>4</td><td>1</td></tr>
<tr><td>1</td><td>4</td><td>2</td><td>1</td><td>3</td><td>2</td></tr>
<tr><td>2</td><td>2</td><td>4</td><td>3</td><td>1</td><td>3</td></tr>
<tr><td>2</td><td>3</td><td>1</td><td>4</td><td>2</td><td>2</td></tr>
<tr><td></td><td>2</td><td>2</td><td>1</td><td>3</td><td></td></tr>
</table>

SKYSCRAPER - 28 (Solution)
Intermediate

<table>
<tr><td></td><td>3</td><td>1</td><td>2</td><td>2</td><td></td></tr>
<tr><td>2</td><td>1</td><td>4</td><td>2</td><td>3</td><td>2</td></tr>
<tr><td>2</td><td>3</td><td>2</td><td>4</td><td>1</td><td>2</td></tr>
<tr><td>1</td><td>4</td><td>3</td><td>1</td><td>2</td><td>3</td></tr>
<tr><td>3</td><td>2</td><td>1</td><td>3</td><td>4</td><td>1</td></tr>
<tr><td></td><td>2</td><td>3</td><td>2</td><td>1</td><td></td></tr>
</table>

SKYSCRAPER - 29 (Solution)
Intermediate

<table>
<tr><td></td><td>3</td><td>1</td><td>3</td><td>2</td><td></td></tr>
<tr><td>2</td><td>2</td><td>4</td><td>1</td><td>3</td><td>2</td></tr>
<tr><td>3</td><td>1</td><td>3</td><td>2</td><td>4</td><td>1</td></tr>
<tr><td>2</td><td>3</td><td>1</td><td>4</td><td>2</td><td>2</td></tr>
<tr><td>1</td><td>4</td><td>2</td><td>3</td><td>1</td><td>3</td></tr>
<tr><td></td><td>1</td><td>3</td><td>2</td><td>3</td><td></td></tr>
</table>

SKYSCRAPER - 30 (Solution)
Intermediate

<table>
<tr><td></td><td>2</td><td>1</td><td>4</td><td>2</td><td></td></tr>
<tr><td>2</td><td>2</td><td>4</td><td>1</td><td>3</td><td>2</td></tr>
<tr><td>3</td><td>1</td><td>3</td><td>2</td><td>4</td><td>1</td></tr>
<tr><td>1</td><td>4</td><td>2</td><td>3</td><td>1</td><td>3</td></tr>
<tr><td>2</td><td>3</td><td>1</td><td>4</td><td>2</td><td>2</td></tr>
<tr><td></td><td>2</td><td>4</td><td>1</td><td>2</td><td></td></tr>
</table>

MAZE

HOW TO PLAY

The aim is to find your way to the exit after entering the maze. You can use your finger or a pen or pencil to trace your path through the maze.

Intermediate

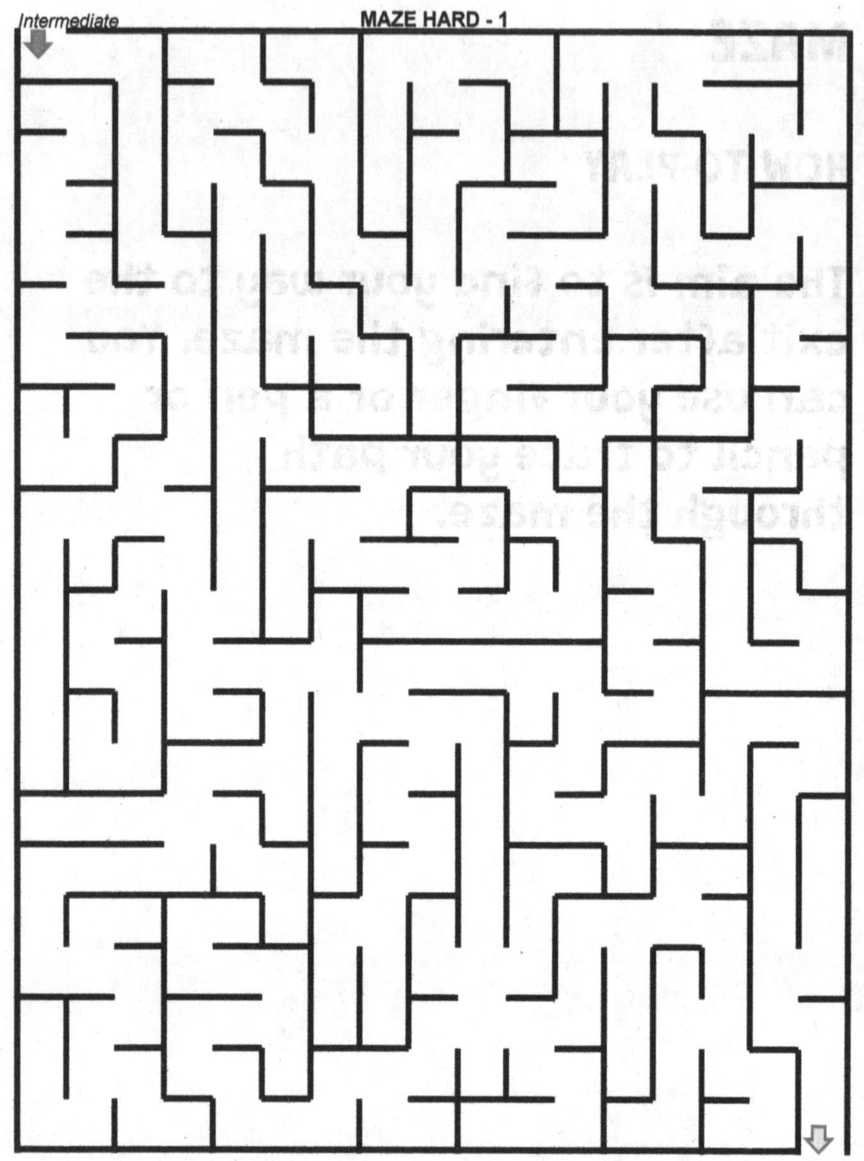

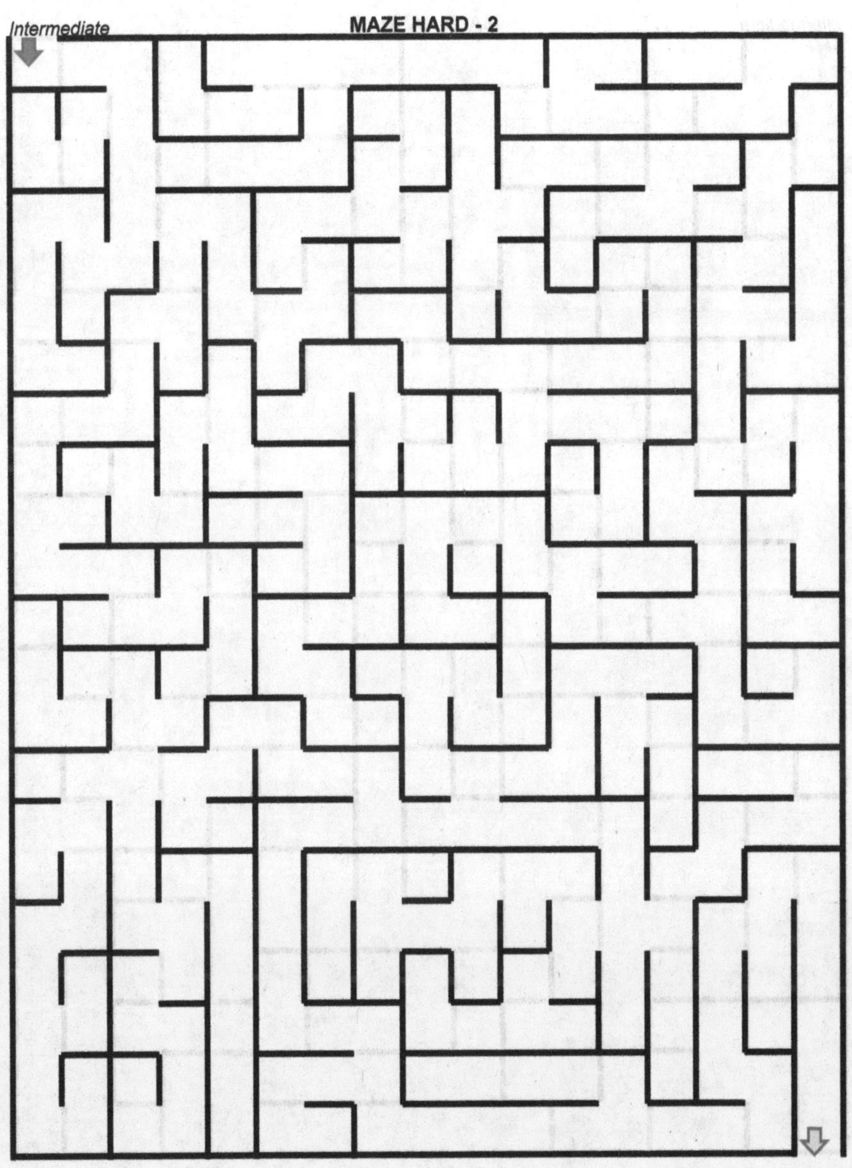
Intermediate

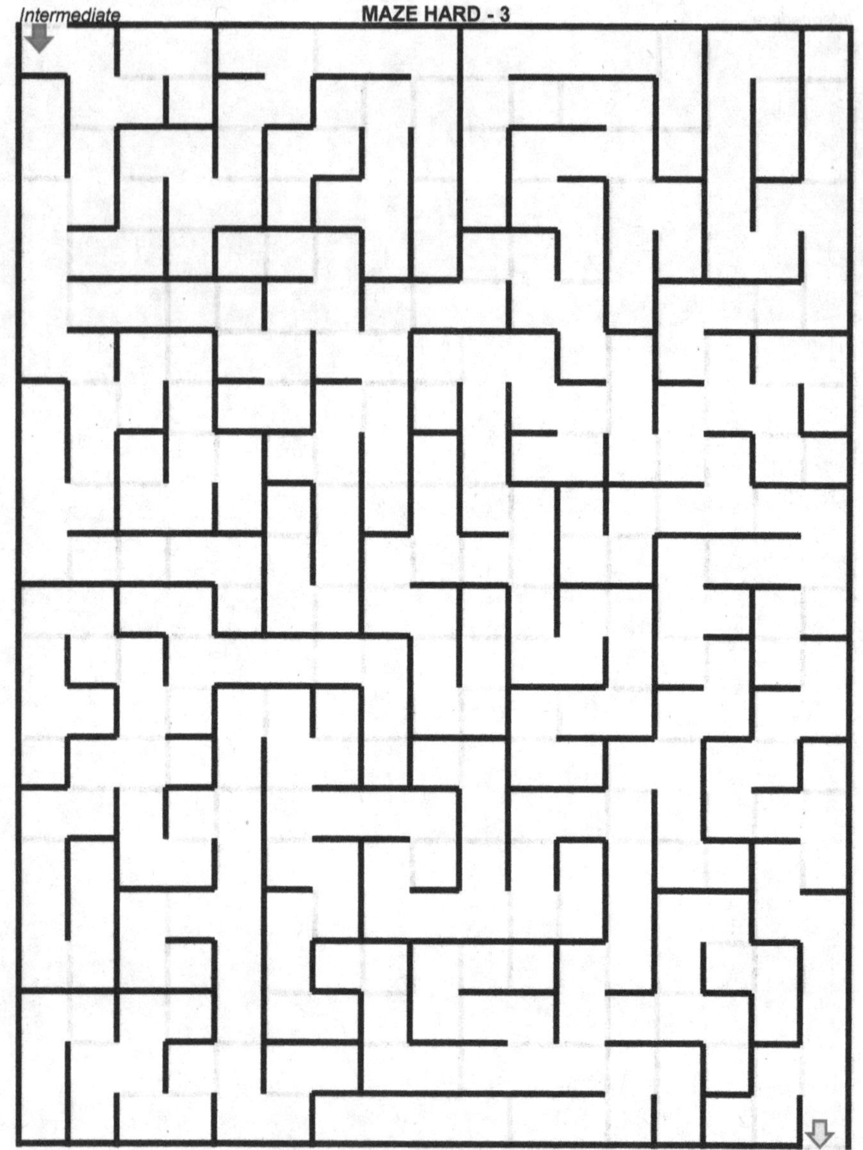

Intermediate

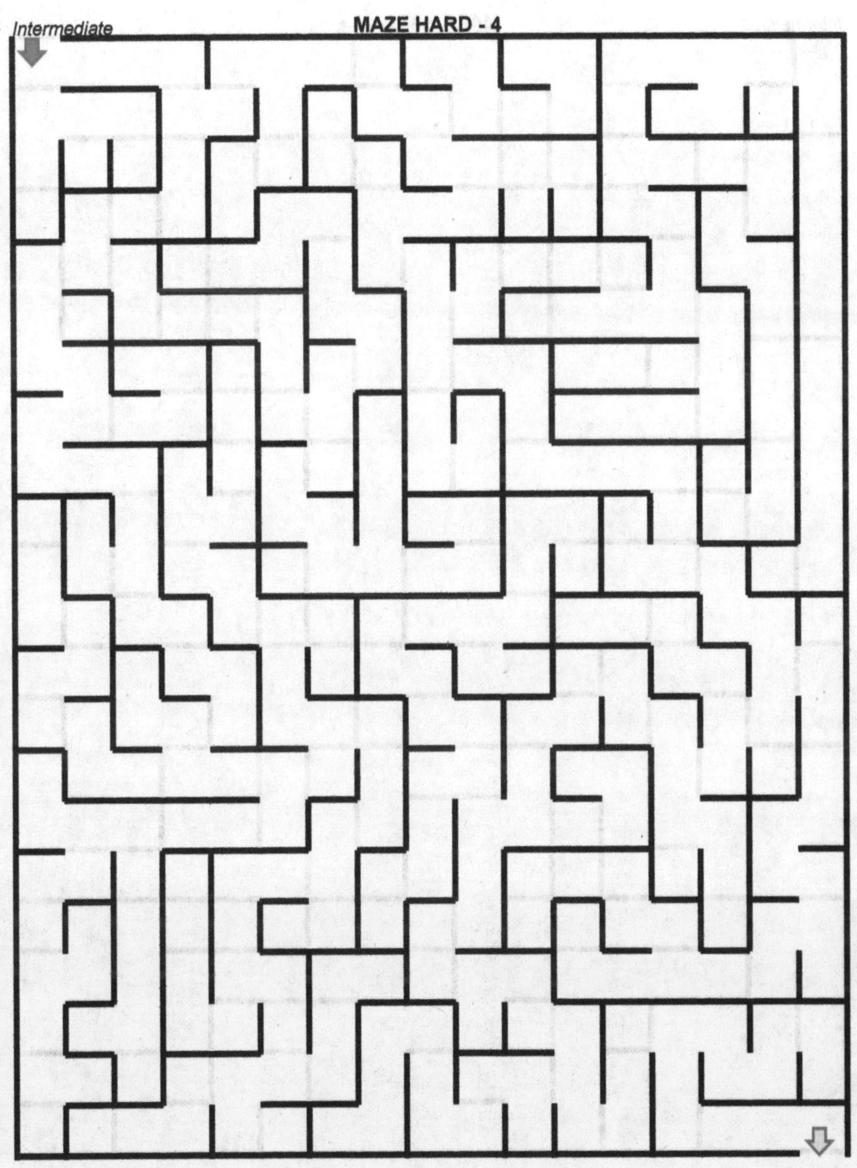

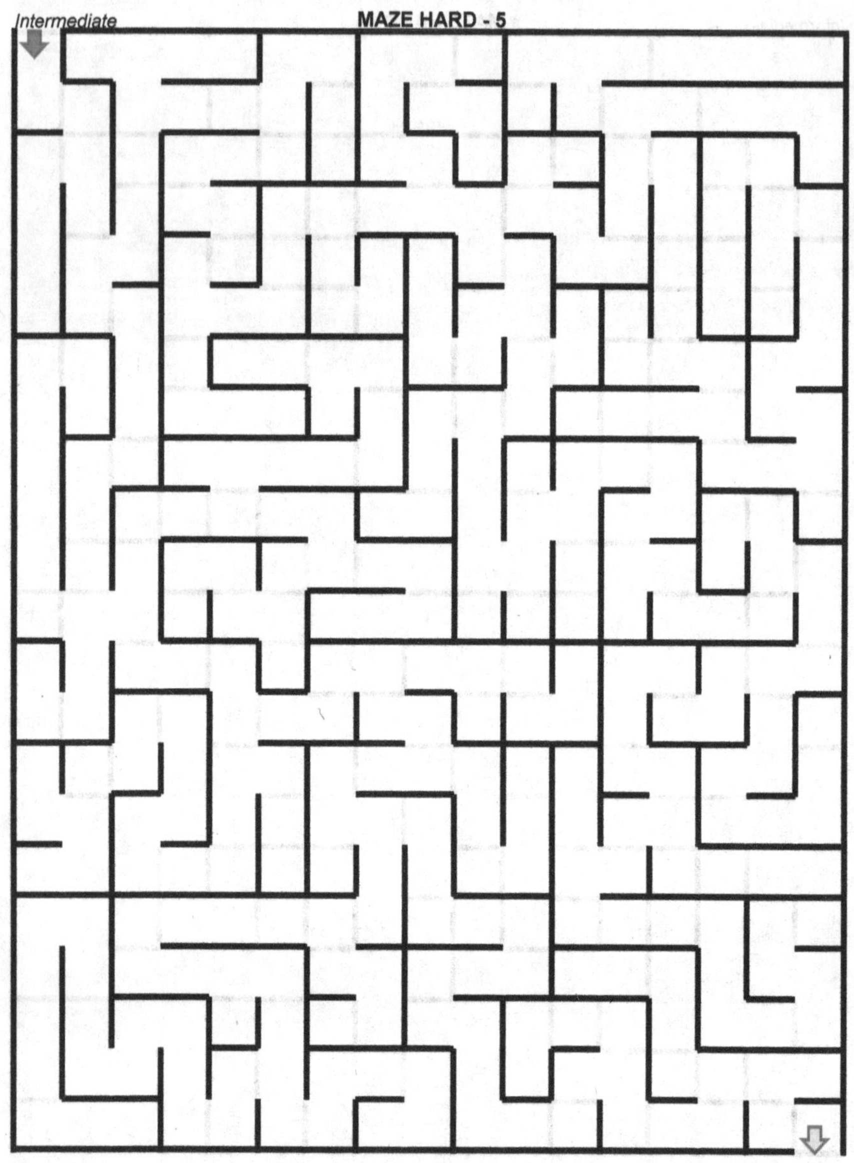

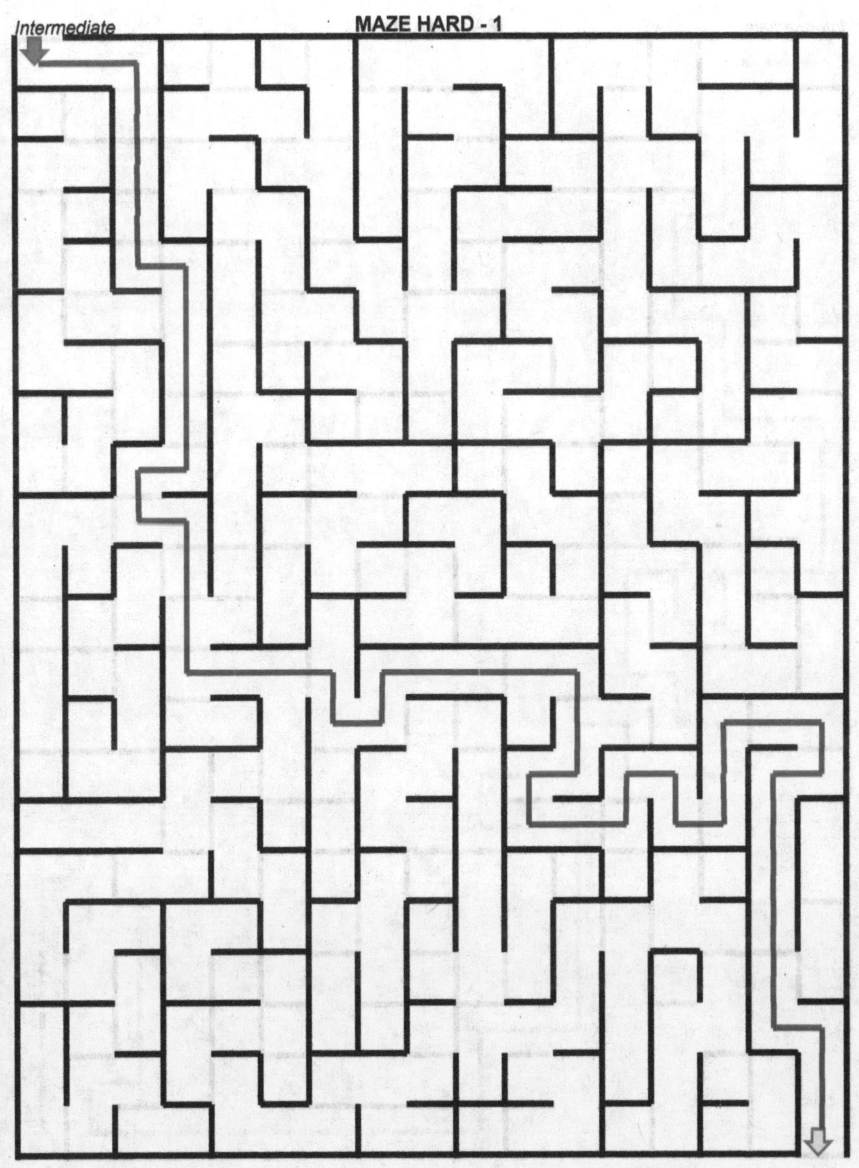
Intermediate

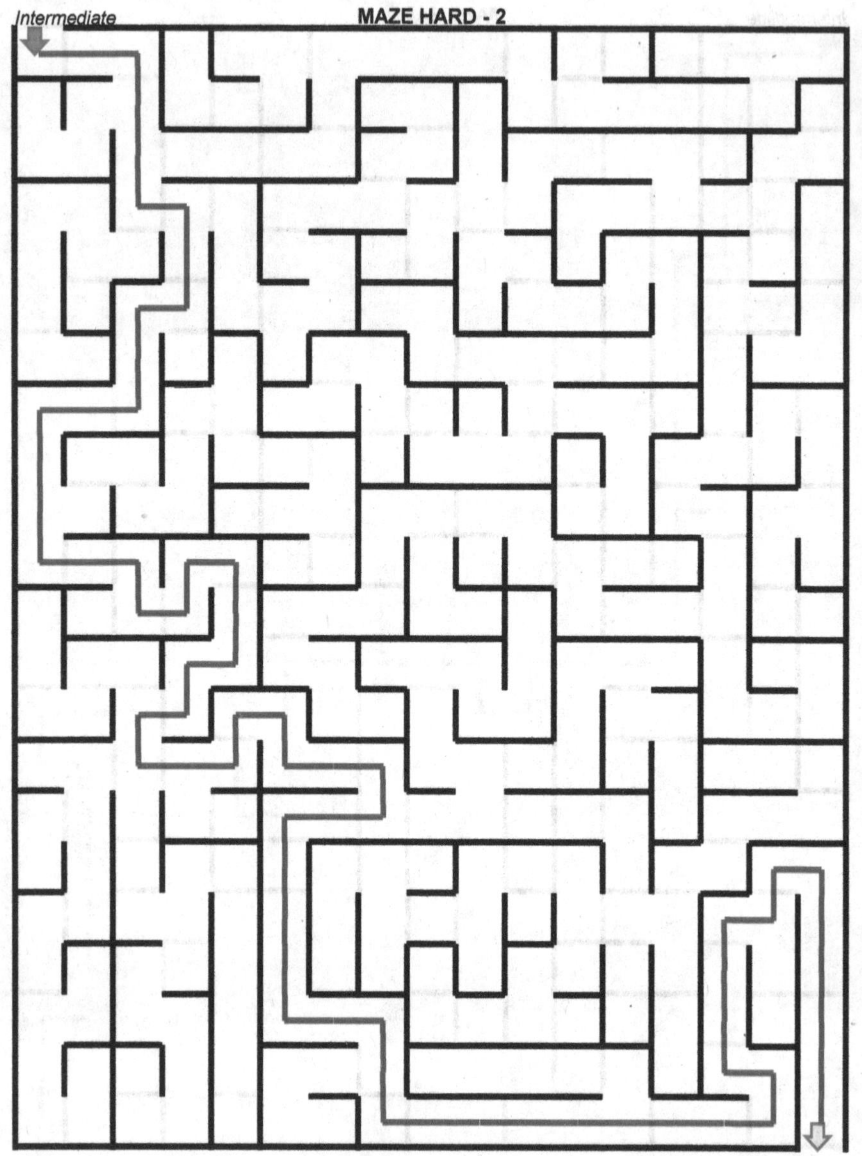

Intermediate

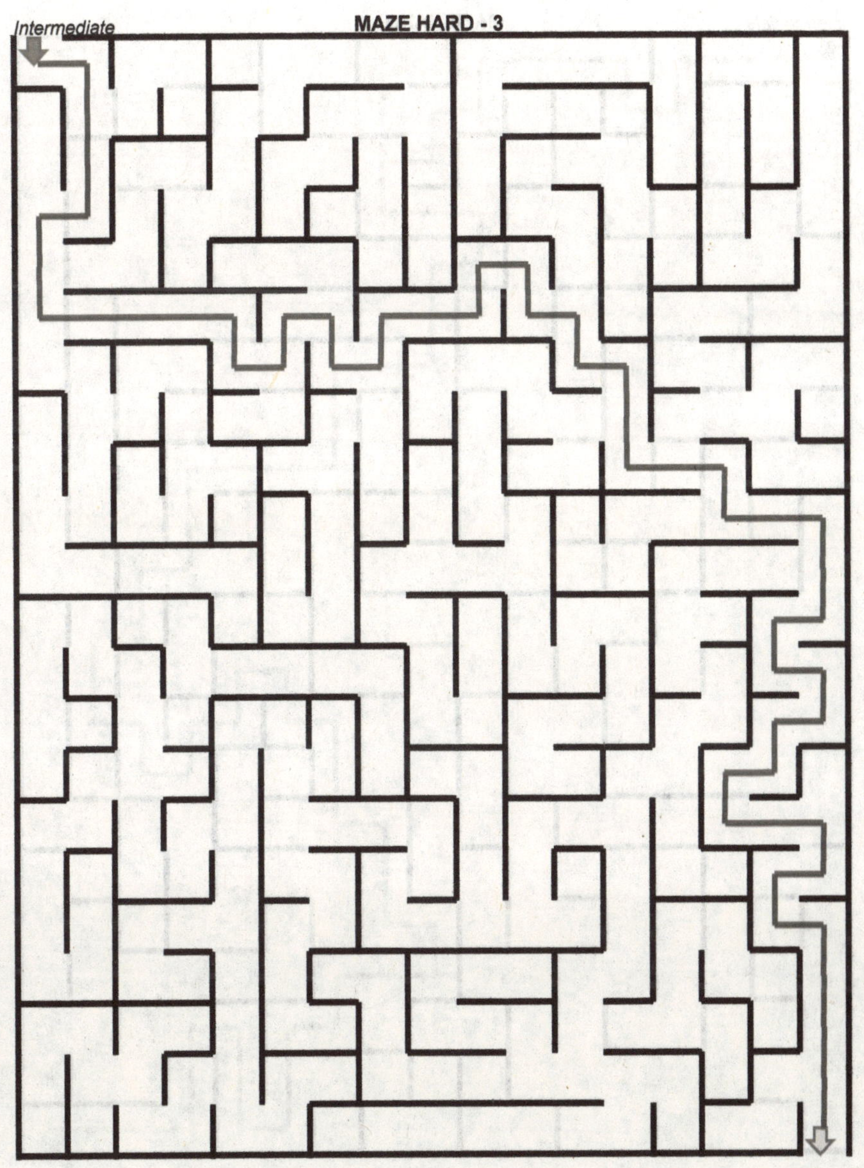

Intermediate

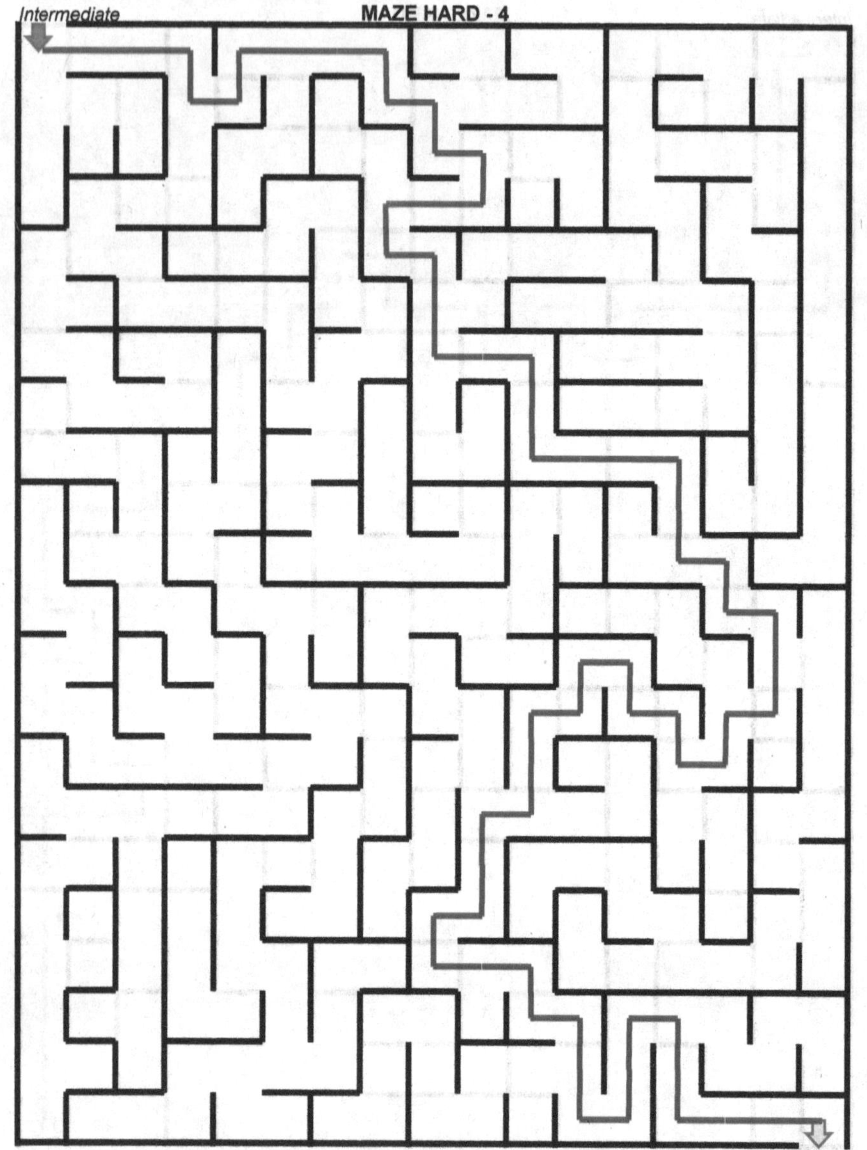

Intermediate

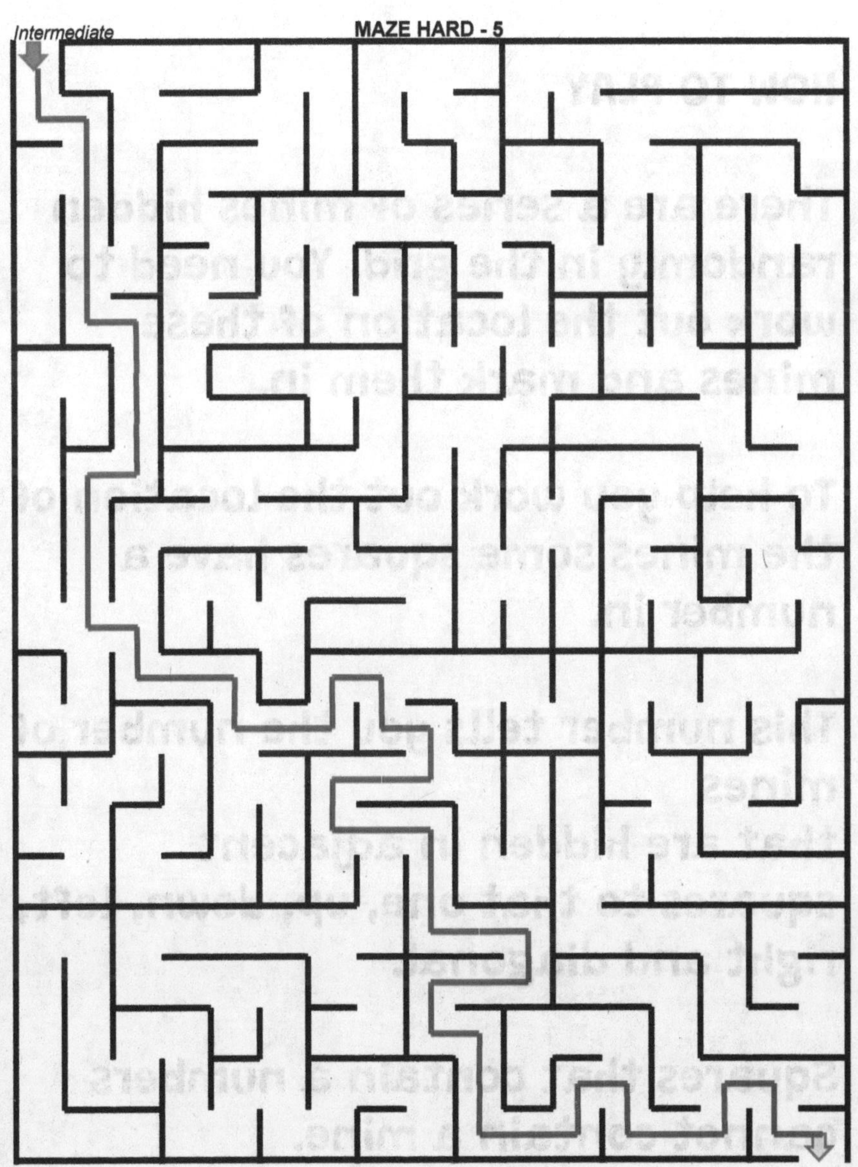

143

MINES FINDER

HOW TO PLAY

There are a series of mines hidden randomly in the grid. You need to work out the location of these mines and mark them in.

To help you work out the location of the mines some squares have a number in.

This number tells you the number of mines that are hidden in adjacent squares to that one, up, down, left, right and diagonal.

Squares that contain a numbers cannot contain a mine.

MINES FINDER - 1

	1			3
1	2	5		
2		5		4
	4			2
2		3	2	1

MINES FINDER - 2

1	3		3	
2			5	3
2		5		
2	2	4		
1		2	2	2

MINES FINDER - 3

2	3	4		3
	6		4	2
	4	2	2	
1	2		1	

MINES FINDER - 4

	2		3	1
1	3		4	
	4	5		3
3				3
2		5		2

MINES FINDER - 5

1	3		4	2
	5			
2			5	2
1	4		4	1
	2			1

MINES FINDER - 6

2				2
2		7		3
2	4			2
	3		3	1
1	2	1	1	

MINES FINDER - 7

2		3		2
	4	5		2
3			3	2
3		5		1
	3		2	1

MINES FINDER - 8

1	3		3	1
2				2
	4	5		2
3	5		3	1
			2	

MINES FINDER - 9

2		3	1	
3			3	1
3			5	
3				2
2		4	2	1

MINES FINDER - 10

1	2	3	3	2
2				
2		7		4
2	3			2
1		3	2	1

MINES FINDER - 11

1				1
3	6		5	2
			4	
	4	3		2
1	1	1	1	1

MINES FINDER - 12

1			2	
2	4		3	1
2		4	3	
3			4	2
	4			1

MINES FINDER - 13

1	1	1		
2		3	2	2
4		6		
2	3	4		3

MINES FINDER - 14

2		3	2	
4		5		2
			3	2
3	5	5		1
1			2	1

MINES FINDER - 15

2	3	3	3	2
4		7		
2		4		3
1	1	2	1	1

MINES FINDER - 16

	2		3	1
1	3			3
1		5		
3	4		4	3
		3		1

MINES FINDER - 17

2	3	2	2	1
			4	
3	6			3
	4		4	
	3	1	2	1

MINES FINDER - 18

3			2	1
		6		2
		4		2
2	3	4	3	2
	1			1

MINES FINDER - 19

1	2	3		1
3			4	2
				2
2	3	5		4
		2		

MINES FINDER - 20

2		3	1	1
2		5		2
3	5			3
				2
3		4	2	1

MINES FINDER - 21

2		3	1	
2			3	1
1	4		6	
1	3			
1		4		3

MINES FINDER - 22

2			1	
4		6	3	1
				1
3		5	4	3
1	1	2		

MINES FINDER - 23

1		3	3	
1	2			3
1	3	4		3
	2		4	
1	2	1	3	

MINES FINDER - 24

2	2	1	1	1
		4	3	
5				3
				2
2	3	3	2	1

MINES FINDER - 25

2	3	3	2	1
				2
3	5	7		3
2				3
2		5		2

MINES FINDER - 26

2	3			1
		6	4	2
				1
4		5	2	1
2		2		

MINES FINDER - 27

	1	2	3	2
2	4			
			7	4
3	5			
1		3	3	2

MINES FINDER - 28

	2		4	
1	4			3
2				3
2				2
1	2	3	2	1

MINES FINDER - 29

2		3	1	1
3		4		1
	5		2	1
		4	2	
3			1	

MINES FINDER - 30

2	2	2	1	1
		4		2
3	5			3
	4		5	
2		2	3	

MINES FINDER - 1 (Solution)

	1	●	●	3
1	2	5	●	●
2	●	5	●	4
●	4	●	●	2
2	●	3	2	1

MINES FINDER - 2 (Solution)

1	3	●	3	●
2	●	●	5	3
2	●	5	●	●
2	2	4	●	●
1	●	2	2	2

MINES FINDER - 3 (Solution)

2	3	4	●	3
●	●	●	●	●
●	6	●	4	2
●	4	2	2	
1	2	●	1	

MINES FINDER - 4 (Solution)

	2	●	3	1
1	3	●	4	●
●	4	5	●	3
3	●	●	●	3
2	●	5	●	2

MINES FINDER - 5 (Solution)

1	3	●	4	2
●	5	●	●	●
2	●	●	5	2
1	4	●	4	1
	2	●	●	1

MINES FINDER - 6 (Solution)

2	●	●	●	2
2	●	7	●	3
2	4	●	●	2
●	3	●	3	1
1	2	1	1	

MINES FINDER - 7 (Solution)

2	●	3	●	2
●	4	5	●	2
3	●	●	3	2
3	●	5	●	1
●	3	●	2	1

MINES FINDER - 8 (Solution)

1	3	●	3	1
2	●	●	●	2
●	4	5	●	2
3	5	●	3	1
●	●	●	2	

MINES FINDER - 9 (Solution)

2	●	3	1	
3	●	●	3	1
3	●	●	5	●
3	●	●	●	2
2	●	4	2	1

MINES FINDER - 10 (Solution)

1	2	3	3	2
2	●	●	●	●
2	●	7	●	4
2	3	●	●	2
1	●	3	2	1

MINES FINDER - 11 (Solution)

1	●	●	●	1
3	6	●	5	2
●	●	●	4	●
●	4	3	●	2
1	1	1	1	1

MINES FINDER - 12 (Solution)

1	●	●	2	
2	4	●	3	1
2	●	4	3	●
3	●	●	4	2
●	4	●	●	1

MINES FINDER - 13 (Solution)

1	1	1		
2	●	3	2	2
4	●	6	●	●
●	●	●	●	●
2	3	4	●	3

MINES FINDER - 14 (Solution)

2	●	3	2	●
4	●	5	●	2
●	●	●	3	2
3	5	5	●	1
1	●	●	2	1

MINES FINDER - 15 (Solution)

2	3	3	3	2
●	●	●	●	●
4	●	7	●	●
2	●	4	●	3
1	1	2	1	1

MINES FINDER - 16 (Solution)

	2	●	3	1
1	3	●	●	3
1	●	5	●	●
3	4	●	4	3
●	●	3	●	1

MINES FINDER - 17 (Solution)

2	3	2	2	1
●	●	●	4	●
3	6	●	●	3
●	4	●	4	●
●	3	1	2	1

MINES FINDER - 18 (Solution)

3	●	●	2	1
●	●	6	●	2
●	●	4	●	2
2	3	4	3	2
	1	●	●	1

MINES FINDER - 19 (Solution)

1	2	3	●	1
3	●	●	4	2
●	●	●	●	2
2	3	5	●	4
		2	●	●

MINES FINDER - 20 (Solution)

2	●	3	1	1
2	●	5	●	2
3	5	●	●	3
●	●	●	●	2
3	●	4	2	1

MINES FINDER - 21 (Solution)

2	●	3	1	
2	●	●	3	1
1	4	●	6	●
1	3	●	●	●
1	●	4	●	3

MINES FINDER - 22 (Solution)

2	●	●	1	
4	●	6	3	1
●	●	●	●	1
3	●	5	4	3
1	1	2	●	●

MINES FINDER - 23 (Solution)

1	●	3	3	●
1	2	●	●	3
1	3	4	●	3
●	2	●	4	●
1	2	1	3	●

MINES FINDER - 24 (Solution)

2	2	1	1	1
●	●	4	3	●
5	●	●	●	3
●	●	●	●	2
2	3	3	2	1

MINES FINDER - 25 (Solution)

2	3	3	2	1
●	●	●	●	2
3	5	7	●	3
2	●	●	●	3
2	●	5	●	2

MINES FINDER - 26 (Solution)

2	3	●	●	1
●	●	6	4	2
●	●	●	●	1
4	●	5	2	1
2	●	2		

MINES FINDER - 27 (Solution)

	1	2	3	2
2	4	●	●	●
●	●	●	7	4
3	5	●	●	●
1	●	3	3	2

MINES FINDER - 28 (Solution)

	2	●	4	●
1	4	●	●	3
2	●	●	●	3
2	●	●	●	2
1	2	3	2	1

MINES FINDER - 29 (Solution)

2	●	3	1	1
3	●	4	●	1
●	5	●	2	1
●	●	4	2	
3	●	●	1	

MINES FINDER - 30 (Solution)

2	2	2	1	1
●	●	4	●	2
3	5	●	●	3
●	4	●	5	●
2	●	2	3	●

RANGE PUZZLE
HOW TO PLAY

The aim is to find the shaded cells, known that
- Each number tells you how many White squares are reachable from that square, horizontally and vertically, in total, including the numbered square (i.e. the range).

- You are not allowed to have two Black squares touching horizontally or vertically (diagonally is ok).

- Any White square can be reached from any other (i.e. they are connected).

RANGE PUZZLE - 1

4			
			2
	6		
		4	

RANGE PUZZLE - 2

		5	
	6		5
	6		

RANGE PUZZLE - 3

	5		
		3	5
4			

RANGE PUZZLE - 4

		3	
	6		6
3			

RANGE PUZZLE - 5

5			
4		5	
		5	

RANGE PUZZLE - 6

6			4
	5		
	5		3

RANGE PUZZLE - 7

		5	3
	6		
	4		2

RANGE PUZZLE - 8

3			
	4		3
		3	

RANGE PUZZLE - 9

	2		
6		5	
4			

RANGE PUZZLE - 10

		6	5
	5	6	

RANGE PUZZLE - 11

4			5
3		6	

RANGE PUZZLE - 12

	5		4
2	5		

RANGE PUZZLE - 13

	3		
4		5	
6			
			2

RANGE PUZZLE - 14

	6		5
		6	
	5		

RANGE PUZZLE - 15

	4	6	
3			2

RANGE PUZZLE - 16

		3	
		6	
4			
			3

RANGE PUZZLE - 17

5			
		3	
			4
2			2

RANGE PUZZLE - 18

		3	
	5		2
	6		

RANGE PUZZLE - 19

RANGE PUZZLE - 20

RANGE PUZZLE - 21

RANGE PUZZLE - 22

RANGE PUZZLE - 23

RANGE PUZZLE - 24

RANGE PUZZLE - 25

RANGE PUZZLE - 26

RANGE PUZZLE - 27

RANGE PUZZLE - 28

RANGE PUZZLE - 29

RANGE PUZZLE - 30

RANGE PUZZLE - 1 (Solution)

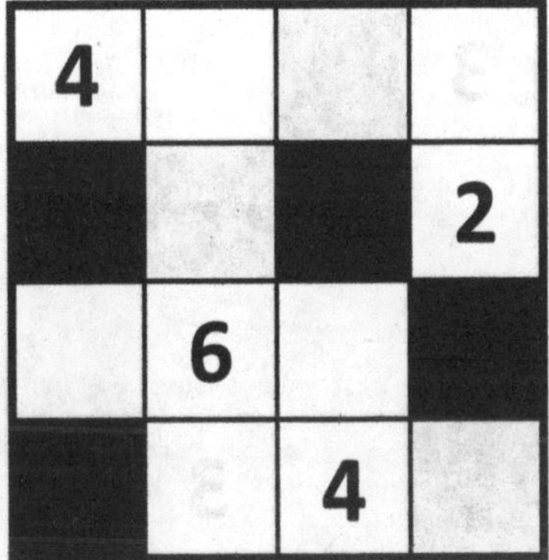

RANGE PUZZLE - 2 (Solution)

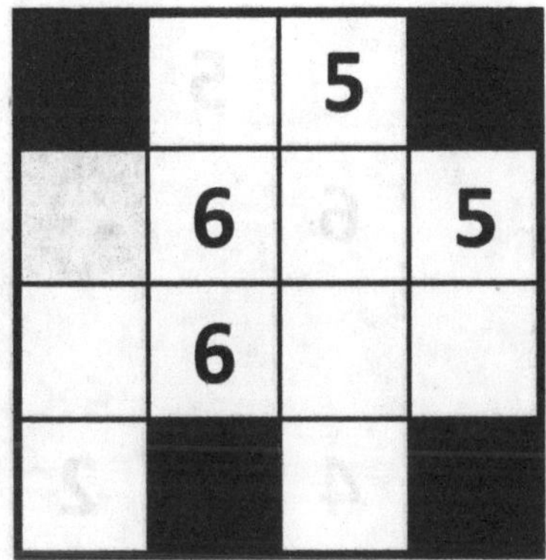

RANGE PUZZLE - 3 (Solution)

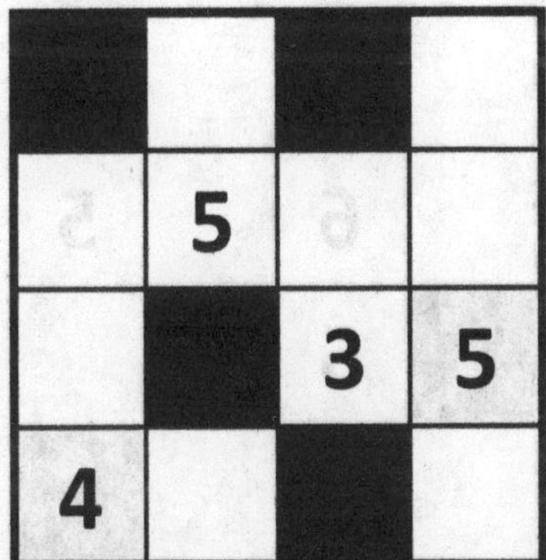

RANGE PUZZLE - 4 (Solution)

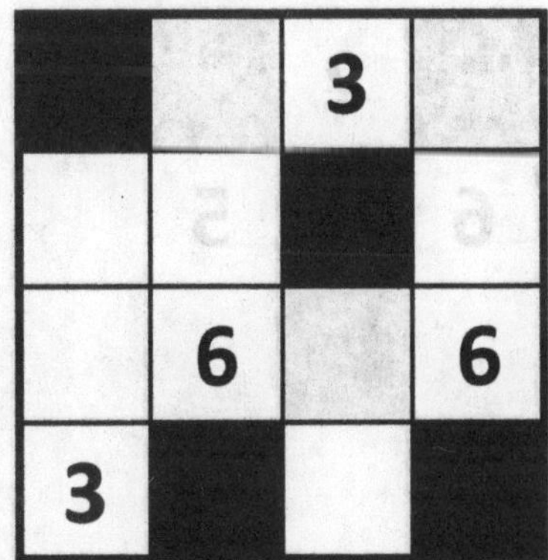

RANGE PUZZLE - 5 (Solution)

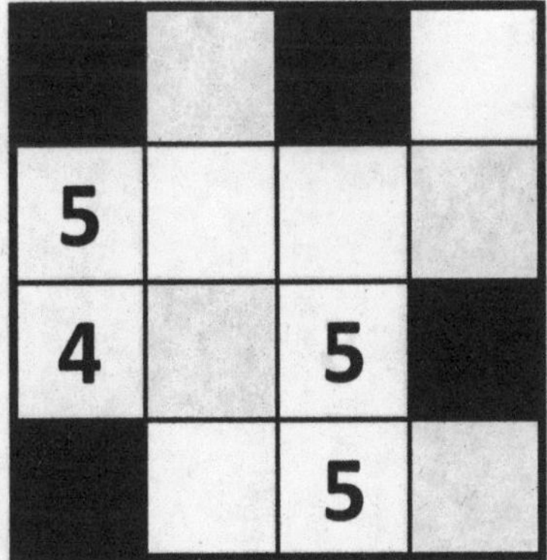

RANGE PUZZLE - 6 (Solution)

RANGE PUZZLE - 7 (Solution)

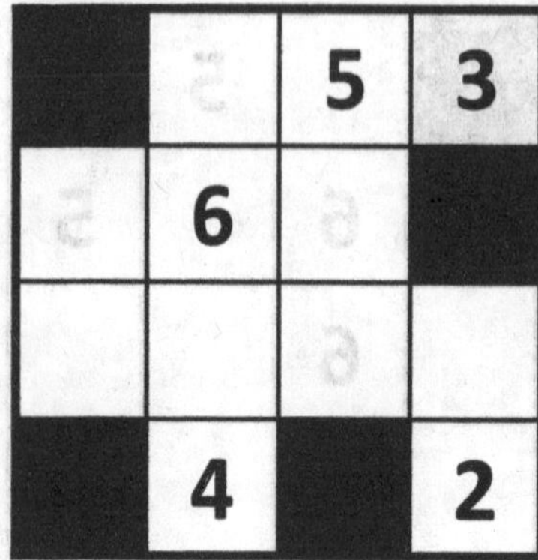

RANGE PUZZLE - 8 (Solution)

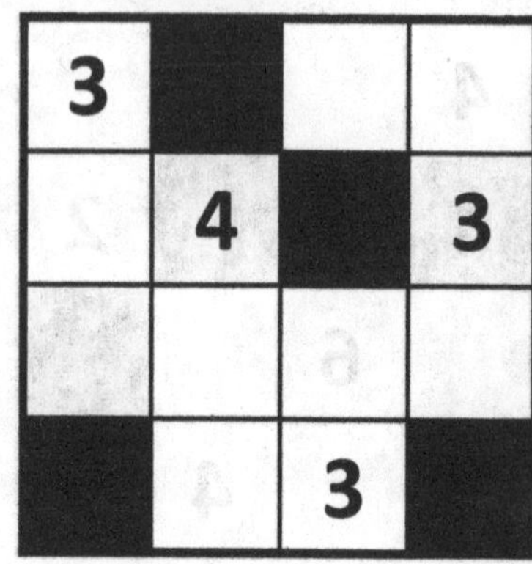

RANGE PUZZLE - 9 (Solution)

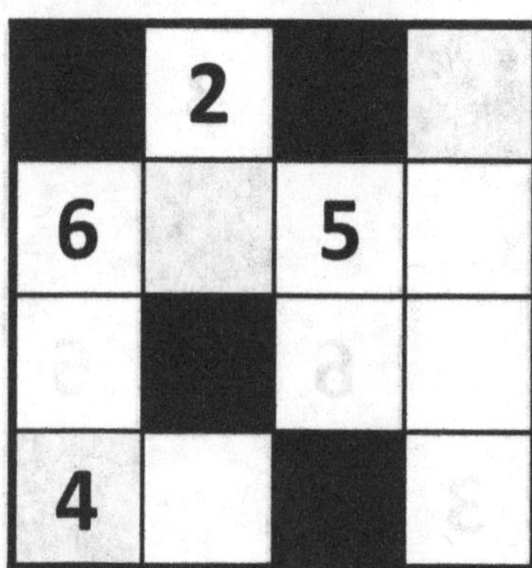

RANGE PUZZLE - 10 (Solution)

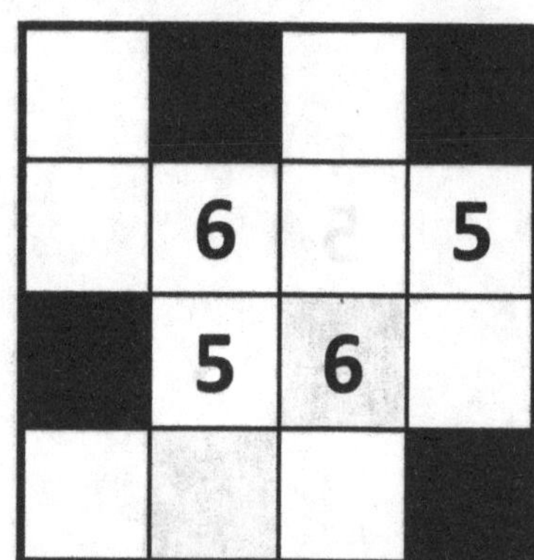

RANGE PUZZLE - 11 (Solution)

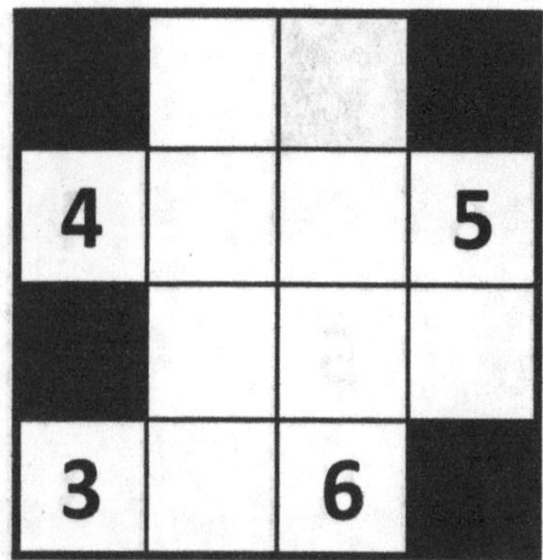

RANGE PUZZLE - 12 (Solution)

RANGE PUZZLE - 13 (Solution)

RANGE PUZZLE - 14 (Solution)

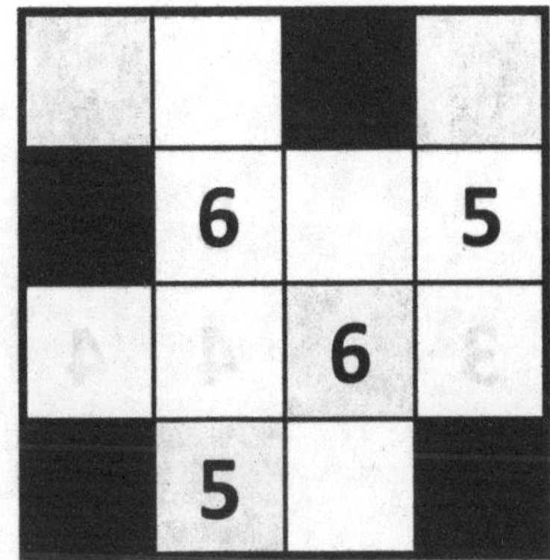

RANGE PUZZLE - 15 (Solution)

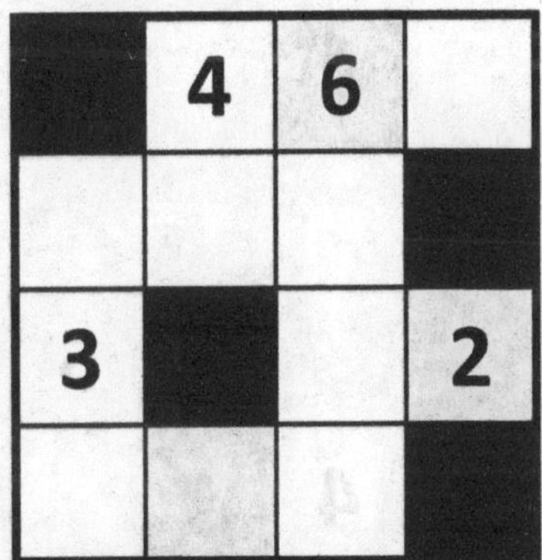

RANGE PUZZLE - 16 (Solution)

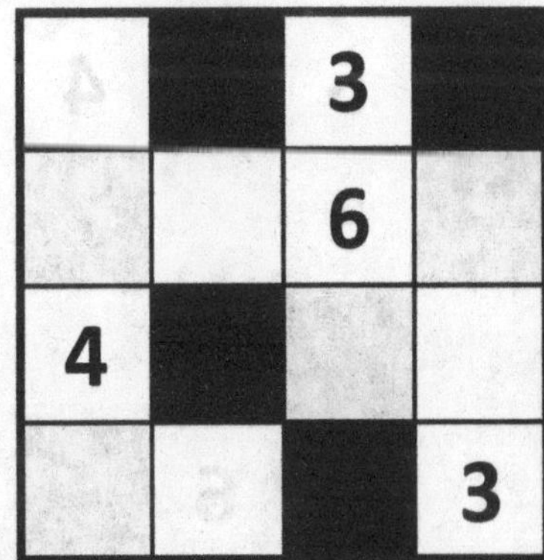

RANGE PUZZLE - 17 (Solution)

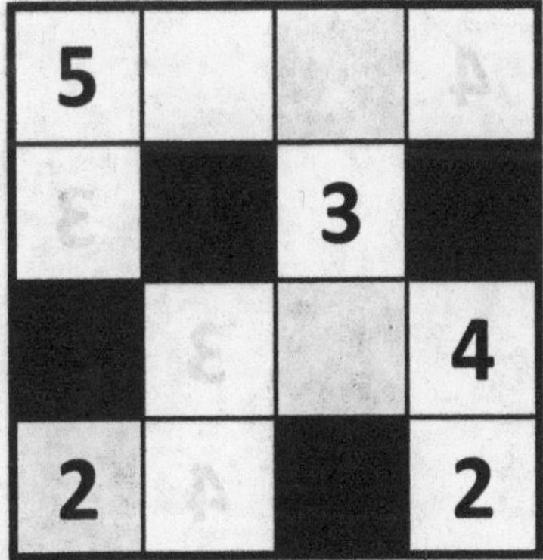

RANGE PUZZLE - 18 (Solution)

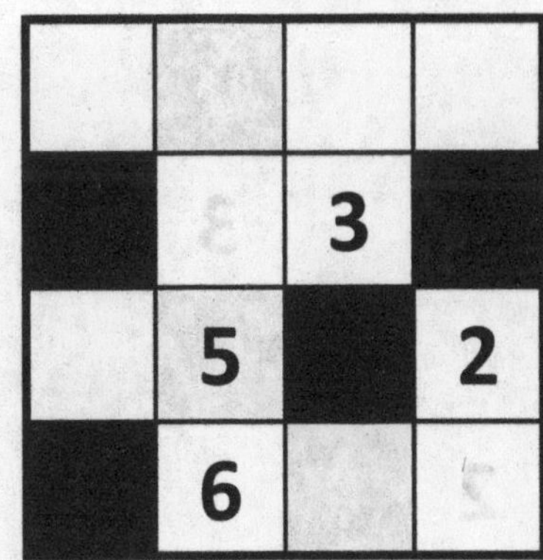

RANGE PUZZLE - 19 (Solution)

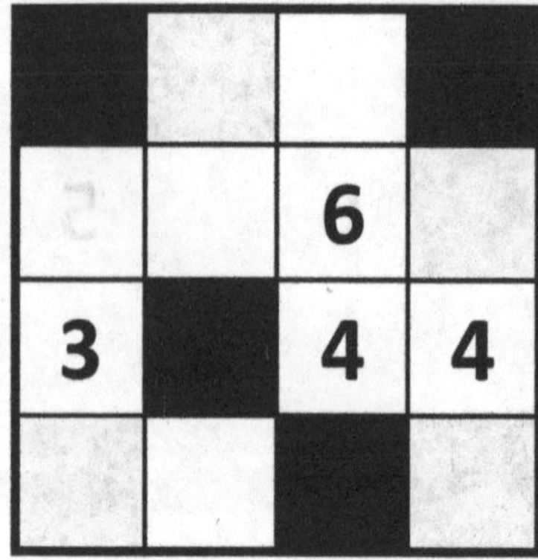

RANGE PUZZLE - 20 (Solution)

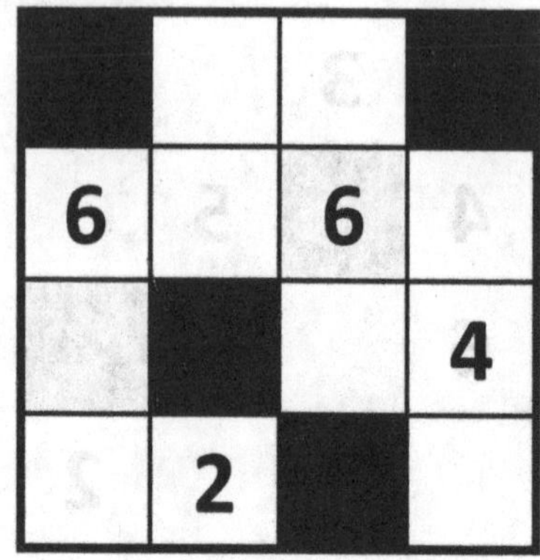

RANGE PUZZLE - 21 (Solution)

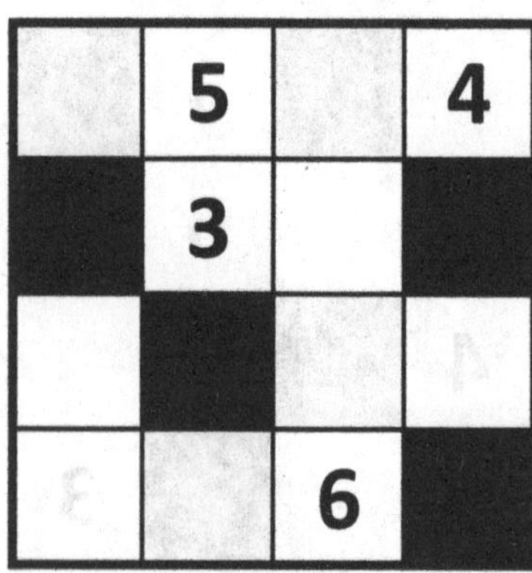

RANGE PUZZLE - 22 (Solution)

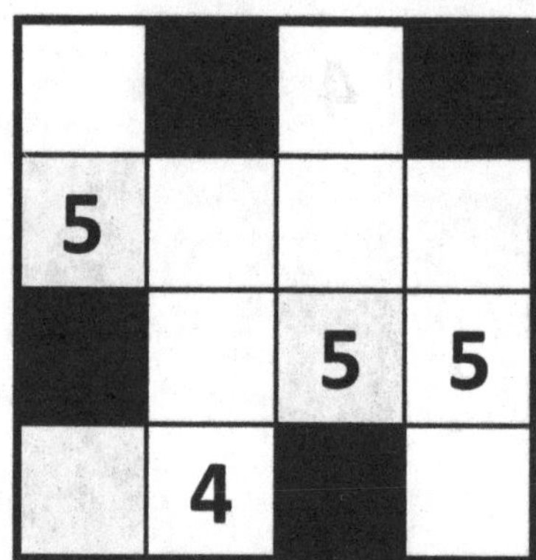

RANGE PUZZLE - 23 (Solution)

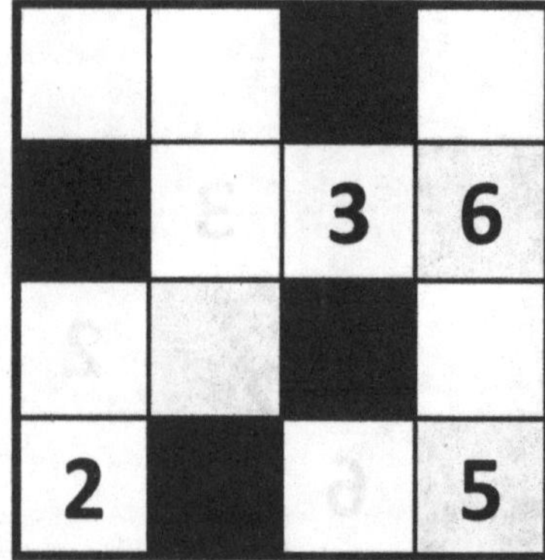

RANGE PUZZLE - 24 (Solution)

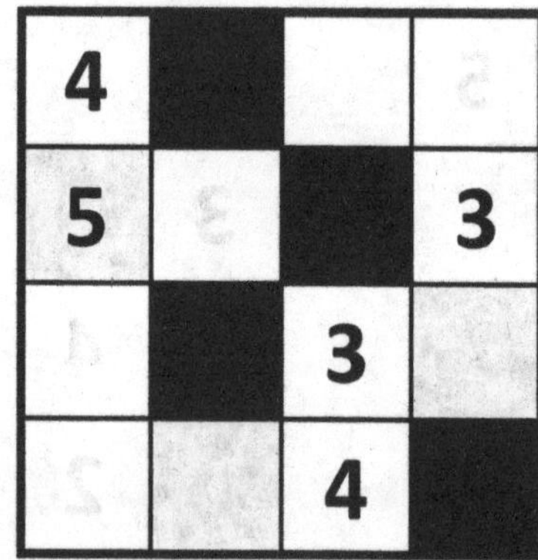

RANGE PUZZLE - 25 (Solution)

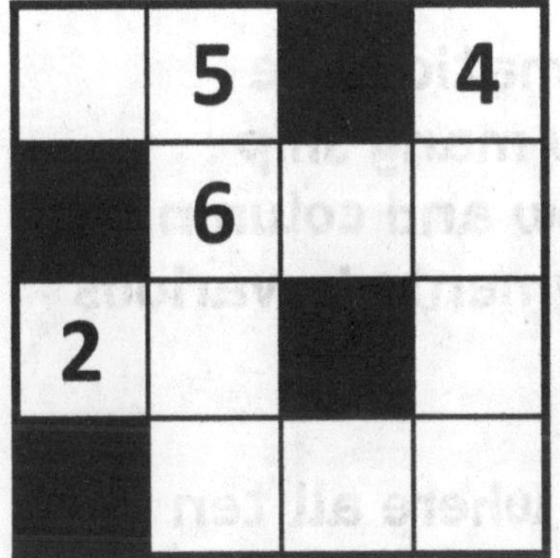

RANGE PUZZLE - 26 (Solution)

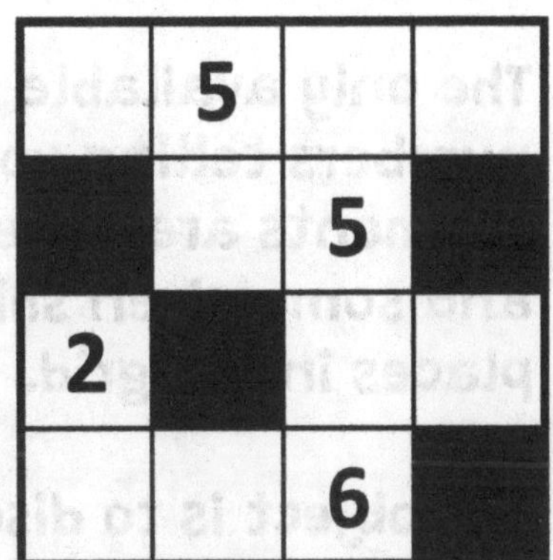

RANGE PUZZLE - 27 (Solution)

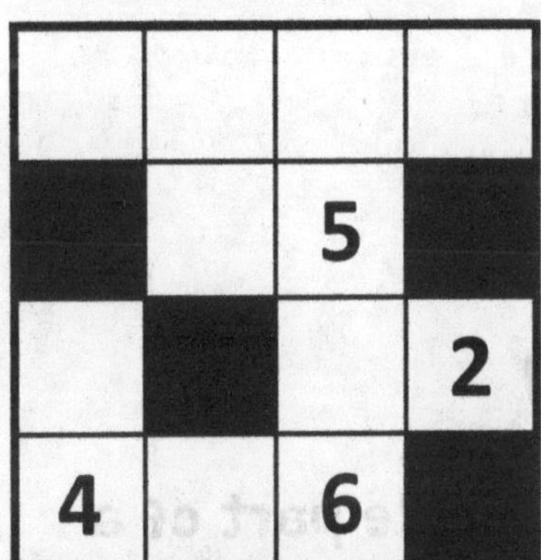

RANGE PUZZLE - 28 (Solution)

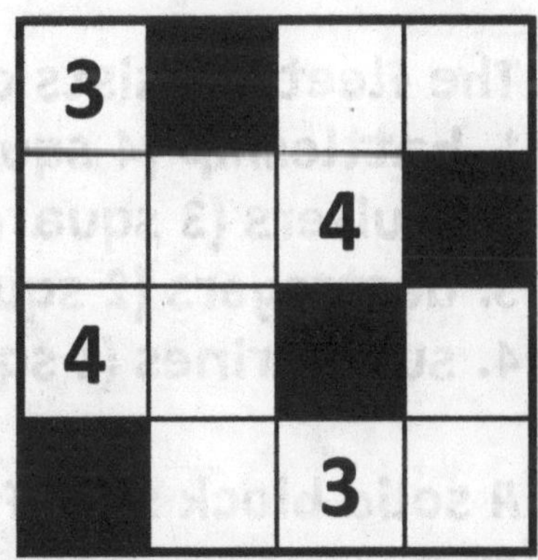

RANGE PUZZLE - 29 (Solution)

RANGE PUZZLE - 30 (Solution)

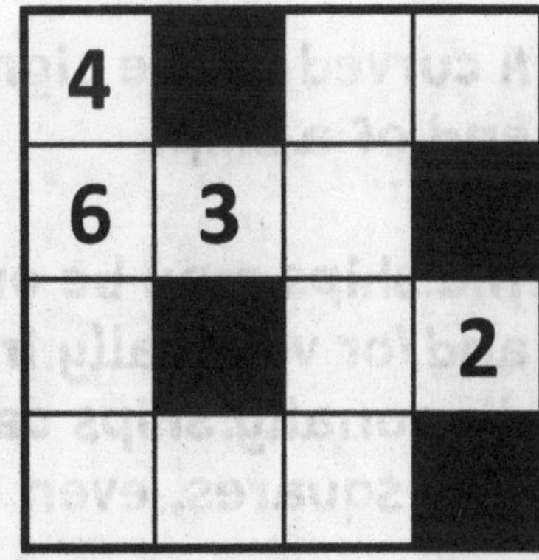

WARSHIP
HOW TO PLAY

The only available information are numbers telling you how many ship segments are in each row and column, and some given ship segments in various places in the grid.

The object is to discover where all ten ships are located in the grid.

The fleet consists of
1. battleship (4 squares)
2. cruisers (3 squares)
3. destroyers (2 squares)
4. submarines (1 squares)

A solid block signifies a middle part of a ship.

A curved shape signifies the start or the end of a ship.

The ships may be oriented horizontally and/or vertically in the grid, but not diagonally.Ships can not occupy adjacent grid squares, even diagonally.

WARSHIPS - 1

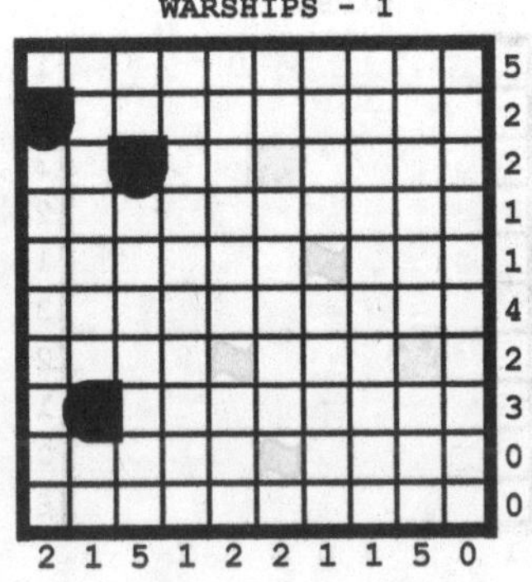

WARSHIPS - 2

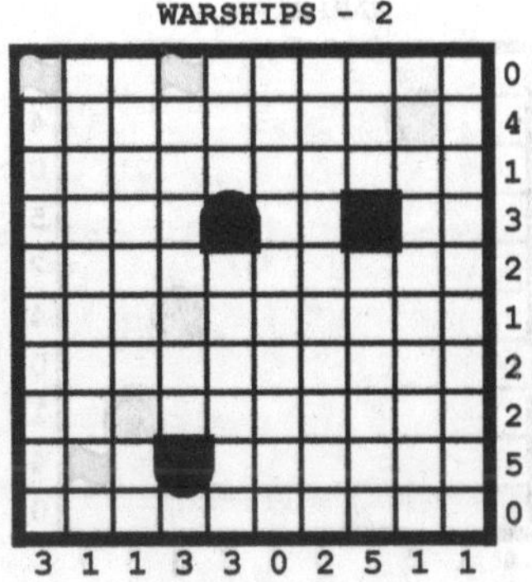

WARSHIPS - 3

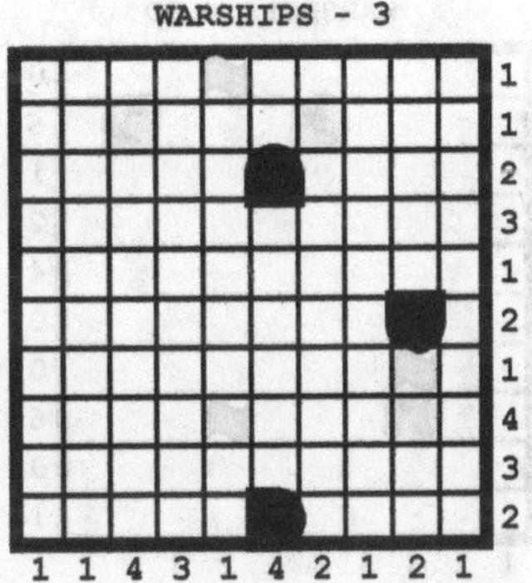

WARSHIPS - 4

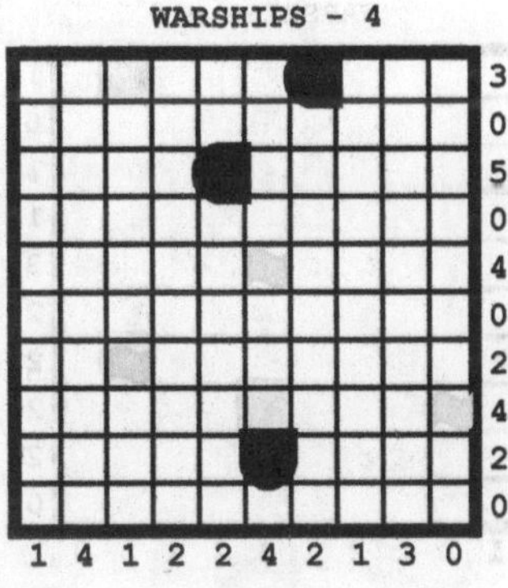

WARSHIPS - 5

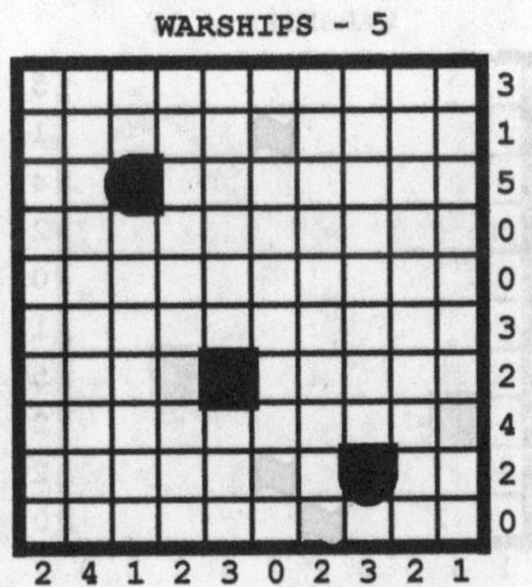

WARSHIPS - 6

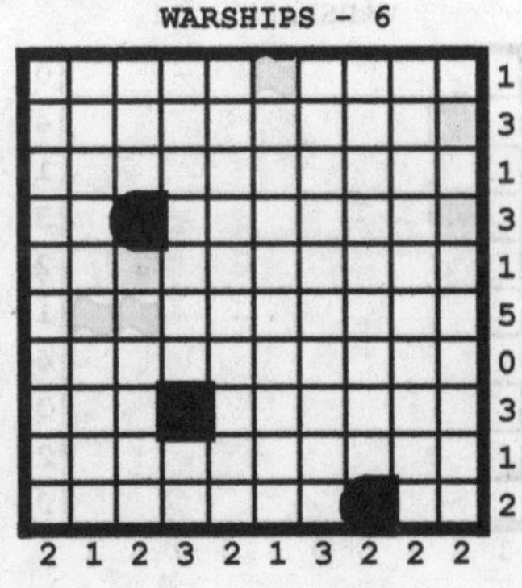

WARSHIPS - 7

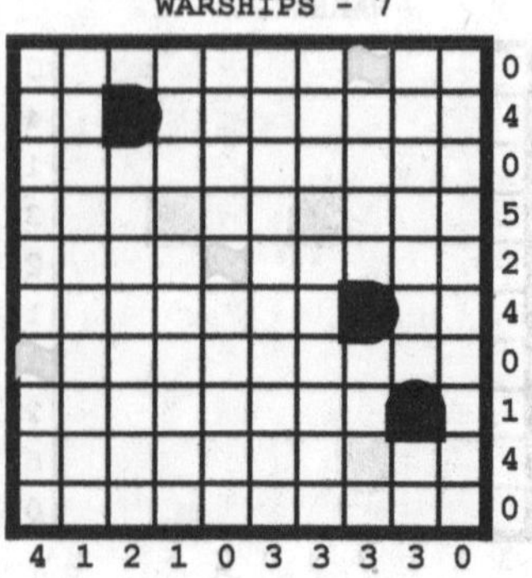

WARSHIPS - 8

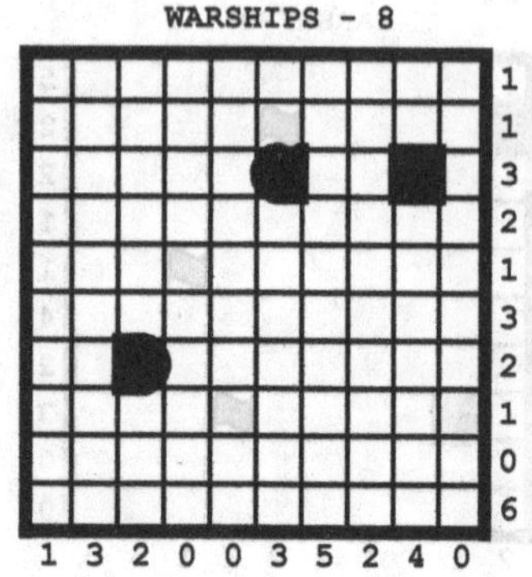

WARSHIPS - 9

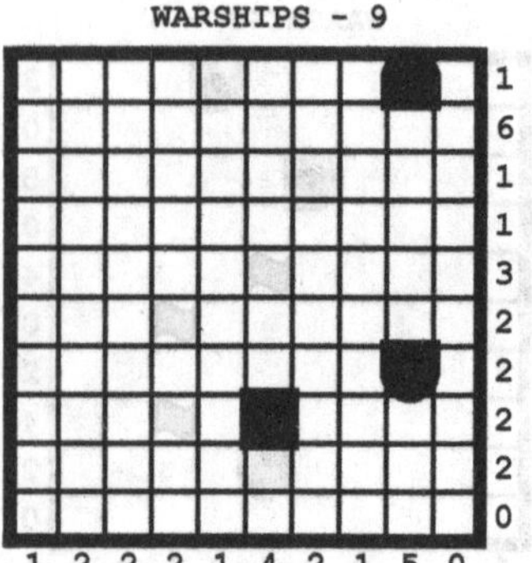

WARSHIPS - 10

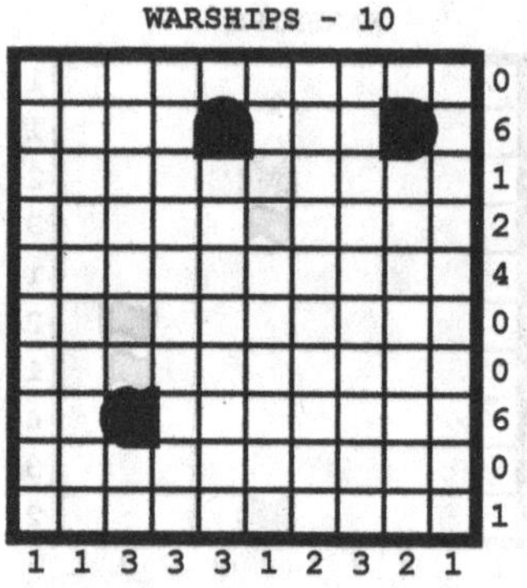

WARSHIPS - 11

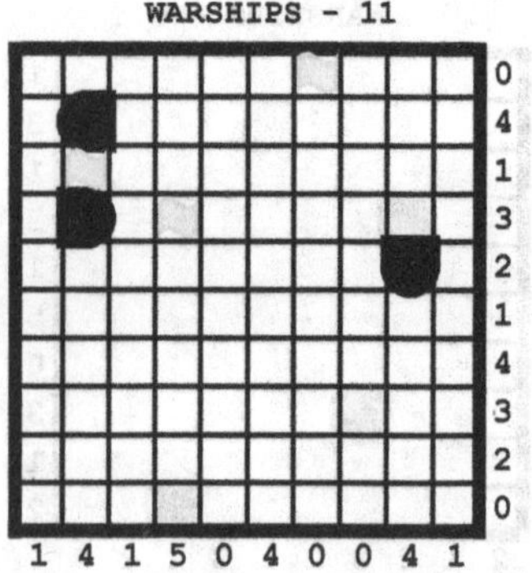

WARSHIPS - 12

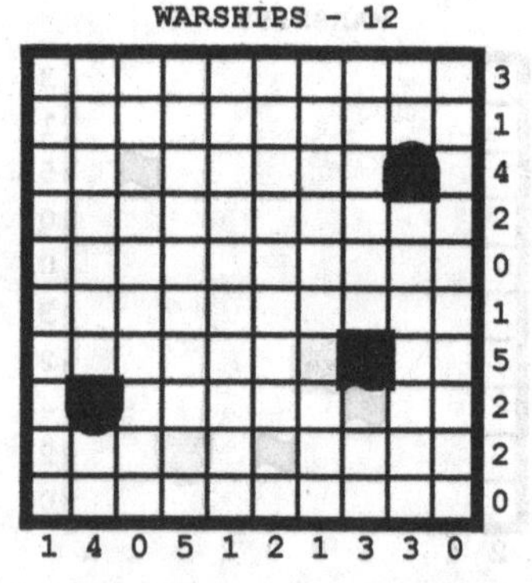

WARSHIPS - 13

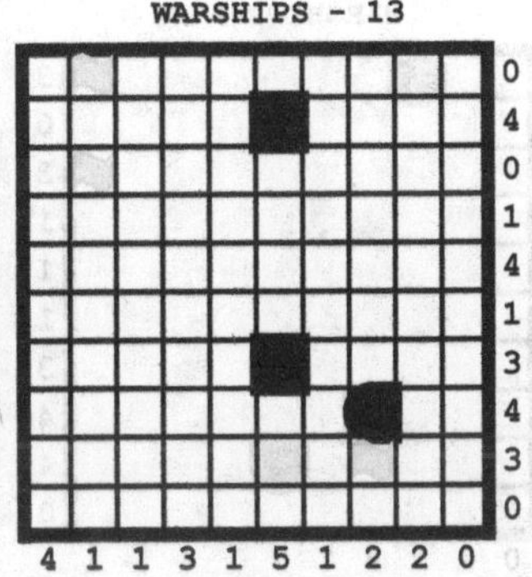

WARSHIPS - 15

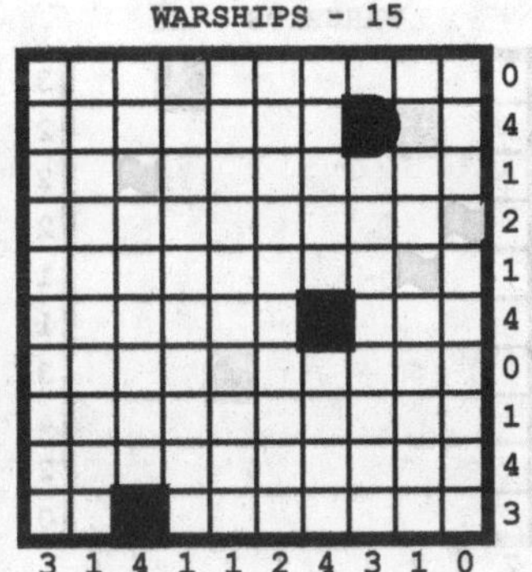

WARSHIPS - 17

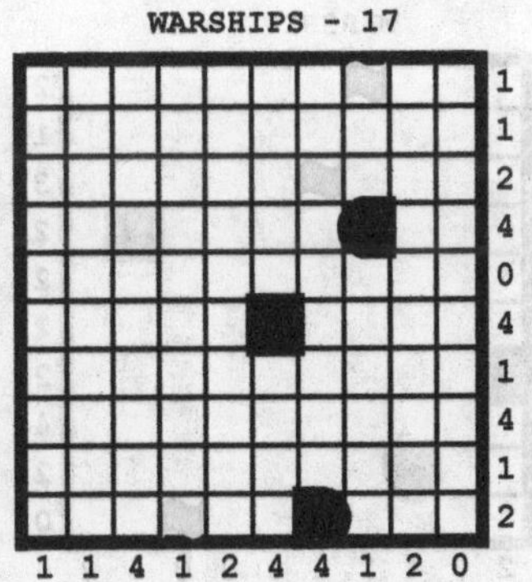

WARSHIPS - 14

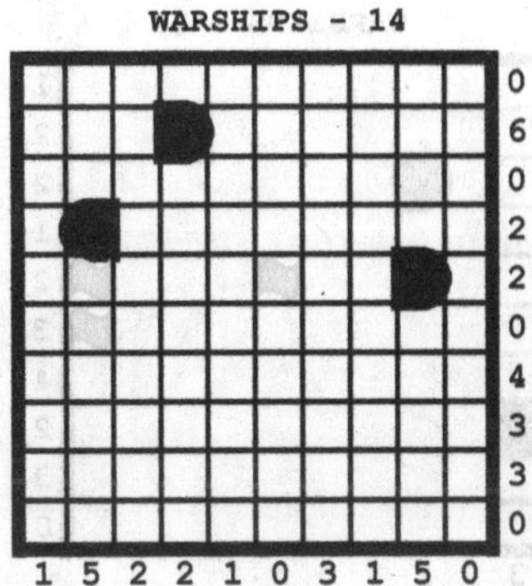

WARSHIPS - 16

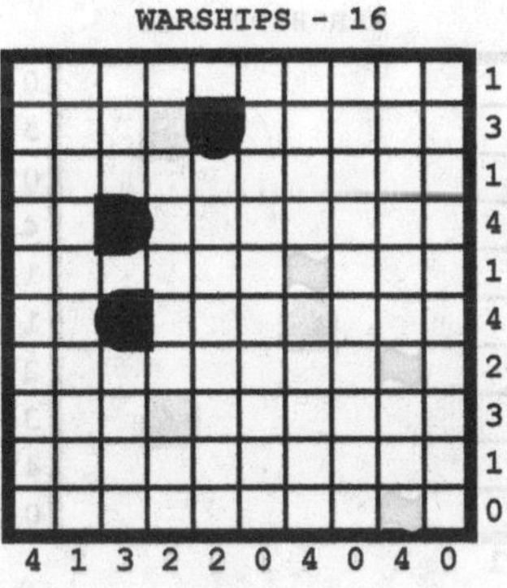

WARSHIPS - 18

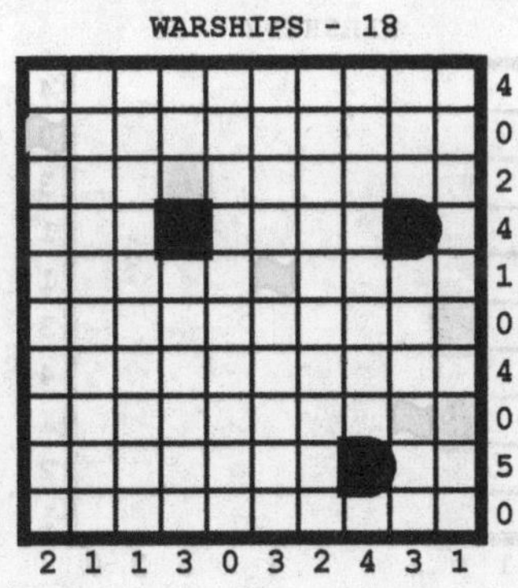

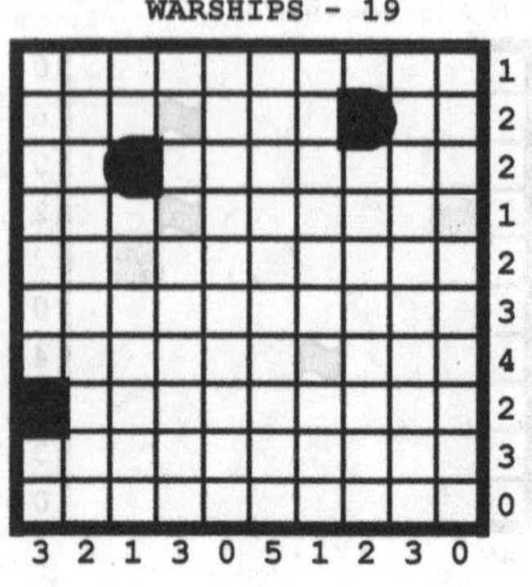

WARSHIPS - 19

Right: 1 2 2 1 2 3 4 2 3 0
Bottom: 3 2 1 3 0 5 1 2 3 0

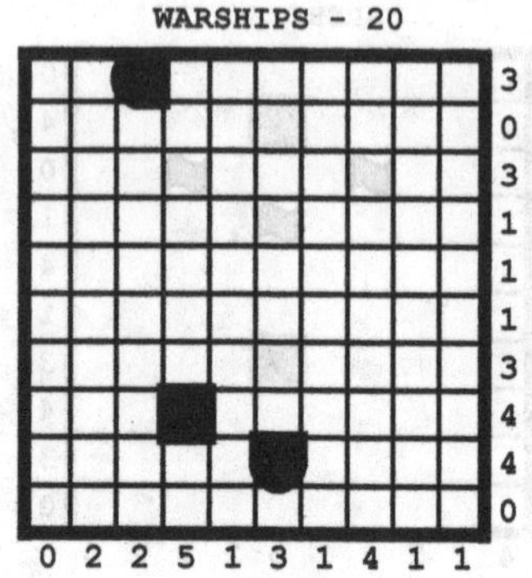

WARSHIPS - 20

Right: 3 0 3 1 1 3 4 4 0
Bottom: 0 2 2 5 1 3 1 4 1 1

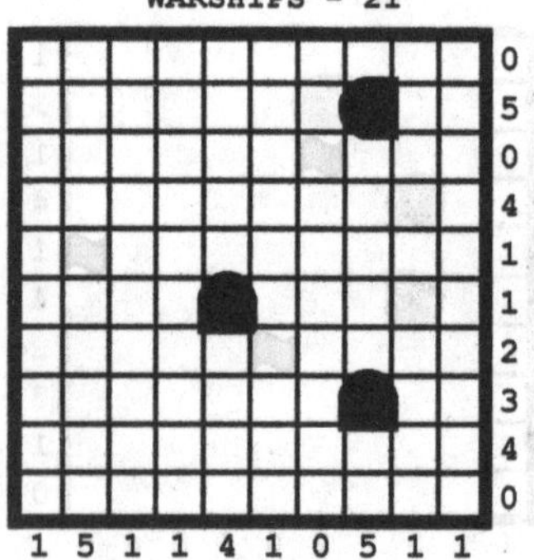

WARSHIPS - 21

Right: 0 5 0 4 1 1 2 3 4 0
Bottom: 1 5 1 1 4 1 0 5 1 1

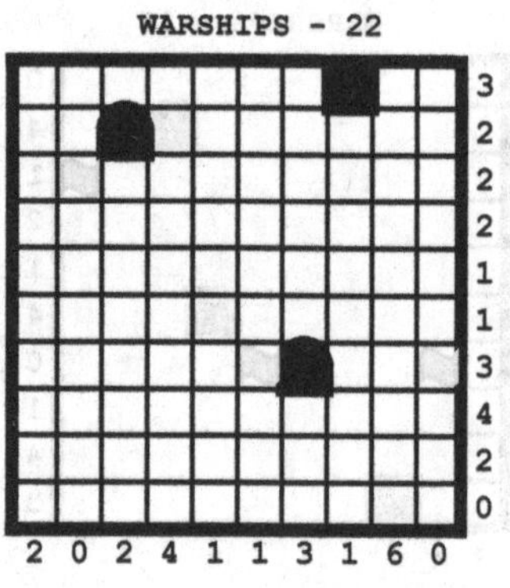

WARSHIPS - 22

Right: 3 2 2 2 1 1 3 4 2 0
Bottom: 2 0 2 4 1 1 3 1 6 0

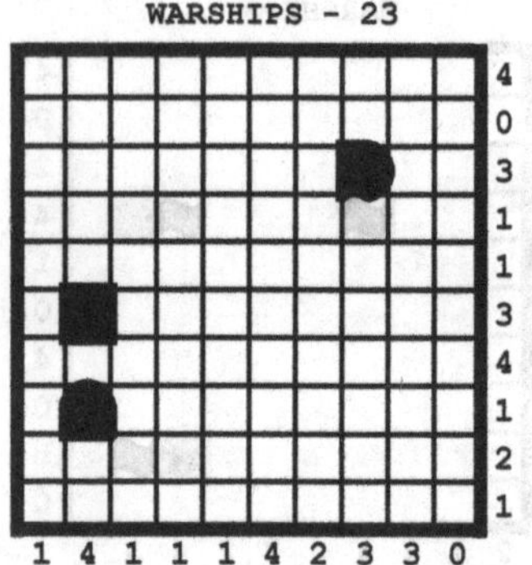

WARSHIPS - 23

Right: 4 0 3 1 1 3 4 1 2 1
Bottom: 1 4 1 1 1 4 2 3 3 0

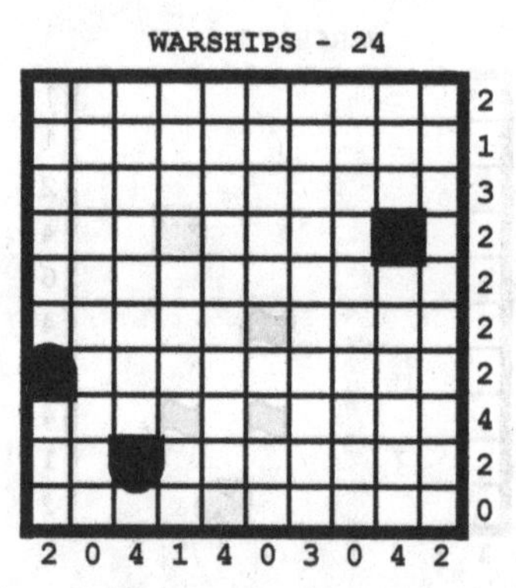

WARSHIPS - 24

Right: 2 1 3 2 2 2 2 4 2 0
Bottom: 2 0 4 1 4 0 3 0 4 2

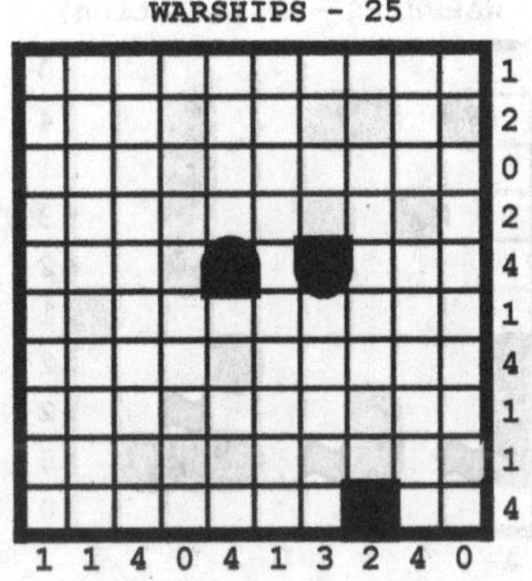

WARSHIPS - 25

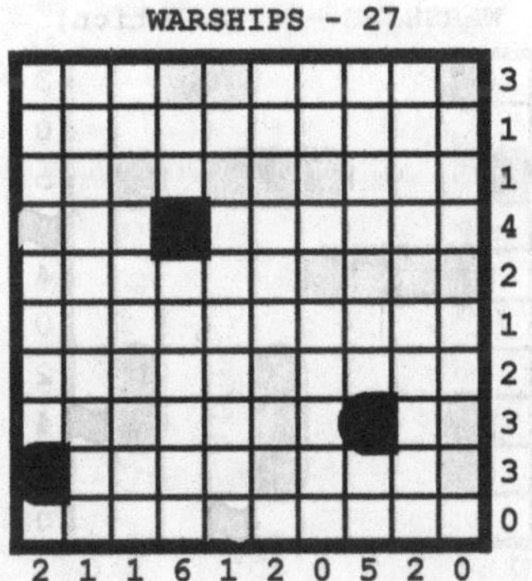

WARSHIPS - 27

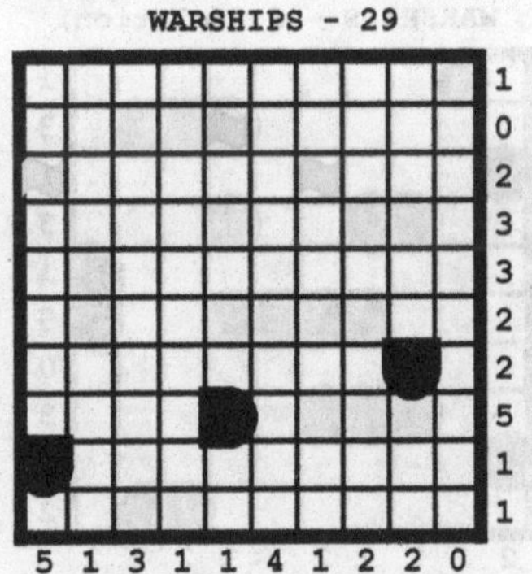

WARSHIPS - 29

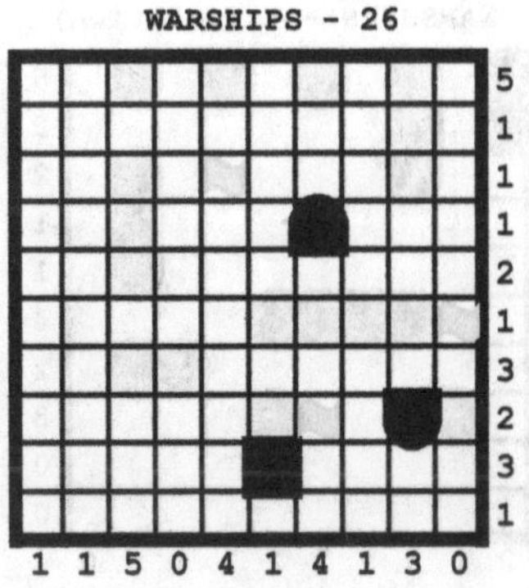

WARSHIPS - 26

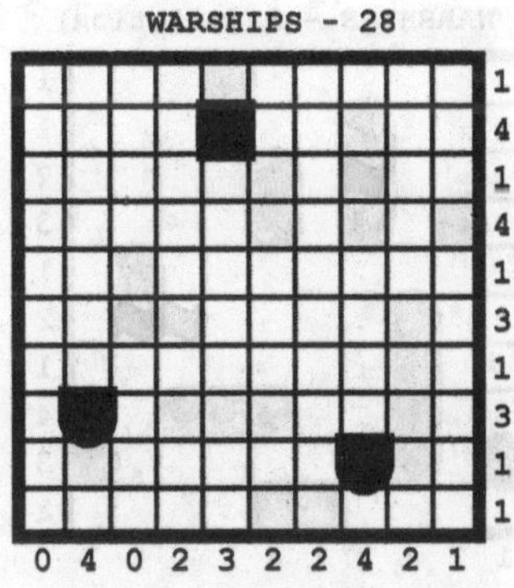

WARSHIPS - 28

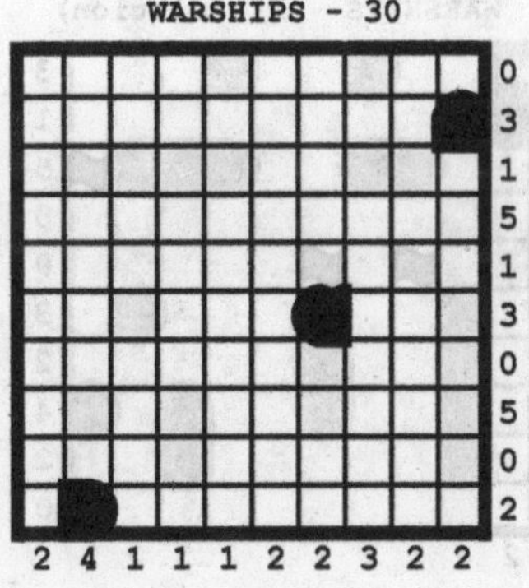

WARSHIPS - 30

WARSHIPS - 1 (Solution)

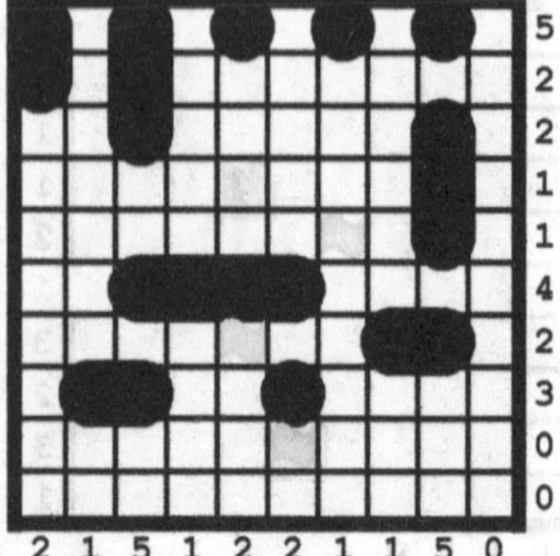

WARSHIPS - 2 (Solution)

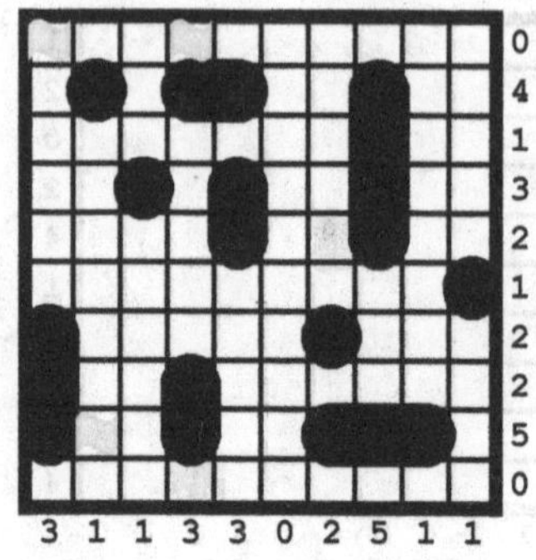

WARSHIPS - 3 (Solution)

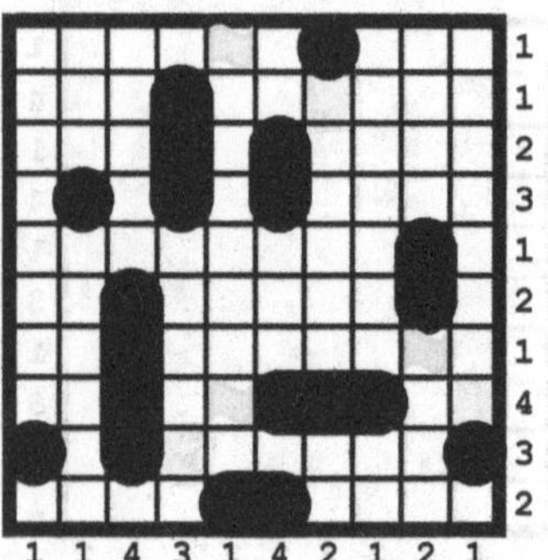

WARSHIPS - 4 (Solution)

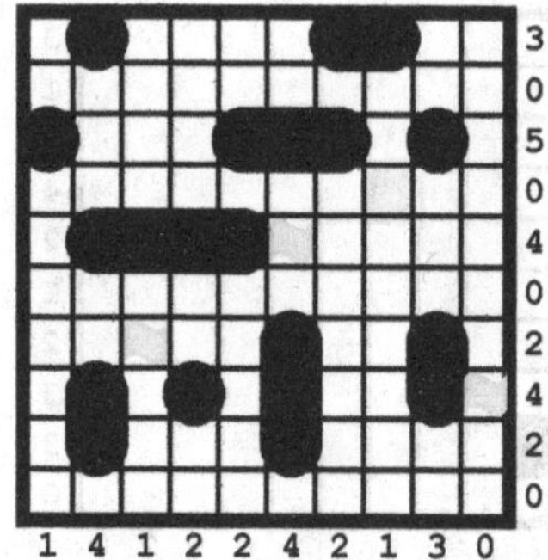

WARSHIPS - 5 (Solution)

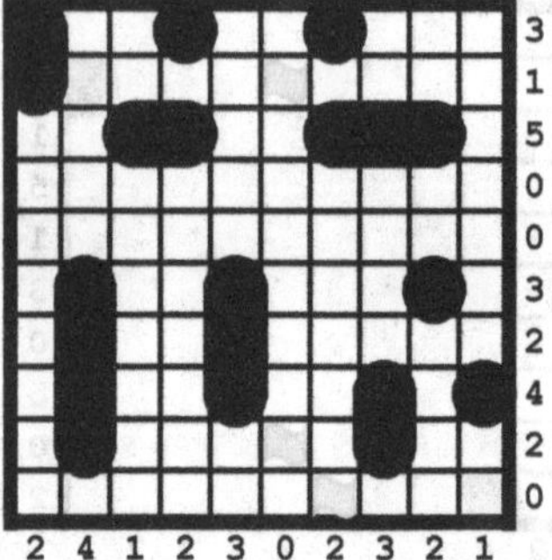

WARSHIPS - 6 (Solution)

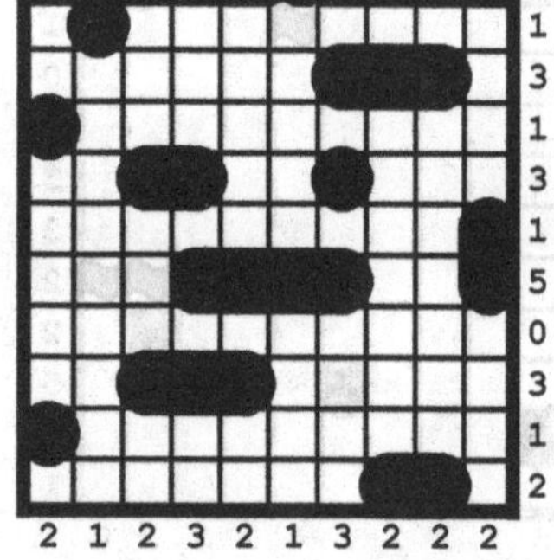

WARSHIPS - 7 (Solution)

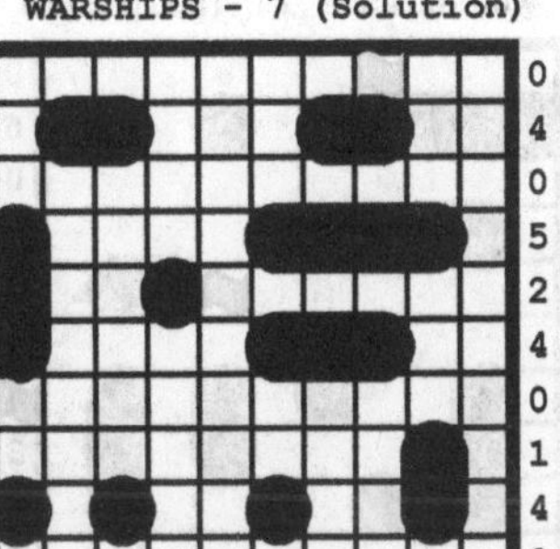

WARSHIPS - 8 (Solution)

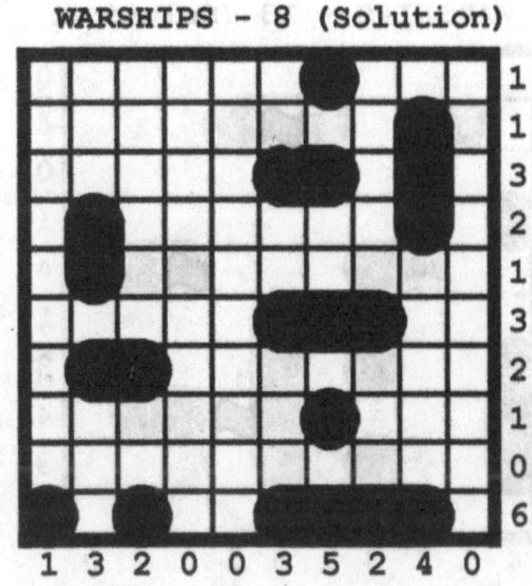

WARSHIPS - 9 (Solution)

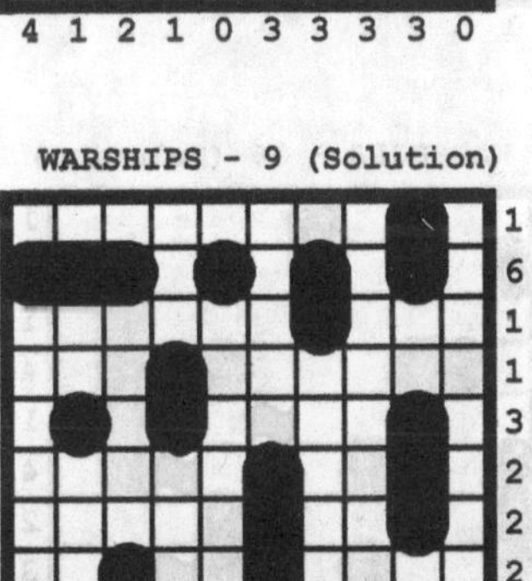

WARSHIPS - 10 (Solution)

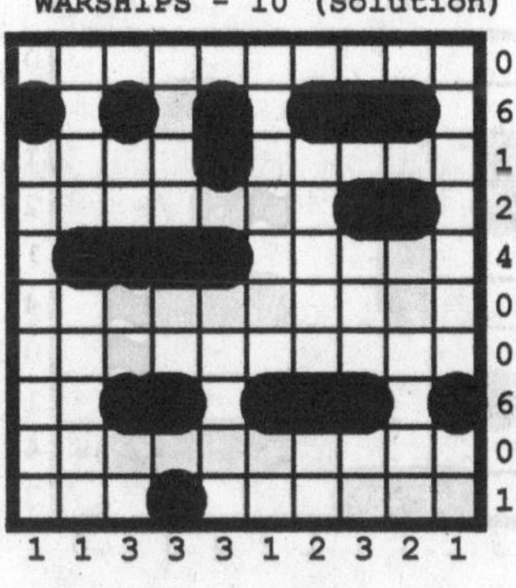

WARSHIPS - 11 (Solution)

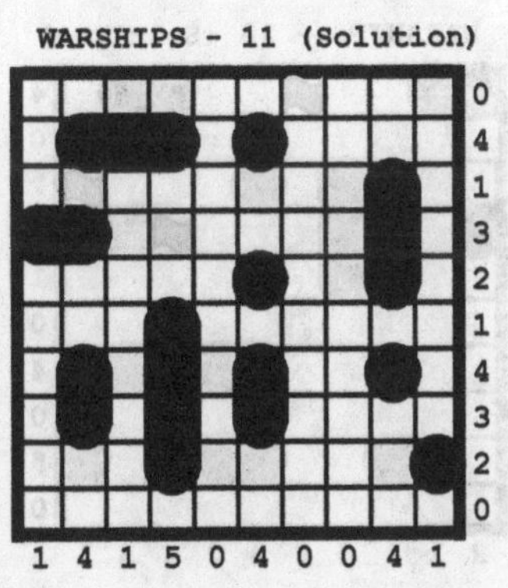

WARSHIPS - 12 (Solution)

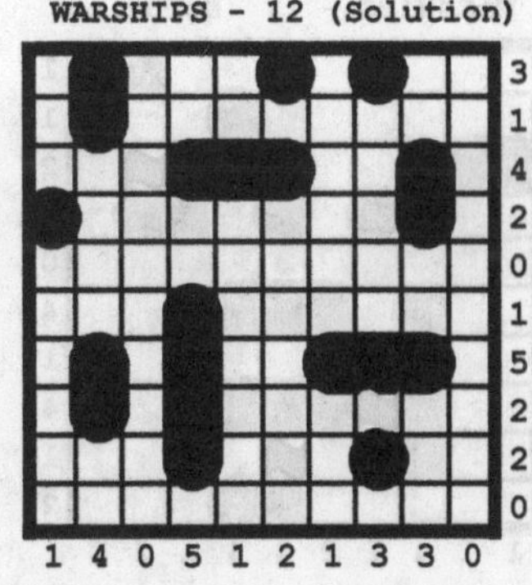

WARSHIPS - 13 (Solution)

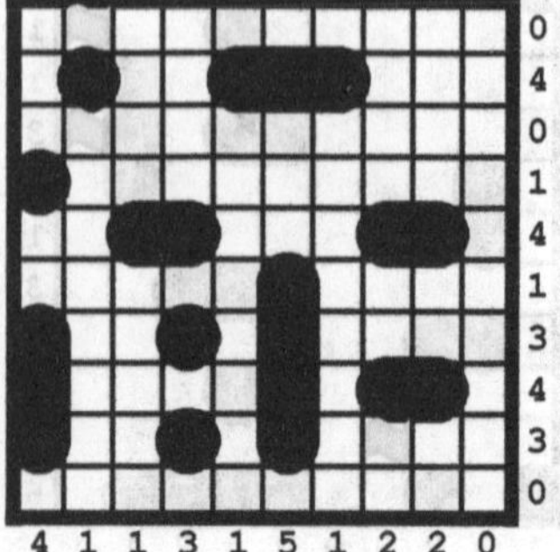

WARSHIPS - 14 (Solution)

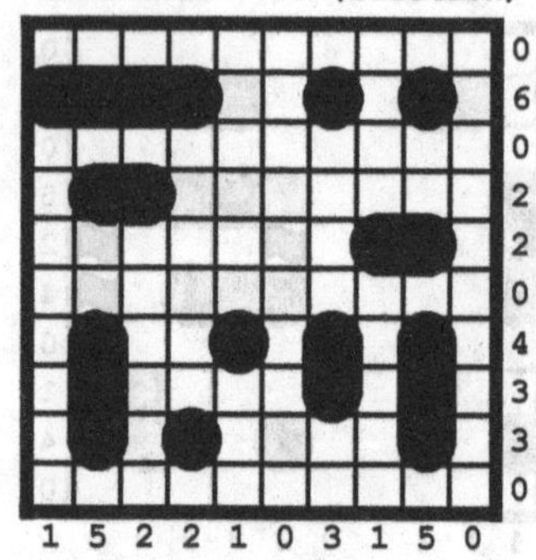

WARSHIPS - 15 (Solution)

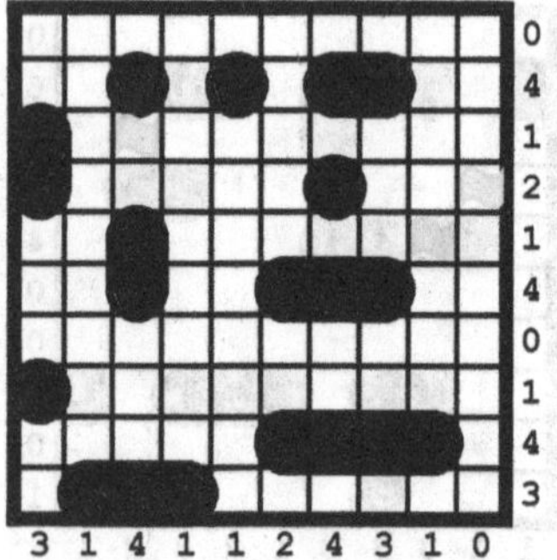

WARSHIPS - 16 (Solution)

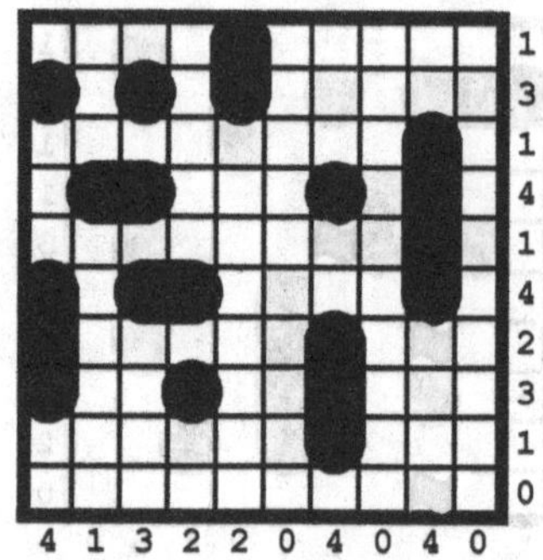

WARSHIPS - 17 (Solution)

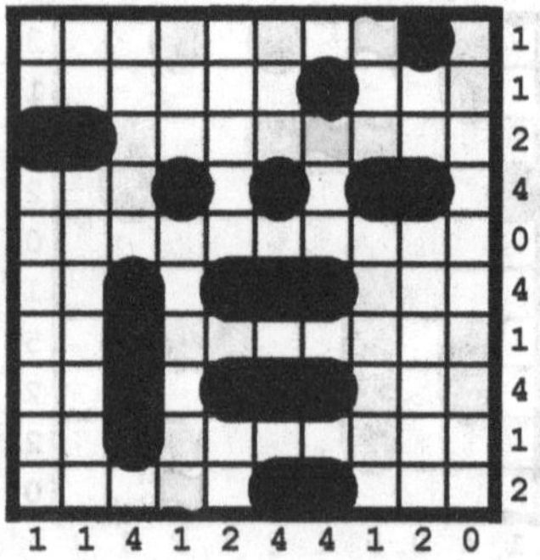

WARSHIPS - 18 (Solution)

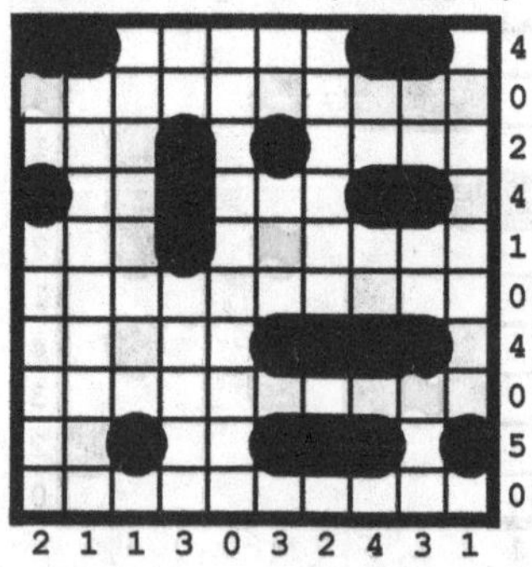

WARSHIPS - 19 (Solution)

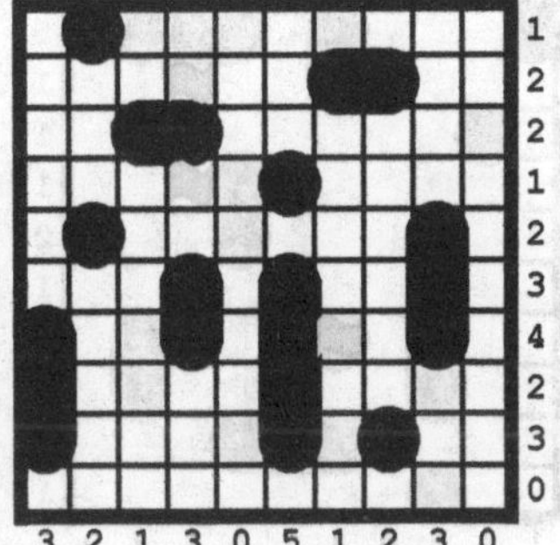

WARSHIPS - 20 (Solution)

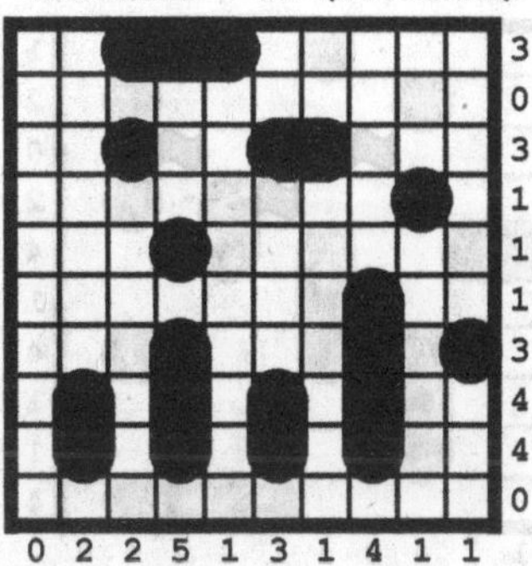

WARSHIPS - 21 (Solution)

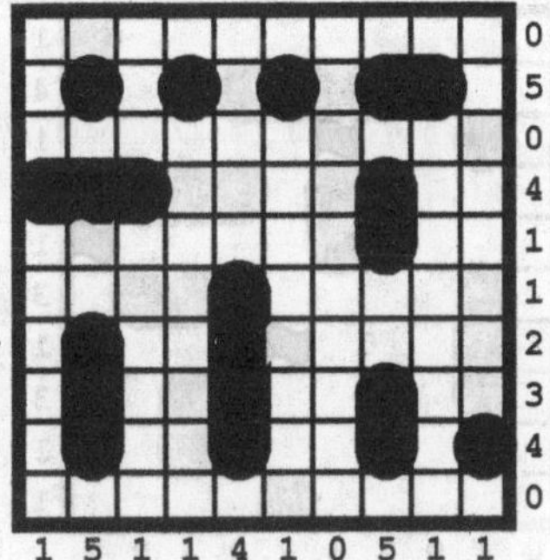

WARSHIPS - 22 (Solution)

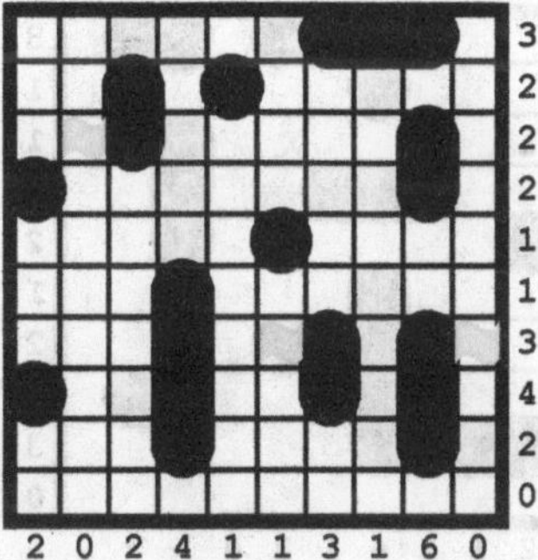

WARSHIPS - 23 (Solution)

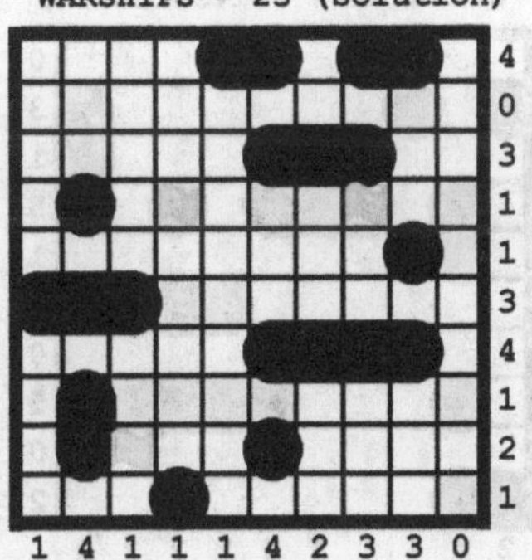

WARSHIPS - 24 (Solution)

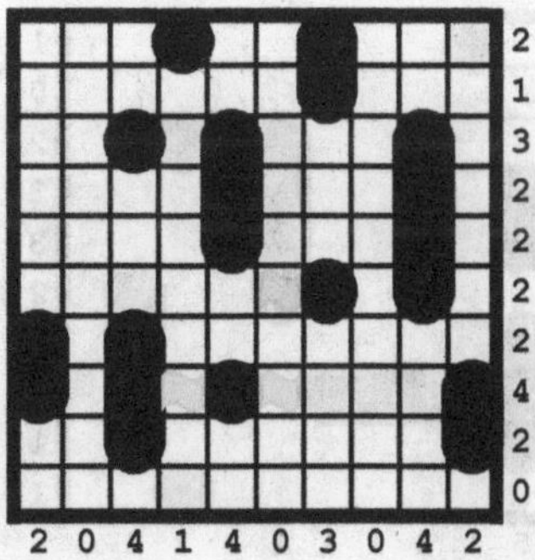

WARSHIPS - 25 (Solution)

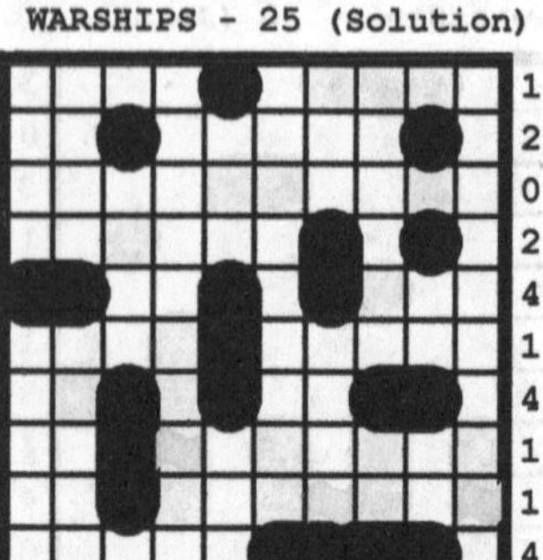

WARSHIPS - 26 (Solution)

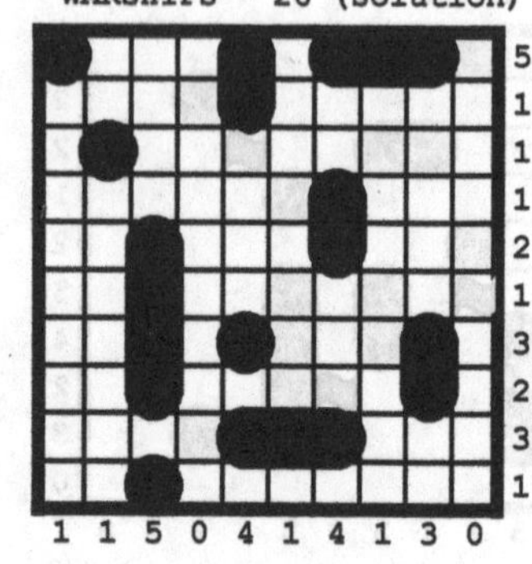

WARSHIPS - 27 (Solution)

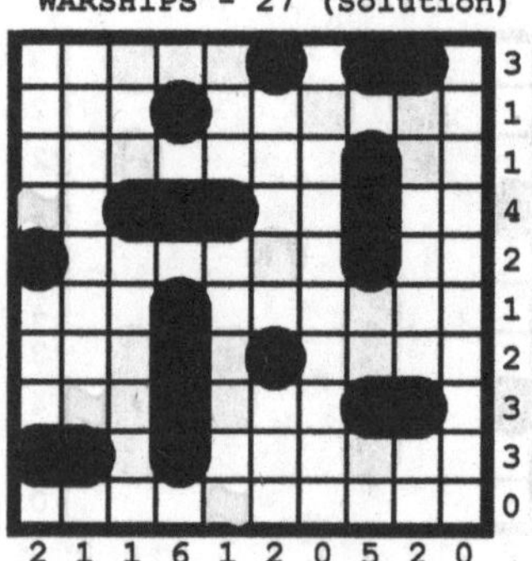

WARSHIPS - 28 (Solution)

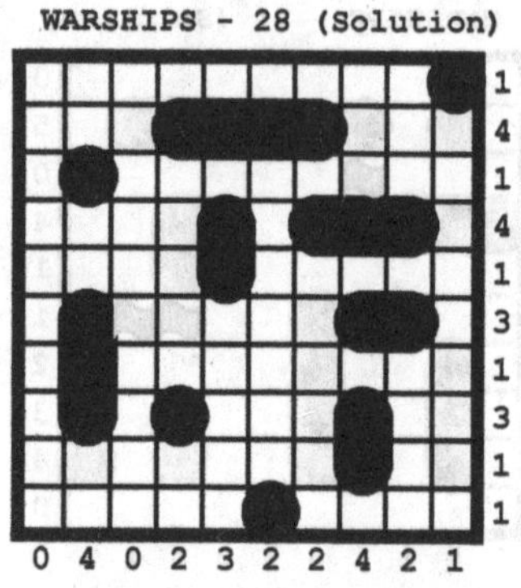

WARSHIPS - 29 (Solution)

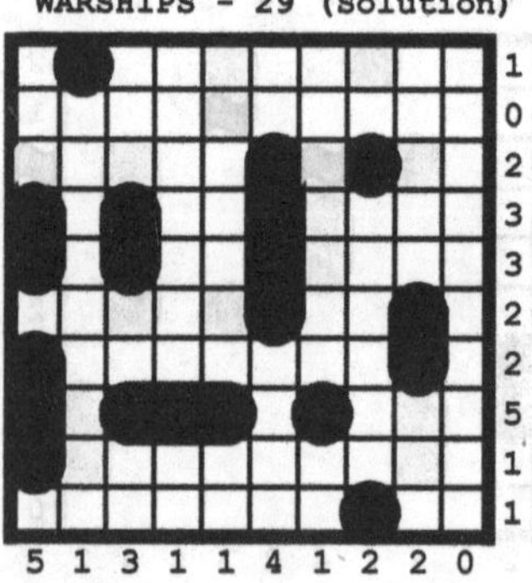

WARSHIPS - 30 (Solution)

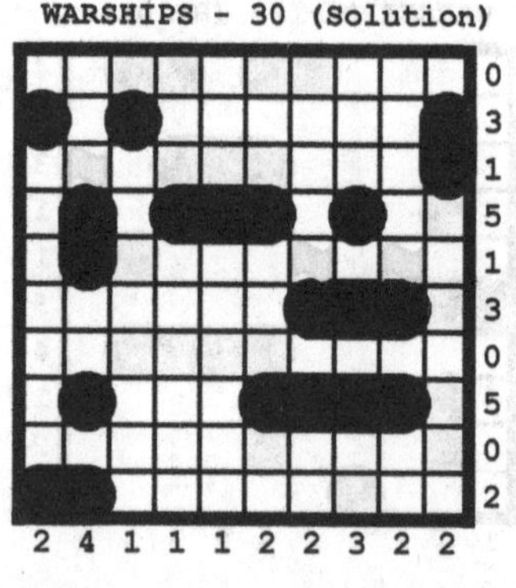

CHALLENGING 100 PUZZLE

HOW TO PLAY

Each puzzle consists of a square grid with numbers appearing in all squares.

The object is to add one additional digit in some cells such as the sum of the numbers in each row and each column equals to the selected sum (100 by default).

ONE HUNDRED - 1

100

1	7	2
6	1	2
2	5	7

ONE HUNDRED - 2

100

4	5	8
6	4	4
5	1	4

ONE HUNDRED - 3

100

7	5	4
4	4	4
4	1	5

ONE HUNDRED - 4

100

6	1	1
2	2	7
6	8	9

ONE HUNDRED - 5

100

6	2	3
3	6	8
9	3	5

ONE HUNDRED - 6

100

8	8	3
8	4	9
5	7	8

ONE HUNDRED - 7

₁₀₀

6	7	2
3	2	7
3	6	4

ONE HUNDRED - 8

₁₀₀

4	9	6
3	4	9
9	6	1

ONE HUNDRED - 9

₁₀₀

4	4	7
1	1	8
5	4	1

ONE HUNDRED - 10

₁₀₀

6	3	2
3	6	5
1	3	6

ONE HUNDRED - 11

₁₀₀

4	9	5
3	6	9
9	3	4

ONE HUNDRED - 12

₁₀₀

6	3	1
3	5	6
1	6	3

ONE HUNDRED - 13

1	4	8
3	8	1
8	1	8

ONE HUNDRED - 14

5	4	5
5	4	4
4	5	8

ONE HUNDRED - 15

4	6	9
9	1	8
5	9	2

ONE HUNDRED - 16

6	5	2
1	2	7
2	7	4

ONE HUNDRED - 17

4	7	1
2	2	6
7	2	2

ONE HUNDRED - 18

2	8	1
4	1	3
5	2	4

ONE HUNDRED - 19

<table>
<tr><td>6</td><td>6</td><td>3</td></tr>
<tr><td>3</td><td>5</td><td>6</td></tr>
<tr><td>6</td><td>3</td><td>3</td></tr>
</table>

ONE HUNDRED - 20

<table>
<tr><td>6</td><td>1</td><td>2</td></tr>
<tr><td>4</td><td>8</td><td>1</td></tr>
<tr><td>2</td><td>9</td><td>6</td></tr>
</table>

ONE HUNDRED - 21

<table>
<tr><td>6</td><td>3</td><td>1</td></tr>
<tr><td>6</td><td>5</td><td>3</td></tr>
<tr><td>3</td><td>9</td><td>6</td></tr>
</table>

ONE HUNDRED - 22

<table>
<tr><td>6</td><td>5</td><td>3</td></tr>
<tr><td>3</td><td>6</td><td>8</td></tr>
<tr><td>8</td><td>3</td><td>5</td></tr>
</table>

ONE HUNDRED - 23

<table>
<tr><td>6</td><td>1</td><td>2</td></tr>
<tr><td>8</td><td>8</td><td>9</td></tr>
<tr><td>2</td><td>2</td><td>7</td></tr>
</table>

ONE HUNDRED - 24

<table>
<tr><td>5</td><td>1</td><td>2</td></tr>
<tr><td>2</td><td>2</td><td>6</td></tr>
<tr><td>1</td><td>7</td><td>6</td></tr>
</table>

ONE HUNDRED - 25	ONE HUNDRED - 26

<table>
<tr><td colspan="3">ONE HUNDRED - 25</td></tr>
<tr><td>1</td><td>2</td><td>6</td></tr>
<tr><td>7</td><td>9</td><td>2</td></tr>
<tr><td>1</td><td>7</td><td>2</td></tr>
</table>

<table>
<tr><td colspan="3">ONE HUNDRED - 26</td></tr>
<tr><td>2</td><td>1</td><td>7</td></tr>
<tr><td>6</td><td>3</td><td>5</td></tr>
<tr><td>7</td><td>6</td><td>2</td></tr>
</table>

<table>
<tr><td colspan="3">ONE HUNDRED - 27</td></tr>
<tr><td>2</td><td>7</td><td>7</td></tr>
<tr><td>1</td><td>2</td><td>7</td></tr>
<tr><td>7</td><td>5</td><td>1</td></tr>
</table>

<table>
<tr><td colspan="3">ONE HUNDRED - 28</td></tr>
<tr><td>3</td><td>5</td><td>3</td></tr>
<tr><td>2</td><td>3</td><td>5</td></tr>
<tr><td>9</td><td>3</td><td>2</td></tr>
</table>

<table>
<tr><td colspan="3">ONE HUNDRED - 29</td></tr>
<tr><td>6</td><td>5</td><td>8</td></tr>
<tr><td>4</td><td>9</td><td>4</td></tr>
<tr><td>9</td><td>3</td><td>7</td></tr>
</table>

<table>
<tr><td colspan="3">ONE HUNDRED - 30</td></tr>
<tr><td>4</td><td>1</td><td>3</td></tr>
<tr><td>4</td><td>2</td><td>5</td></tr>
<tr><td>9</td><td>8</td><td>5</td></tr>
</table>

ONE HUNDRED - 1 (Solution)

100

19	79	2
60	16	24
21	5	74

ONE HUNDRED - 2 (Solution)

100

40	52	8
6	47	47
54	1	45

ONE HUNDRED - 3 (Solution)

100

7	52	41
49	47	4
44	1	55

ONE HUNDRED - 4 (Solution)

100

69	13	18
25	2	73
6	85	9

ONE HUNDRED - 5 (Solution)

100

61	2	37
30	62	8
9	36	55

ONE HUNDRED - 6 (Solution)

100

8	89	3
87	4	9
5	7	88

ONE HUNDRED - 7 (Solution)

100

67	7	26
3	27	70
30	66	4

ONE HUNDRED - 8 (Solution)

100

4	90	6
3	4	93
93	6	1

ONE HUNDRED - 9 (Solution)

100

49	44	7
1	16	83
50	40	10

ONE HUNDRED - 10 (Solution)

100

69	3	28
30	65	5
1	32	67

ONE HUNDRED - 11 (Solution)

100

4	91	5
3	6	91
93	3	4

ONE HUNDRED - 12 (Solution)

100

67	32	1
32	5	63
1	63	36

ONE HUNDRED - 13 (Solution)

100

16	4	80
3	85	12
81	11	8

ONE HUNDRED - 14 (Solution)

100

5	45	50
54	4	42
41	51	8

ONE HUNDRED - 15 (Solution)

100

4	6	90
91	1	8
5	93	2

ONE HUNDRED - 16 (Solution)

100

69	5	26
10	20	70
21	75	4

ONE HUNDRED - 17 (Solution)

100

4	78	18
20	20	60
76	2	22

ONE HUNDRED - 18 (Solution)

100

2	80	18
43	18	39
55	2	43

ONE HUNDRED - 19 (Solution)

100

6	62	32
30	5	65
64	33	3

ONE HUNDRED - 20 (Solution)

100

69	11	20
4	80	16
27	9	64

ONE HUNDRED - 21 (Solution)

100

64	35	1
6	56	38
30	9	61

ONE HUNDRED - 22 (Solution)

100

62	5	33
30	62	8
8	33	59

ONE HUNDRED - 23 (Solution)

100

64	15	21
8	83	9
28	2	70

ONE HUNDRED - 24 (Solution)

100

56	19	25
29	2	69
15	79	6

ONE HUNDRED - 25 (Solution)

100

19	21	60
71	9	20
10	70	20

ONE HUNDRED - 26 (Solution)

100

29	1	70
64	31	5
7	68	25

ONE HUNDRED - 27 (Solution)

100

22	71	7
1	24	75
77	5	18

ONE HUNDRED - 28 (Solution)

100

3	58	39
2	39	59
95	3	2

ONE HUNDRED - 29 (Solution)

100

6	5	89
4	92	4
90	3	7

ONE HUNDRED - 30 (Solution)

100

49	12	39
42	2	56
9	86	5

RECOMMENDATIONS from The Same Author

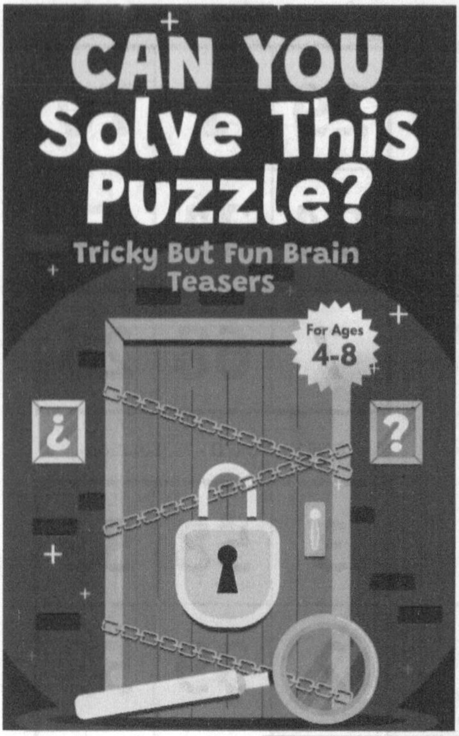

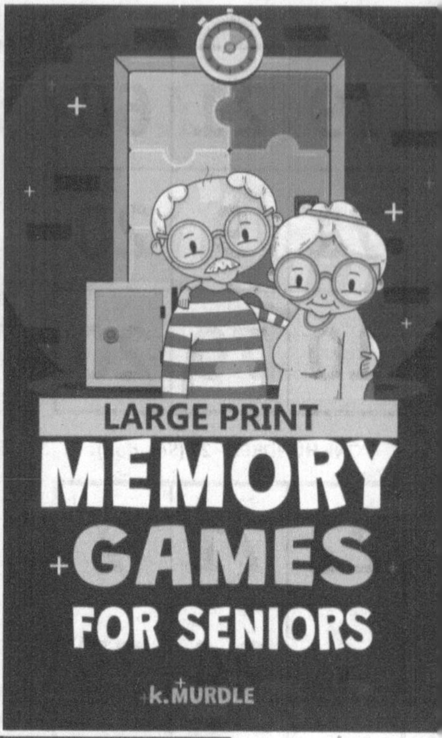

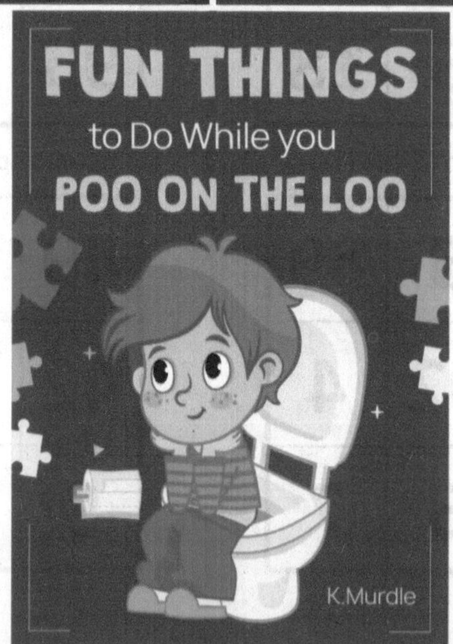

www.ingramcontent.com/pod-product-compliance
Lightning Source LLC
Chambersburg PA
CBHW021803130726
47987CB00008B/2995